Storming the Heavens

VOICES OF OCTOBER

EDITED AND INTRODUCED BY MARK JONES

LONDON   ATLANTIC HIGHLANDS

First published in 1987 by Zwan Publications
11-21 Northdown Street, London N1 9BN
and Zwan Publications at Humanities Press Inc
Atlantic Highlands, New Jersey 07716, USA

Foreword and introduction © Mark Jones.
The extract from *My Life*, by Leon Trotsky,
is reproduced by permission of Penguin
Books and Pathfinder Press, USA; the
extract from Clara Zetkin, *Selected Writings*,
by permission of International Publishers,
NY; the Debate in the Council of the
Republic is reprinted from *The Russian
Provisional Government, 1917*, ed. Browder
and Kerensky with the permission of
Stanford University Press. The editor is also
grateful to Roger Pethybridge, editor of
Witnesses to the Russian Revolution, published
by Unwin Hyman Ltd.

Cover design: Adrian Yeeles/Artworkers
Typesetting: 'The Works', Exeter, Devon.
Printed and bound in the UK by
Billings & Sons Ltd, Worcester

**British Library Cataloguing in Publication
Data**

Storming the Heavens: the Russian
Revolution through contemporary eyes.
1. Soviet Union – History – 1917-1936
I. Jones, Mark
947.084′1   DK266.5
ISBN 1 – 85305 – 020 – 2

**Library of Congress Cataloging-in-
Publication Data**
Storming the heavens.
    1. Soviet Union – History – Revolution, 1917-1921 –
Personal narratives. I. Jones, Mark.
DK265.69.S76   1987   947.084′1   87 – 14748
ISBN 1 – 85305 – 020 – 2 (U.S.)
ISBN 1 – 85305 – 025 – 3

Contents

Foreword

In July 1917, as the First World War entered its third year, the fourteen-million strong Russian army launched its summer offensive. It was a disaster which marked the end of the Tsarist military tradition. After it, the Eastern Front disintegrated, to the point where further resistance became impossible. Three months later the Bolsheviks came to power, but the national collapse continued. Then, in the winter of 1918 the working class of Petrograd – the shock troops of October – began to desert the city, succumbing at last to the hunger and mass unemployment which their own workers' government proved powerless to alleviate. The Bolsheviks themselves abandoned the capital, moving the government to the relative safety of Moscow. The country slid into a chaos of epidemic disease, darkness and death.

Undaunted, the Bolsheviks set about improvising a new army. Their soldiers, sometimes equipped only with wooden, silver-painted bayonets, marching upright into the attack (crouching was thought at first to show lack of proletarian spirit), went on to defeat armies from fourteen different countries during the War of Intervention. Between five million and seven million died in that conflict, which ended in 1920. By its end Lenin and his followers had restored the country more or less behind its Tsarist borders.

The Bolshevik victory, compounded of mass fervour and energetic leadership, forestalled national disintegration. The scale of their achievement is evident from comparison with the fate of the Habsburg Empire. While Austria-Hungary was shattered, the Bolsheviks hung on to almost everything. Only Poland and Finland were lost and, temporarily, the Baltic states of Latvia, Lithuania and Estonia. Yet powerful nationalist movements operated across the whole of the old Empire, in the Ukraine, Georgia, the Caucasus, in Central Asia and in the Far East.

The external difficulties they faced, though enormous, do not tell the whole story. The dearth of statecraft among the Bolsheviks must also be acknowledged. Months before seizing power they were still a scattered, despised sect. Until the very eve of the revolution Lenin had to remain in hiding, monitoring events only with difficulty. The Bolshevik leader had no military experience and was not a statesman (much of his working life had been spent inside libraries). There was nothing to suggest that this conspiratorial leader and his small party would be capable of holding power and of resolving the problems which had destroyed Tsarism and three successive Provisional Governments. Yet the Bolsheviks were to do all this and more – they were to create a new state, built on historically-innovative principles, with its own unique ideology and civil culture. More than this, they created a new nation, built of the shards left by Tsardom – with its more than 100 restive subject nationalities.

The discomfiture Bolshevik successes produced in Western chancelleries was made worse by the prevailing ignorance of their origins and goals. Almost nothing was known of Lenin outside Russia (before the revolution, *The Times* mentioned the presence in Petrograd of a 'pacifist-agitator'). The first Soviet government was (like its bourgeois predecessors) announced as 'provisional'; few even among its supporters expected it to last much longer than they. Lenin himself, although subsequently one of the most written-about leaders in history, remains something of an enigma. His abilities as a military and political leader are recalled in Nikolai Podvoisky's invaluable memoir of the October rising, included in this collection. Podvoisky's insights into Lenin's leadership style retain a capacity to surprise; even now Lenin is not generally regarded as a military strategist, a role more usually ascribed to Trotsky.

The Soviet state's astonishing survival was only partly due to Bolshevik skill in organising military victory. The struggle for Soviet power was above all one for the hearts and minds of millions of ordinary people. This put a premium on other skills: of agitation, and of propaganda. Sometimes (as with Lenin) all these attributes were found in the same person. Larisa Reisner was another such. An avant-garde writer in Petrograd's literary demi-monde, renowned for her beauty, she became a commander of the Bolshevik Volga flotilla. Reisner's *The Front* is a brilliant evocation of Bolshevik *eclat* in the civil war period, and adds much to our understanding of the mass dynamics of the October Revolution.

If the preservation of Russia was a feat of arms and of ideological and moral suasion, it was also an irony. Alone of all the parties, socialist, bourgeois or monarchist, the Bolsheviks had not sought to prevent the destruction of Russia in the First World War. They were self-conscious 'defeatists' who believed in World Revolution rather than national revival. They considered that October had opened the socialist epoch, and this was the belief which sustained them in their subsequent bitter struggles with the Whites and the Interventionists, when defeatism gave way to sacrificial heroism.

In the period of the October Revolution, millions of people became persuaded of the imminence of World Revolution. This was a primary Bolshevik achievement. World Revolution became a universal totem, although when Lenin announced the doctrine to his shocked supporters, in his first speech on returning from exile, in April 1917, it seemed he was was the only person in Russia who believed in such a thing. But as the First World War dragged ruinously on, the notion began to acquire mass resonance, for the second, socialist revolution, constantly hailed by the Bolsheviks, offered perhaps the only hope of peace. Then mass despair began to fuse with evangelical hope. The salvation of Russia would be but the prelude to universal peace; in the chiliastic tones characteristic of the period, Lenin said they would 'put an end to the reign of capitalism and hired labour. Then will begin the kingdom of socialism, the kingdom of peace, the kingdom of the toilers.' As the Bolsheviks grew from a despised sect to a mass party in the spring and summer of that year, such vistas grew seductively plausible.

Utopian fantasy ran like a red thread through 1917, and Lenin was not immune. But the concept of World Revolution had a long and respectable pedigree among 'scientific' socialists, wherein lay much of its fascination in 1917. Its origins lay in Karl Marx's conception of the historical limits to capitalism, a theoretical implication of the entire corpus of Marx's work. It was a notion which Marx himself scarcely elaborated, however: it smacked of speculation. The brief extract from Volume III of *Capital*, contained in this collection, is one of the few references to the idea to be found throughout that work. Nevertheless, this terminus of Marxism was to be the starting-point for Leninism. In 1917, the collapse of capitalism no longer seemed a matter of speculation.

Marx had prophesied the breakdown of the capitalist world order. For this he was vilified. 'Throughout the civilised world', Lenin said, 'the teachings of Marx evoke the utmost hostility and hatred'. But no matter; 'the Marxist doctrine is omnipotent because it is true.' Marxism was a science. This meant that, for the first time, social emancipation was the subject of conscious practice, not, or not only, of a mystical yearning. Marxism (especially in the hands of Lenin, in the Russia of 1917) could speak to the most fundamental needs, the most sacred goals and the most generous human instincts. It could pre-empt religion, proposing to create Utopia in the here-and-now, not the hereafter. Marxism, Lenin said, is 'comprehensive and harmonious, and provides men with an integral world outlook irreconcilable with any form of superstition, reaction or defence of bourgeois oppression'(Lenin [1969] p. 20).

The transcendental imagery of the world's first proletarian revolution, and the inflated expectations it aroused, may have served to embarrass (as well as incite) subsequent generations of the constructors of Soviet socialism. But there was a justification for it in Marxism. For capitalism itself was, according to Marx, endowed with supernatural qualities: 'There appears', he wrote, 'nothing higher in itself, nothing legitimate for itself' outside capital, which:

> creates bourgeois society, and the universal appropriation of nature as well as of the social bond itself by the members of society. Hence the great civilising influence of capital; its production of a stage of society in comparison to which all earlier ones appear as mere local developments of humanity and as nature-idolatry. For the first time, nature becomes purely an object for humankind, purely a matter of utility; ceases to be recognized as a power for itself; and the theoretical discovery of its autonomous laws

appears merely as a ruse so as to subjugate it under human needs. (Marx [1973] p. 409)

Thus capital seemed imbued with Faustian powers; but in reality these fantastic capabilities were only the social form taken by human activity. What was capital? In itself, nothing, a shadow on the cave-wall. Its protean content, and true creator, was the proletariat. And since capitalism was merely the form taken by social labour, that is, by the collective appropriation of nature, it was the proletariat which contained mankind's potential for transcending its species-specific limitations, in the very act of subjugating nature 'under human needs'. Under socialism, the vast human powers unlocked during the development of capitalist production, would no longer take the form of capital – of an alien being standing opposite mankind, and oppressing its creators. Then the proletariat would become the conscious master of its social destiny, which would truly be the 'kingdom of socialism'.

Marx argued that the capitalist *mode* of production is governed by laws of motion which are both inherent and contradictory. Thus the pursuit of profit entailed a limitless expansion of production. This, the accumulation of capital, constantly threatened to overwhelm wage-labour – the historical foundation of capitalist production. The result of the contradiction between labour and capital was the incessant crises which 'are always but momentary and forcible solutions of the existing contradictions. They are violent eruptions which for a time restore the disturbed equilibrium' (Marx [1974] p. 249). Since capitalist production is really the *expanded reproduction of its contradictions*, its growing instability and its inherently crisis-prone nature doom it to social and political upheavals whose end-point must be proletarian revolution and the transition to socialism.

In 1916 Lenin had already argued, in *Imperialism, the Highest Stage of Capitalism*, that the World War was the expression of a fundamental crisis of capitalism. It was 'an annexationist, predatory, war of plunder', fought for 'the partition and repartition of colonies and spheres of influence of finance capital' (Lenin [1969] p. 171). The war had brought the world to 'the eve of the social revolution of the proletariat'.

When Lenin wrote *Imperialism*, he was an isolated figure in the international socialist movement. Almost everywhere, socialists in the belligerent countries had rallied to the flag. 'Alone against the whole world', Alexandra Kollontai said, Lenin 'pitilessly analysed and laid bare the essence of imperialist war and, more importantly, clearly indicated the ways and means of transforming this war into civil war and revolution' (Kollontai [1984] p. 72). So when, in February 1917, news seeped out of the momentous events in Petrograd, culminating in the fall of the Tsar, Lenin was ready. With total conviction and absolute clarity, he began to preach the need for a second, socialist revolution to follow the February bourgeois revolution.

Lenin returned to Russia in April, and events soon seemed to confirm the

Marxist–Leninist doctrine which he put forward in the April Theses. The country was in the grip of a fatal dilemma, which the propertied government set up in February shared excruciatingly with the Tsarist regime it replaced. The war could not be won, nor even long continued. Yet no peace was on offer which would permit the creation of a viable postwar capitalist Russia. At the same time the Central Powers were too weak and over-extended to force capitulation on the new regime. The defeated state could not impose internal order, yet the victors were unable to occupy the country and impose their own order either. It was a situation without historical precedent. While the Provisional Government flailed in desperation the country sank ever-deeper into chaos and turbulent revolt. Russia had become a point of singularity in the colossal crisis embroiling the capitalist world.

Between the iron certainty of a faith declared rational by confirmatory events, and the grandiose visions of human freedom conjured up by Lenin's vast and dangerous dreams (not least the freedom from prosaic cares offered by devotion to a worthy cause), lay a rich seam of psychological and emotional energy. Despising 'petit-bourgeois' self-indulgence, the newly-enlisted comrades rushed forth to do battle with age-old enemies who were suddenly, unexpectedly vulnerable. The magic of October clothed lives beset with every kind of difficulty and privation, making them perhaps the envy of more privileged times. It is hard, even now, to resist the engaging earnestness of the schoolgirl Bolshevik, Lusik Lisinova: 'Democracy', she wrote to her sister, 'has as yet too little under its control ... No, Anaid, I am not satisfied by events.' Plunged headlong into the vortex of October, Lusik's letters show her sharing what seemed a pervasive regret for the lost occasions of youth, but in that strange interlude between two revolutions, she had time to revel as well in the 'insinuating, consuming warmth' of a Moscow spring. This sadness, her 'faithful companion', is the entitlement of those who, yielding up the present, yearn for a future they will never see.

Lenin also surrendered himself to dreams in the summer of 1917, and there are few more evocative memorial sites to October than Razliv, overlooking the Gulf of Finland, where Lenin hid for 26 days and nights in a straw hut, a *shagash* ... and wrote *State and Revolution*, that astonishing utopian reverie which, he said, was 'interrupted' by the Bolshevik revolution. *State and Revolution* exists somewhere between February and October – between the fall of capitalism and the final victory of socialism. It betrays Lenin's yearning for a utopian future and, like every good utopia, its prescriptions contain many departure-points in the present.

By contrast, the grey realism of Malyantovich, the Provisional Government Minister of Justice and a hostile witness, has an oddly modern feel, perhaps because revolutions and risings have become commonplace, *deja vu*. As the Provisional Government finally collapsed, his principal feeling was one of relief. Malyantovich was glad to get away: 'A thought, sudden and persistent, flashed in my mind: Is this not your last day?' This was in strong contrast with the behaviour of Alexander Kerensky: the Minister-President's speech to the Council of the Republic on 24 October (the eve of the Bolshevik rising), was full of hysterical recriminations – as was the subsequent debate. The centre parties which had been dominant since February were sliding towards extinction.

Malyantovich was arrested by the Bolshevik leader, Antonov-Ovseenko, who thus saved him from the mob. But in a characteristic reversal of fortunes, Antonov-Ovseenko was himself then arrested by counter-revolutionaries, as the American journalist, Albert Rhys Williams, reports.

No social underclass in Russia was so affected by the emancipatory impulse of the Bolshevik revolution as that of women. In what was still predominantly a patriarchal, peasant-based society, the difficulties endured by women were taken particularly seriously by the Bolsheviks. Alexandra Kollontai, head of the legendary *Zhenotdel* (Women's Department), set up by the Party after the revolution, argued for separate work among women (though bitterly contesting the quite different separatism preached by bourgeois feminists). The articles excerpted here concisely summarise the pre-revolutionary experience of the Russian women's movement, as well as its problems in the immediate aftermath of October.

Bukharin and Preobrazhensky's *ABC of Communism*, written in 1919 at the height of the civil war, amongst other things was an early demarcation of the line between socialist and communist parties, arising out of the disintegration of the Second International and the triumphant rise of the Third. It could not have been written two years earlier, but, with only slight modifications, could easily have appeared at almost any time since. This is an instance of October shaping the politics of the twentieth century. More fundamentally, perhaps, October marked the end of deference, at least as a fundamental social principle. Henceforth no state and no ruling class anywhere in the world has been able to count on the social resignation of the underprivileged. Since 1917 there has permanently existed in human society the mass psychology, the theory and the practice of revolution.

Year of Two Revolutions

MARK JONES

In the autumn of 1916 the Allied cause began to founder in the mayhem of the trenches. In October, 620,000 British and French casualties were lost in a futile offensive on the Somme which put paid to hopes of early victory, and brought popular discontent in France. In Britain rising food prices and a strike wave in the arms industries followed the shock of the Easter Rising, which was crushed only after five days of bloody fighting in Dublin. But in the East a disaster altogether different in magnitude seemed about to overwhelm the Russian Empire.

The Allies had been saved that summer by the sacrificial gallantry of General Brusilov's great offensive in Galicia, the preparations for which had strained the Russian army and war industries to the uttermost. The appalling losses sustained in that struggle destroyed the Russian ability to fight on. As chaos deepened in the rear and on the fronts, the Empire slithered towards a defeat which threatened to destroy Tsarism.

The British and French, desperately worried about their Eastern ally, found scant reassurance in the behaviour of an obscurantist court. ('Am I to regain the confidence of the people or are they to regain my confidence?' Tsar Nicholas asked Sir George Buchanan, the British Ambassador, when the latter suggested confidence was a problem). As unrest in the capital grew, even Alexander Guchkov, the right-wing leader in the Duma,[1] began to discuss the alternatives: better a palace coup than an elemental upsurge on the streets of Petrograd which might destroy the government and finish off the army. When the Allies began to encourage the constitutional schemes of highly-placed reformers like Pavel Miliukov, the Cadet[2] leader in the Duma, it seemed the fate of the Romanovs was sealed.

War was to be the midwife of a revolution which the allies hoped to prevent by pushing the country in the direction of constitutional reform. But the causes of the revolution lay elsewhere, in a society riven with contradictions which were nowhere more apparent than in the capital city itself. Petrograd, situated on the western seaboard of an immense Empire, was unlike any other Russian city. Founded in 1703 to be Peter the Great's 'window on the West', the city was built on malarial marshes, but had served its purpose, and in 1917 its population of 2,400,000 made it the fifth largest in Europe. With its great canals and broad River Neva, spanned by graceful bridges, it was also one of the most beautiful. Peter had made it the focus of Russian culture, as well as the seat of government. Petrograd's straight avenues and magnificent stone buildings contrasted with the disorderly wooden buildings more usual in Russian towns. Aristocratic palaces neighboured huge barracks like the Peter-Paul Fortress (home of the Tsar's secret police, the Okhrana) and administrative complexes like the Admiralty. The city's broad central squares housed the fine mansions of the nation's bourgeoisie.

Petrograd's capitalists had connections throughout the national economy. Their fabulous wealth, which supported the capital's theatres, orchestras and its famous ballet, came from the metallurgical and coal industries of the south, from the Baku oilfields which supplied half the country's oil, from Siberian gold, Ukrainian sugar, Volga shipping, and from the vast cotton production of Central Asia. Petrograd's private banks held three-quarters of all Russia's capital. This concentration of wealth and power made what was still a raw, youthful city – the birthplace of Bolshevism – a magnet which sucked in labour from every corner of the Empire.

Finance poured in from France and Britain, fusing with Russian private capital and with the gigantic resources of the state. Giant enterprises sprang up; the decade before the war saw the creation of electro-technical, engine-building, precision machine, marine engineering and chemical industries. The mass-production of armaments and vehicles was beginning. The huge Putilov arms factory, employing 30,000, and the Nevsky shipyard (6,000) were both state-controlled but privately-owned. Plants like these made Petrograd an island of technological sophistication in the sea of Russian backwardness; their scale and modernity had no parallel except in Germany and in the heavy industry of northern Italy. Working conditions were often appalling. So great was the risk of explosion in one of the most modern Artillery Administration plants that the factory director always crossed himself and muttered a prayer before entering the factory; but shop stewards in Tsarist industry could do little to help matters: the law confined them to such duties as refilling the factory icon-lamps.

The new industries were mostly arms-related. The capital city had undergone a forced, lop-sided development which would make it vulnerable to the social and economic crisis of the war-years. This arms-economy straddled a city whose traditional occupations drew on settled relations with the countryside, rather than the capital and commodity markets of the West. More than half the workforce were peasant recruits or marginalised women, deepening the poverty and squalor of the capital's proletariat. Industrially-advanced Petrograd was in some respects still in the eighteenth century – a 'ruralised town' lacking urban amenities. Tsarism muffled but did not defuse the explosive contradictions which resulted. The peasant tradition of anarchic violence and brawling was sustained in the new urban environment.

Driven in to the capital by land scarcity, debts and poverty, the new arrivals replenished a populace ravaged by epidemic diseases. In the poorer quarters houses which lacked running water stood in cesspools, and the unlit streets were quagmires in winter. The chairman of Vyborg Duma sanitation committee said the overcrowded residents had less space than those buried in a nearby cemetery.

Petrograd's heavy industry was the foundry in which the industrialised Russia of the future was being forged. The Bolsheviks strove, with some success, to cultivate in the city's 400,000 industrial workers a sense of their future social importance. Contemporary diarists record watching these grim-faced, grimy men and women pouring in their thousands from the factories at the end of the shift. Many had a strong desire for self-improvement, and after the working day they went to improvised schools, to learn or pass on basic literacy, hygiene and domestic economy. Voluntary teachers, often Bolsheviks with a burning commitment to 'the emancipation of labour', risked prison to teach them about Russian history, or about atheism, or how to organise. A Petrograd worker said: 'We will not learn from any but ourselves. We, the conscious working people, have no right to be like the bourgeois.' In the years of underground struggle they had created a labour movement quite unlike that in the West, one imbued with a sharp revolutionary spirit.

The war sharpened all the contradictions besetting Russian society. Those who bore its burdens had no say in the decision to fight Germany. The government's own policy created fertile grounds for subversion. Trade union activists and Bolshevik agitators were among the first to be conscripted and sent to the front – where they carried on their organisational work among the peasant-soldiers instead. Meanwhile soldiers and sailors drafted into the great factories on the Vyborg Side soon made common cause with the workers of this traditional Bolshevik stronghold.

Nicholas ignored the ferment seething in the lower depths. Alone among his brother-monarchs, the Tsar led his armies into battle. This quixotry was not rewarded with military success. Nicholas blamed his people: five million soldiers had been killed or wounded, but almost a million more had deserted (often sacking country manors on the way home). People had not conducted themselves in the old way; Russia stumbled to defeat, the secret police were increasingly all Tsardom could rely on.

The Tsar had abandoned the government to his wife, the Empress Alexandra. Disliked equally by the middle classes and by the capital's burgeoning industrial proletariat, and isolated from the country, she ruled with the advice of Grigory Rasputin and the aid of a ouija-board. Miliukov accused the Empress of high treason in a speech in November 1916, and a few weeks later Rasputin was murdered – by a monarchist hoping to save the Romanovs from themselves.

The war had cut down the flower of Russian manhood, and ravaged the economy. There was chaos on the railways, resulting in food shortages in the cities and industrial decline. The loss to Germany of Poland's industrial and coal-producing regions aggravated the difficulties.³ This had especially serious effects on Petrograd's heavy industry, which was internationally-oriented and dependent on the flow of foreign capital, parts, machinery and technology. The great arms factories had already been hit as war industries in the West diverted their production elsewhere, and by the loss of land routes. Germany's successful deployment of submarines made the supply situation much worse. The crisis in Petrograd's industry deepened. Desperate to import armaments, the government was unable even to find means of payment and was reduced to paying debts literally in blood, by exporting soldiers to France to fight on the western front.

The collapse of manufacturing industry meant a shortage of goods for the home market, causing a further worsening in the supply of food to the cities, as peasants withheld their produce (since there was nothing to buy in exchange). The absence of the 15 million peasants conscripted to the army had already resulted in agricultural production falling by a fifth. The countryside was sliding back into pre-commodity production, as the towns started to fill with starving unemployed.

All this was a far cry from the heady days in August 1914, when the crowds in the capital had fallen to their knees to greet the Tsar, and the endless columns of peasant conscripts had hailed their 'Little Father' as they left for the fronts. The war, hated by the workers and the soldier-masses squatting half-starved in verminous trenches, became unpopular with the employers. They had seen industrial production grow by three-quarters in the decade before the war, and in the heavy industries by nearly half during the war itself. But its prolongation now spelt crisis and ruin from which only the speculators associated with the court could gain.

As the Court's inanition deepened and turmoil grew in the cities, a trickle of exiled revolutionaries made their way back to the capital; Alexander Shlyapnikov, Peter Zalutski and Vyacheslav Molotov arrived and set up an underground Russian Bureau of the Bolshevik Central Committee. In his memoirs, Shlyapnikov left a remarkable record of the mood in the capital at the time:

By the end of 1916 the idea of 'war to the end', to 'the final victory', was largely undermined. Anti-war feelings were rampant ... Despair and hatred gripped the labouring masses ... The government ... stepped up their repressive methods of fighting isolated manifestations of protest. Intensive agitation was conducted against us in the press and through the Voluntary Organisations. Every canard was employed: we were accused of being German agents, provocateurs, bribe-takers. But no slander could halt the workers' movement; just like all the ploys of the bourgeoisie, the proletariat could not be aroused to fight ...⁴

Shlyapnikov spent months in hiding, never sleeping more than a single night under the same roof. The Russian Bureau raced to rebuild the party apparatus while the mounting fury of the Vyborg and the capital's other great proletarian bastions threatened to spill into the streets at any moment. Savage new strikes began in the autumn of 1916 as workers began to link their demands for food supplies, and for wages to match rampant inflation, with opposition to the war. On 17 October they marched to the Finland Station singing the (illegal) *Marseillaise*, and were joined by soldiers from the 181st Infantry Regiment as the strike spread to the huge Kronstadt naval base.

Hoarding, speculation and rocketing prices fuelled popular anger (potatoes, bread, sausages and milk rose five times in price during the war). In savage cartoons and satire,[5] the busy underground press portrayed greedy courtiers profiting from hunger and despair. As the crisis deepened, short-time working caused by lack of fuel and raw materials, and industrial bankruptcy, brought 1916 wages below starvation levels. By the New Year of 1917 the capital was on the point of explosion.

Petrograd was on a northerly latitude, and it was hardly the season for rioting. Winter clamped an Arctic darkness on the town 19 hours in 24. Trams groaned through biting fogs, and the capital's deserted streets were rivetted with ice. But in the winter of 1917, as the fuel ran out, the citizenry emerged in their tens of thousands to stamp their anger on the capital's broad squares. A strike movement of unparalleled ferocity exploded in Petrograd, and the Romanov dynasty shook to its foundations.

On 9 January 1917, 300,000 demonstrated on the anniversary of Bloody Sunday.[6] In February 30,000 workers at the giant Putilov arms factory went on strike. Police reports plotted the public's growing anger. There were rumours of a palace coup in the offing, and a few days later Miliukov's Progressive Bloc called for a government of national confidence (Nicholas would respond by dissolving the Duma). But still nobody expected a revolution. In the streets cold and hungry women queued for bread. Contemporary reports testify to the feverish atmosphere of the time, as even normally-acquiescent office workers complained about food shortages and the manifold difficulties of everyday life. Warehouses were looted, and the disorders on the Vyborg Side grew in scale. There, the wives of the locked-out Putilov workers had taken to the streets along with the *soldatki* – war-wives and widows, who were treated with contempt by the government. Turning the stagnant bread queues into demonstrations, they improvised placards which read 'Down with the War!', 'Our Children Are Starving!' or simply 'Bread!'

On 22 February tens of thousands of these women surged across the Neva bridges and into the city centre. They were joined by women workers from the Vasilievski Island tramway terminus, who pounded on the huge wooden doors of the 180th regiment's barracks, calling on the soldiers not to shoot them down in the streets. The proletarian bastion of the Vyborg was seething, as women workers in their thousands came pouring from the great textile mills, taking up the cry of 'Bread!'

But when Kayurov, a Bolshevik Central Committee member, was asked by a group of women textile workers for advice on how to mark International Women's Day (23 February, old-style)[7] he urged them to avoid striking. Kayurov and Shlyapnikov feared the response of Russia's inscrutable peasantry to an attack on Tsardom in wartime and were more cautious than the Duma politicians who sought only a change of monarch, not the overthrow of the Romanov dynasty. With numberless troops at the fronts and – also waiting on events – 300,000 in the Petrograd region alone, the regime did not look broken.

Kayurov's instructions were ignored (in any case, the police had suppressed the party press) and the mass demonstrations traditionally marking International Women's Day launched the four-day February Revolution. Women textile workers came pouring out of factories like the Bolshaya Sampsionevskaya. They threw snowballs through the windows of neighbouring works, calling on those inside to join them. Already the police estimated 197,000 were on strike (more than half the industrial workforce).

Then on Friday 24 February the movement erupted over Petrograd. Nevsky Prospekt and the adjoining squares filled with workers. Mounted Cossacks armed with *nagaykas* (rawhide whips) arrived, but contemporary accounts speak of their unusual tolerance; when voices from the crowds shouted 'if you want to destroy the revolution, shoot me first!' they were answered 'We do not shoot our brothers.' Significantly, one of the few 'Cossack excesses' reported was when a trooper slashed the hand off a mounted police inspector who had threatened the demonstrators.

Next day workers in 13 columns penetrated to the city centre. The Russian Bureau decided to engage the support of the soldiers, but the Bolsheviks were running behind events; the garrison revolt had already begun. During the morning workers, students, party activists and delegates made their way through streets littered with torn-down proclamations, to begin a great round of mass meetings, party caucuses and conferences of workers' movement organisations. At a meeting of Duma representatives, trade unions and cooperative societies, F.A.Cherevanin, an old Menshevik, proposed calling elections in the Petrograde factories for a 'Soviet' ('Council') of workers' deputies. Ever-larger crowds filled the streets, the police were unable to disperse the unauthorised meetings, and Cossacks were fraternising. Petrograd was in turmoil. The spontaneous strike movement had paralysed the city. The police vanished from their posts. The factories stopped, then the trams. Troops cordoned off the streets but the crowds sallied through anyway. The city centre was now one continuous mass meeting. News reels of the day conjure up the scene, as tens of thousands of people swirled around Znamensky Square, where socialists denounced the war from the statue of Alexander III. Troops and Cossacks in great numbers, many on horseback, pushed slowly through the crowds, without interfering in any way, except for occasionally removing red banners. Many among the garrison had wives and friends in the crowds; others were wounded veterans of the front, or militant workers conscripted as a punishment.

The troops were increasingly unwilling to crush the revolt. Police reports grew more alarmist. Nicholas, in his headquarters at Mogilev, heard of the latest disturbances from the Empress at Tsarskoe Selo, and her news contrasted starkly with the bland optimism of the city governor.

The Tsar cabled to 'put an end, as from tomorrow, to all disturbances in the streets of the capital'. A warning was issued to the population that troops would shoot to kill, and promising to send strikers (most of the populace) to the front. The proclamation was simply scattered in the streets during the night; the government had run out of glue to paste it up.

On the evening of 25 February a special counter-insurgency unit opened fire on demonstrators in Kazansky Square; but this was seen as an act of desperation by the authorities, not firmness, and incensed the people still more. Fights began, bloody encounters often in back-to-backs, in the muddy, dank, ill-lit alleys of the Vyborg, where small groups of workers fought off marauding policemen, answering pistol-shots with volleys of half-bricks, cobbles, lumps of ice. Tramcars were overturned and telegraph poles knocked down for barricades.

On Sunday, 26 February, with the city now an armed camp, the Red Cross set up a headquarters. The Bolshevik 'Petersburg Committee' was arrested along with many other revolutionary leaders. More than ever, the revolution was to be the work of the people alone. It seemed that the government was belatedly taking decisive action. The crackle of small-arms fire echoed round the city. Working-class suburbs were sealed off, factories besieged, the bridges over the canals cordoned off. At one o'clock Nevsky Prospekt was swept with rifle fire. The police hastily cleared away dozens of bullet-riddled bodies.

The streets emptied. By 5 o'clock the city governor concluded that, as on other occasions, the display of exemplary force had quelled the 'disorders'. But as night fell people began to tear the Romanov's double-headed eagle from walls and railings. Next day, soldiers surrendered en masse to the crowds. Workers collected up their weapons and took them to their factories.

Women left the bread queues, buttonholing soldiers in friendly argument. When agitators spoke to the cheerful Grenadiers guarding the Peter-Paul their officers simply turned away in disgust. It was clear that the garrison was dissolving; for all its strength on paper, the absolutist state was crumbling. Incidents occurred which represented a fundamental escalation of the disturbances. A detachment of mounted police, ordered to disperse a crowd by the Catherine Canal, fired on it from the opposite bank. Answering fire came from soldiers of the Pavlovsky Regiment passing through the crowd. This episode, a detail in the huge scale of events, had important repercussions.

Mutineers had hitherto only passively resisted their officers. Opening fire on other units committed them to the outcome of the rising. Since its suppression would mean summary execution for participants, mutineers now had nothing to lose, and no reason not to crush the regime. Exchanges of fire between mutineers and loyal troops represented an equivalent raising of the stakes for the garrison command and the government. They, too, were committed by events to the maximum use of force to crush the rising and began to rush reinforcements from the front.

The die was also cast for the vacillating businessmen, bankers and liberals locked in debate in the Duma. News of what seemed the onset of civil war brought an immediate halt to the talk of forcing 'minor concessions' from Nicholas. It was no longer possible to use events in the capital as a pretext for imposing constitutional reform on the monarchy. If, after all, the rising should still be crushed, then anyone, even respectable Duma deputies, who had sought to profit from the actions of mutineers, would be at risk of losing their own lives or liberty. Faced with a full-scale revolution, the Duma men had to decide – either denounce the insurgents and affirm their oath of allegiance, or reject the Tsar, and try to place themselves at the head of the revolution. In practice, the bourgeois politicians had little choice but to repudiate Nicholas,[8] although this scarcely meant an end to public vacillation and private intrigue by the democrats of the Duma.

The climax approached. Crowds returned to the streets in greater numbers than before. Mutineers shot Colonel Ecksten, commander of the Pavlovsky Regiment, in the street by the barracks. Next day, 27 February, the whole garrison rose up; they had been ordered to 'shoot to kill'. The revolt began in the special training unit of the Volynski Guards, whose members had opened fire on the crowds the previous day. Two sergeants shot the regimental commander from a barracks window, then ran round neighbouring barracks to win support. Officers were shot, and the rebellion grew.[9]

By now the factories were deserted for the streets, where workers lynched any policemen they came across. The arsenal was captured, and city prisons emptied of political and common criminals. The Bicycle Battalion resisted for a day, was crushed and its officers shot. On the morning of 27 February, there were 10,200 rebel soldiers. Their numbers grew until by 1 March 170,000 out of 180,200 troops in the city had joined the insurrection.

The crowds who invaded the city centre that decisive Monday, 27 February, were no longer content passively to demonstrate their disaffection by holding mass meetings. Mutineers pressed down to the Tauride Palace to make their demands on the Duma. A torrent of red banners poured down the Sadovaya and Nevsky Prospekts and into the palace square. Marching behind their regimental colours, without an officer in sight, the garrison soldiers were cheered on by the watching multitude. Troops passing down Liteiny Prospekt released from the Kresty prison some right-wing Mensheviks jailed on 14 February after calling for a representative government.

These middle-class socialists, who later fiercely resisted the call for 'All power to the Soviet', now were most active in setting it up. They saw it as a little more than a glorified strike committee, as it had been in the 1905 revolution.

Nor did they suppose it would play more than a temporary role, serving to restrain the forces unleashed in the rising until a bourgeois government could be installed and a constitutional democracy inaugurated (Marxism decreed that only the bourgeoisie was fitted to rule during Russia's impending capitalist epoch).

But the reflexive dogma which informed Menshevik actions in February was falsified from the start. They were surprised to discover that the crisis of authority extended into the Duma, which they had confidently expected would create the new government. Even the Progressive Bloc liberals were frightened by the mass eruption onto the streets of the capital. From day one, much against their will, the parliamentary socialists were face to face with the problem of power.

Fearing that mass anger might at any moment turn on them, the Duma men had begun to repent of their attacks on the monarchy. While the crowds invaded the Tauride's left wing (appropriately enough) to begin their noisy deliberations, the Duma deputies were meeting in their quiet offices in its right wing. They did not reach any conclusions. Nothing in their experience had prepared them for this moment.

The Tauride's left wing soon became the centre of a vortex which seemed to draw in the entire population of the capital. Contemporary reports describe the frenzy inside its Catherine Hall, resembling a village assembly when the tillers redivided the communal land. Amidst the din of a yelling mob, small knots of people wrangled and argued: the capital's writers, intellectuals, fugitive revolutionaries, working-class agitators, trade unionists and officials from the flourishing cooperative movement, who had come to the Tauride as much to find out what was going on as to contribute.

The begetters of the Soviet faced tasks on which the immediate fate of the rising depended. They were besieged by tens of thousands of people, with new columns of soldiers marching down Shpalernaya and Basseinaya to offer support. They had no idea what counter-measures the government might take, or how to react to them. The leaders of the workers' and peasants' parties had no time even to ask the question, 'To whom shall go the power?' (Shlyapnikov, the Bolshevik leader, refused to discuss questions of such import in the absence of the exiled party leaders). The spontaneous nature of the revolution meant there were no plans for life after it. There were no arrangements even to secure the building where the Soviet was to meet; meanwhile the Treasury, posts and telegraphs, the High Command, even the Secret Police were still in the hands of Tsarist functionaries.

The arrest of the government had to be organised. The railway network serving the city had to be secured against the deployment of counter-revolutionary troops from the front. Fires raged unchecked and a huge column of smoke rose over the city where the notorious Litovsky prison had been burned down. The revolution would inherit hunger, and this was not a matter of long-term policy, but of finding grain for the next three days; the collapse of food distribution was a primary cause of the rising. In the streets the endless crowd, leavened with tens of thousands of cold, hungry and now homeless mutineers moved and stirred in a thickening February afternoon.

By noon the assembly in the Catherine Hall, with its embryo cliques and caucuses, had somehow formed a committee to convoke the Soviet; messengers were sent to the factories and barracks, and within five hours working-class Petrograd began electing its first delegates: one per 1,000 workers, and one for each company of soldiers or sailors. The Petrograd Soviet of Workers' Deputies – 'Petrosoviet' as it was dubbed – was struggling into life.

As evening came the crowds surrounding the Tauride impatiently awaited the opening of the first session. Pressing through the enormous thronged ante-chamber and into the Catherine Hall, still (according to Nikolai Sukhanov, the great Menshevik chronicler of the revolution) clad in their furs, proletarian caps and army greatcoats, many bearing arms, the delegates began to arrive, waving their credentials and with loud, cheery voices, demanding to 'report to the Soviet'. Meanwhile in the right wing of the palace, a rump of the Duma elected a 'Provisional Committee', headed by Mikhail Rodzianko (1859–1923), a Tsarist statesman and large landowner, who still hoped to save the monarchy despite itself.

Rodzianko insisted on a Provisional 'Committee' rather than fully-fledged government. He considered that for the Duma to form a government would be in breach of his oath of allegiance to the Tsar. Miliukov rejected this idea for the opposite reason. He did not consider that the Duma could form a Provisional Government acceptable to the nation; it 'was clamped in a vice by the prerogatives of autocratic power ... what part could such an institution play in the new situation?' This was the beginning of the bourgeois revolution. Rodzianko spent the afternoon of 27 February closeted in his study in the right wing of the Tauride, trying to arrange secret negotiations with Grand Duke Michael, whom he hoped would become a constitutional monarch after Nicholas's abdication. Nothing came of this; public opinion resolutely opposed it, as did Nicholas, who was suspicious of his brother (the latter had entered a morganatic marriage).

Rodzianko telegraphed the front commanders to ask their support, and his messages to the generals show the apprehension of the Duma men. To Alekseev, the Chief of Staff, he wired about 'the most fearsome of revolutions'. The people, he said, 'are murdering their officers ... I fear the same fate may overtake me'. To General Ruszky, who was gathering forces to crush the rising, Rodzianko said 'My heart bleeds at the sight of what is happening', and implored him to 'stop sending troops – they will not take action against the people. Prevent unnecessary bloodshed.'

Hoping to gain control of the army, the Provisional Committee established a Military Commission. In the days which followed the February Revolution, the Military Commission won the allegiance of many officers. But among the millions of trench and garrison soldiers a process had begun which eventually destroyed not only the Military Commission, but the Provisional Government itself and the bourgeois world on which it rested.

The furnace of revolt had forged its own weapon: the Soviet. At 9 p.m. the first session of the Petrosoviet was called to order, but before the chairman, Skobelev, could even get a Credentials Committee elected, the floor was taken by the first of many soldier delegates, amid riotous cheering and foot-stamping. A stream of delegates from the Volhynian Regiment, the Pavlovsky, the Lithuanian, the Keksholm and other ancient and battle-honoured regiments which had now made a revolution – told the same story, of officers in hiding and of illegal mass meetings where the soldiers voted never again to fight for the Tsar or oppress the people. Sukhanov describes how a simple private with the raw, bony hands of a peasant, stood on a chair and announced:

> We had a meeting, and the lads told me to say that we are joining the Soviet and refuse to serve against the people any more – that we're joining with our brother workers, all together, to defend the people's cause, and we'll die for it if need be![10]

As all these disconnected episodes of revolt and mutiny came together the realisation grew that Tsarism had been destroyed: there could be no going back. It was decided to issue proclamations to the capital and the provinces, and the meeting turned to detailed matters, but the interruptions did not cease, as new soldier-delegates from time to time burst in and told of yet more regiments adhering to the Soviet: the Semyonovsky (which in 1905 had won notoriety in the bloody suppression of the Moscow rising), the Cossacks, the machine-gun regiments, an armoured division – all traditional enemies of the people.

While the Soviet continued its noisy deliberations, outside the Catherine Hall a good-natured pandemonium reigned. Thousands of people swirled in and around the great palace. Groups of ragged workers were locked in fierce debate in the rooms and galleries; women organised tea and bread for the milling soldiery, and peasants in army greatcoats thrust their way through carrying enormous sacks of flour and meal, or dried herrings, or ammunition cases and weaponry, which they dumped unceremoniously in huge piles on the muddy marble floors. Beside the entrance stood two duty guards. Bewildered and frightened, they were the last sentries of the old regime, and no one had told them to go off duty.

Outside, new groups of workers struggled across the frozen Neva to the Tauride. Contemporary accounts vividly describe the scene as armoured cars with red flags roared in and out of the palace yard and shadowy groups of Red Guards and soldiers huddled around braziers, standing guard over their revolution.[11]

Information scarcely existed about events at the front or in Moscow or the provinces. In its death-throes the old order still kicked. The Black Hundred death squads were unleashed. *Provokatsy* shot at passers-by from high windows; there were assaults on women, the burning of Jewish premises, a wave of looting began. The electricity supply grew erratic. To restore order, the Soviet adopted delegate Braunstein's suggestion that 'Commissars' (the first time the word was used) be appointed in the districts. A Supply Commission was elected, and left at once to find offices and start work. Its first head, A.V. Peshokhonov, heard of a large food depot still held by Tsarist authorities and sent two guards to take it over. (Next day a huge crowd gathered, began arguing with the sentries, then broke into the depot. Loading the food onto commandeered lorries, they took it down to the Food Commissariat, where everything was triumphantly handed over to Peshokhonov.)

The Secret Police was destroyed by the people. Sukhanov relates a dramatic episode, when Shcheglovitov, the feared police minister and sponsor of the Black Hundreds, was arrested by a student who persuaded a group of soldiers to help him. They took him amidst angry crowds to the Catherine Hall where they were met by Kerensky, who, hoping to prevent a lynching, said: 'Mr Shcheglovitov, I arrest you in the name of the people!' Less tactfully, Rodzianko pushed through and said to Shcheglovitov with a smile, 'Ivan Grigorievich, do please enter my office!' But the student protested and Shcheglovitov was led away.[12]

Armed resistance to the revolution ended with the surrender of the besieged Admiralty (the garrison commander thought the building – a fine piece of architecture – should be preserved). The Council of Ministers cabled its resignation to Nicholas. The end had come.

Almost overnight, the vast edifice of Tsardom had vanished. Later, the Soviet announced that nearly 2,000 had died in the rising, about half of them workers; more than 100 officers were killed by their men, including the Admiral of the Black Sea Fleet. Nicholas II, soon a virtual prisoner of his own elite troops in Mogilev, abdicated 20 minutes before midnight on 2 March. 'All around me', he told his diary, 'treason, cowardice and deceit.'[13] He exchanged heart-rending messages with the Empress, who was preoccupied with tending the royal children (they were ill with measles).

The question of power, raised by the fall of the autocracy and seemingly neglected by those at the epicentre of revolution, loomed much larger to observers at a distance. As news of events in Petrograd seeped out, US President Woodrow Wilson was quick to welcome the Revolution. He thought it would mean the displacement of a barren autocracy by Western-style democracy. In his declaration of war on Germany, made weeks after the fall of the Tsar, Wilson was to mention of 'the wonderful and heartening things that have been happening in the last few weeks in Russia'.[14]

In Switzerland, Lenin, the exiled Bolshevik leader, observed the formation of the Provisional Government, scantily reported though it was, with different feelings. When Alexandra Kollontai wrote from Stockholm for advice (she was on the point of returning to Petrograd), Lenin could only reply:

Fancy asking for 'directives' from here, where we're completely in the dark! All the leading Party comrades are in Peter [Petrograd] now ... A week of bloody workers' battles, and Miliukov, Guchkov and Kerensky are in power! Well, so be it. This 'first stage of the revolution', born of the war, will not be the last ...[15]

The February Revolution had come as a complete surprise to the revolutionary diaspora. One evening Lenin had given a lecture to a youth meeting at the Zurich People's Hall. Subject: the 1905 revolution. Many in the audience were war-resisters from France and Germany. Lenin wanted to explain what a revolution feels like. The coming European revolution would be both proletarian and socialist: 'Only stern battles, only civil wars, can free humanity from the yoke of capital',[16] Lenin had said. And it would be class-conscious workers who would come forth to lead the masses in titanic struggles.

But he could not say when these events might begin: 'We of the older generation may not live to see the coming decisive battles.' That was on 22 January – just six weeks before the revolution. Yet Lenin was in constant touch with events. Letters were sent to Berne from all over Russia.

Lenin's *Letters From Afar*, sent to *Pravda* (now openly published in Petrograd) were the first evidence of Lenin's uncanny anticipation of the problems thrown up by the revolution. He discussed the nuts and bolts of a socialist state – the possibility of which still seemed not merely remote, but completely unreal, to the Bolsheviks in Petrograd.

What, for instance, would be the role of the future proletarian militia? The police had disappeared overnight after the February Revolution (and were never replaced). Lenin wanted a general arming of the citizens, with a workers' militia not only keeping order but distributing bread and acting as *sanitarki*, (lay health workers), to see that every family was provisioned and 'each child given a bottle of good milk', rich and poor alike. And the militia would ensure that the palaces of the rich were not left unoccupied while the poor were destitute.

'Who can carry out these measures except a people's militia, to which women must belong equally with men?[17] he wrote. And then, while arguing about whether militiamen delivering infants' milk was 'socialism' or not, Lenin characteristically struck at the question which was to dog the Russian revolution: was the bourgeois revolution (which had now happened) the beginning of a capitalist era, as traditional Marxist theory seemed to suggest? Or could the proletarian revolution follow, in an unbroken process? Lenin said:

It is not a matter of finding a theoretical classification. We would be committing a great mistake if we attempted to force the complex, urgent, rapidly unfolding tasks of the revolution into the procrustean bed of a narrowly conceived 'theory', instead of regarding theory first of all and above all as a guide to action.[18]

And he went on to reject the theory of revolutionary 'stages', which said the socialist parties would be no more than the legal opposition during a prolonged period of capitalist development. There was no reason why the bourgeois should not be followed immediately by the proletarian revolution. The institution of the Soviet – a spontaneous creation of the working class – was the harbinger of the workers' state: therefore the Bolshevik slogan should be 'All Power to the Soviet!' Lenin's *Letters From Afar* were mostly published posthumously – his cautious Petrograd comrades decided Vladimir Ilyich had gone mad. But the questions he raised in them were to prove central to the Bolshevik rising, and Lenin would refer to them again and again, particularly in *State and Revolution*.

Could a backward country like Russia build socialism in isolation? This, too, was a key question if world revolution should turn out to be a chimera. At this stage, at any rate – when the main thing was somehow to get back to Russia – (from where Lenin had been absent for 15 years) Lenin allowed no room for doubt. World capitalism had entered a period of dramatic crisis. The struggle, the horrors, misery, ruin and brutalisation caused by the imperialist war had opened an era of proletarian socialist revolution.

And the Russian proletariat had led the way. To talk of confining the tasks of revolutionaries to being the midwives of Russian capitalism stood history on its head, and ignored everything that was happening in the world outside. 'Imperialist war is the eve of socialist revolution', Lenin said.

Judge for yourselves, can the war continue, can the capitalist domination continue on earth, if the Russian people, always sustained by the living memories of the great Revolution of 1905, win complete freedom and transfer all political power to the Soviets of Workers' and Peasants' Deputies?[19]

Soon, Lenin's call to arms would ring out in Russia itself:

We are out to rebuild the world. We are out to put an end to the imperialist world war into which hundreds of millions of people have been drawn and in which the interests of billions and billions of capital are involved, a war which cannot end in a truly democratic peace without the greatest proletarian revolution in the history of mankind.[20]

Petrograd was drunk on revolution. In the icy depths of March a holiday was declared, and Nevsky Prospekt flowed with banners and bunting, blood-red against the snow. Workers scrambling on perilous roof-tops decanted the symbols of Tsarism into the streets below. One morning deputies arriving for a session of the Soviet watched two soldiers climb on the platform and take their bayonets to Repin's portrait of Tsar Nicholas. The great gilt frame would gape down on the Catherine Hall until October. Outside, groups of armed workers, soldiers and sailors stood by cheery braziers on the corners of streets, watching for Black Hundreds and greeting with loud 'Hurrahs!' new detachments marching under their red banners. It seemed that nothing could break the revolution. An elemental force had been freed, its energy surprising no one more than the insurrectionists.

Telegraphed across the country, the February Revolution everywhere led to a joyous outburst. From sleepy provincial towns and great river ports, from arid steppes and the fertile Ukraine, and from the regions of ice and the fiery deserts, came a tumult of greetings to the 'fighters of the capital', support for the Soviet 'to the last breath', and ardent requests not to give up until the last relics of Tsardom were swept away. Soon delegates from local soviets (which sprang up overnight in every city and village, and throughout the war fronts) began arriving in Petrograd. To cater for this flood of visitors, the Soviet plenum (now in continuous session) was moved from the cramped Tauride to the huge White Hall. Everything had to be improvised. Since there were no typists, secretaries or printers, no telecommunications or transport, and no support staff of any kind, the newly-elected officers had to go out into the blistering cold and agitate among soldiers and workers to carry out whatever had just been decided. Cajoling troops to guard premises, printers to publish *Izvestia* (the Soviet's newspaper), catering workers to organise food, and a hundred and one other things, they began to create a fledgling bureaucracy.[21]

Petrograd's factories, barracks and suburbs were still electing their deputies. Men and women straight from the workplace were dazzled by the brilliant, fractious oratory of the Soviet, and bewildered by the tide of proclamations, pamphlets and newspapers which some were unable even to read. These makers of the new Russia were soon joined by the representatives of the professional classes – teachers, doctors, lawyers, radicalised officers, engineers and Zemstvo functionaries. In the electric atmosphere of the White Hall it seemed that each new deputy, worker or intellectual, peasant or soldier, arrived with some scheme for the future of Russia. Working for days on end in the vortex of the Soviet, snatching rest when they could, they were possessed by dreams which one by one became real or were broken, as the first weeks of freedom passed and the vast sweep of the revolution unfolded. Tsardom, buttressed by Church and Land (atavistic symbols of the national destiny), and by immense reserves of patronage and corruption, had seemed impregnable. Its fall opened glittering prospects for the middle classes. In speeches and articles liberals used their new freedom to speculate on the enticing vistas which had opened up. A coherent 'bourgeois programme' emerged, one from which it seemed all Russia's social classes and national minorities could hope to gain. The destruction of the pro-German court, which cleared the way for the installation of a popular government, could lead the country to victory.

Then, strong and free, the new republic would end the war consolidated within the boundaries of the old Empire, perhaps even extending them at the expense of the Central Powers. A parliamentary democracy, uniting the social classes and national minorities, and freeing business from the petty tutelage of the autocracy, might (they dreamed) usher in a golden age of prosperity and progress for Russia. Political and business leaders were quick to try to use the Soviet to further these ends.

In the mood of national joy after February, it was possible to ignore the underlying social divisions. The war was a fount of unity and only the 'bourgeois programme' offered a chance of avoiding ruinous defeat. As yet no political force existed which put forward a credible alternative. Even the Bolsheviks were caught in the undertow of 'conciliationism', the Menshevik goal of a 'sacred union' in the interests of victory and the postwar consolidation of capitalism.

The most probable outcome to the war was the victory of the Allies. This would consolidate the supremacy of the leading capitalist powers, ruling out the transition to socialism, to the dreamed-of 'world revolution'. Postwar Russia would be capitalist, its constitution thrown round property like a rampart. The land would not go to the tiller. Production would not be socialised. Menshevik arguments that this was, in any case, in line with the Marxist theory of 'revolutionary stages', seemed unanswerable, Lenin's notion of transition to a communist utopia, incomprehensible. The consensus around the 'bourgeois programme' was immensely strong. Cadets who had been pre-eminent in the Tsar's Duma found political bed-fellows among Socialists who still had Tsarist arrest-warrants outstanding. Even Plekhanov, the founding father of Russian Marxism, supported the 'bourgeois programme'. There might be disagreement about war aims, but there could scarcely be argument about the fundamental issue of support for the war.

The self-confidence of the bourgeois revolution was manifest in Pavel Miliukov's Note to Russian ambassadors, announcing the government's 'determination to strictly observe the international obligations undertaken by the Old Regime and its will to fight the war to a victorious end' and adding that 'the exaltation which now moves the entire nation would increase its strength and would bring the final triumph of Russia and its glorious allies much closer.' The vision of 1789, moving but anachronistic, seemed to hover above the well-to-do revolutionists of the Tauride's right wing – the bankers, lawyers and industrialists in their sleek black cassocks and gleaming starched shirt-fronts.

They were helped by the fact that the first leaders of the Soviet would not have been revolutionaries in a parliamentary country. They had no programme for power, and were fatally trapped by their attitude to the war. Some amongst the delegation which negotiated the establishment of a Provisional Government were 'patriotic' socialists in favour of the war. This was particularly true of Alexander Kerensky, the Trudovik (Labour Party) leader destined to play a key role in the months ahead. Despised by Miliukov for his

Bonapartist pretensions, Kerensky argued that a separate peace with 'Butcher Wilhelm' would leave the country abandoned by the West, to be torn to pieces by the Germans. The leaders of a successful revolution thus felt themselves hopelessly trapped from the start. As Sukhanov said, they 'furled the banner of Zimmerwald' in order to create a propertied government. But, Sukhanov added, they were under 'a restraint and submission to circumstances which to the outsider's eye might look like a betrayal of their basic principles and be misunderstood by the masses they were leading'.[22] The bourgeois slogan of the day was 'A Ministry responsible to the Duma' – and the socialists agreed.

In his remote exile Lenin, on the other hand (like Molotov on the spot in Petrograd), was left in no doubt by the news of the revolution about the issues at stake. It was the moment of truth, not just for the autocracy, but for Russian capitalism itself. The flower of Russian manhood lay in bloody trenches. The Germans advanced and no one knew how to stop them. The countryside was sliding into chaos. How was bread to be brought to the hungry cities, without first reconstructing the rural economy? Lenin was to laugh such day-dreams to scorn: the best they would achieve was 'hunger organised with genius' – on the German model. Even that meant a peasantry ground under the heel of forced grain collections. Meanwhile, in the great industrial centres, where enslaving ignorance still chained millions to hopeless labour, the tribunes of the Soviet could only offer freedom in a fantasised future, in exchange for intensified exploitation in the present. All depended on a quick end to the war, but the Soviet Executive Committee would only 'call on' the government it now created, to 'renounce' a war of annexation, a meaningless demand since the only annexations going on were of Russian soil. They had no peace policy.

If this was the reality of the 'bourgeois programme', then for the Soviet to collude in it could only be, as Lenin said, 'a nonsense, a crying mockery'.

On 1 March, in the immediate aftermath of the fall of the Tsar, a delegation from the fledgling Soviet turned up in the right wing of the Tauride to negotiate the creation of the first bourgeois government. Miliukov received them in his elegant chambers. There, amongst handsome men of business and sleek officers, the exhausted members of the Soviet's Executive Committee, who had not eaten since the previous day, sipped tea and talked of Russia, while Miliukov's silent aides produced plates heaped with rich foodstuffs. After prolonged negotiations the Soviet delegation agreed to support a propertied government. As the Soviet's deferential deputies, whose lives had been a wasteland of police wanted lists, exile and prison, now (in Lenin's words) 'voluntarily surrendered the power', Miliukov said in an undertone: 'Yes, I was thinking as I listened to you, how far our working class movement has advanced since 1905.'[23]

Next day the Menshevik paper *Rabochaya Gazeta* said: 'Members of the Provisional Government, the proletariat and the army await your orders to consolidate the revolution and make Russia a democracy' ...

Miliukov's victory was easier because of the disarray in the Bolshevik camp.

Not until 27 February did the party begin to address the enormity of the event which had eclipsed Tsardom, and only on 5 March did Molotov bring out the first legal issue of *Pravda*, which sold 100,000 copies; it called the world war a 'civil war' between the capitalists of the belligerent countries. But this position was not sustained; the party was already moving towards the conciliation of the bourgeoisie preached by the Mensheviks.

Rodzianko's Provisional Committee anticipated the new government's struggle to restore traditional discipline in the armed forces by issuing a decree on its own behalf, scarcely before the dust had settled after the collapse of the autocracy. On 1 March an angry Soviet plenum listened as the wealthy lawyer Sokolov, a Bolshevik sympathiser, stood up and, surrounded by soldiers, read their reply. They had come straight from the Tauride's Room 13 where for an hour the lawyer sat taking notes while the soldiers spoke as they felt, without agenda or formalities. The result, which entered history as 'Order No.1', was published by *Izvestia* the next morning. It was a momentous event in the revolution. It destroyed the omnipotence of officers in the army and the spirit of servility they fostered. It was also the first nail in the coffin of Menshevik 'conciliationism'. Its eight points included the election of Army Committees, which would take control of weaponry and supervise the officers, and the election of deputies to the Soviets, which would exercise a final say in military policy. While on duty strict discipline would be observed, but off-duty soldiers would have the same rights as other citizens. Honorific titles like 'Your Excellency' were abolished and all coarse conduct by officers to men was forbidden – especially the demeaning use of the familiar 'thou'.

Order No.1 bound the mass of soldiery to the Soviet, but the initiative for it came from the people and from their directly expressed anger, rather than from any party's programme or manifesto. The order destroyed any chance of the Provisional Government asserting its authority over the army. This was confirmed in the days that followed, as the capital filled with tens of thousands of soldiers, who came pouring in along every road, and by every train. They had been sent from the front to crush the rising. Obediently they arrived, were met at the railway stations by garrison soldiers and workers, heard about Order No.1, and changed sides en masse.

On 6 March, the Soviet heard that Nicholas II was fleeing to England; the Provisional Government had negotiated with the British, and Kerensky decided to let him go. But the Soviet EC intervened, and the Tsar and his family were taken into 'protective custody' at Tsarskoye Selo. Later the British Government decided that because of 'strong feelings hostile to the Tsar in working-class circles, asylum was not possible'. The unwanted Romanovs remained in Russia.

But symbolic problems were easier to deal with than the fundamental crisis gripping the country. The bread queues were as long as ever, and in them disgruntled women (according to Sukhanov) said 'liberty-flibberty, it's all the same, there's nothing to be had. It's just the same, the rich keep on fleecing the poor. The shopkeepers are the only ones making money.'[24] A deputation of working-class women went to see the city governor to complain about high prices and food shortages; a huge crowd gathered in the street to hear him and his Menshevik deputy, Nkisky, explain the laws of economics. The crowd shouted about greedy shopkeepers and the meeting dispersed, no one satisfied. The bread ration was cut from 800 grammes to 500 grammes per day; in the countryside the peasants were spending more time settling accounts with landlords and moneylenders than providing food for the hungry cities. The Soviet EC established an 'Economic Department' to begin economic planning and regulation.

Despite the crisis of everyday life, the mood of national euphoria did not abate overnight, and the revolution continued to deepen. The great national upswelling continued without let-up. Every day hundreds of mass meetings took place as trade unions, cooperatives, clubs and women's societies were set up; soviets mushroomed everywhere. The newspapers were full of appeals, proclamations, announcements, dates of meetings and classes, invitations. The working-class parties frenziedly organised and propagandised, to the unconcealed dismay of the Provisional Government and the middle classes. Russia was, in Lenin's words, 'the freest land in Europe'.

Trench-soldiers bombarded the Soviet with requests and pleas for a solution to the land question, without waiting for a Constituent Assembly. Mostly they wanted to hear of peace talks. None of this was welcome to the Menshevik Executive Committee which was often absent from Soviet sessions on 'urgent business' – usually discussions with government ministers. But day by day the work of the Soviet broadened, taking on more and more of the tasks of the government its leaders did not wish it to become. It issued an appeal on the preservation of monuments and works of art, which Maxim Gorky penned:

> Citizens! The old rulers have gone, and a great heritage is left behind. Now it belongs to the whole people.
> Citizens, take care of this heritage, take care of the palaces – they will become palaces of your national art; take care of the pictures, the statues, the buildings – they are the embodiment of the spiritual power of yourselves and your forefathers.
> Art is the beauty which talented people were able to create even under despotic oppression, bearing witness to the strength and beauty of the human spirit.
> Citizens, do not touch one stone; preserve the monuments, the buildings, the old things, the documents – all this is your history, your pride ...

While soldiers and sailors acted on Order No.1, shaking out the Tsar's officer corps like moths from an old coat, the workers quickly smashed the 'absolutist' order in the great engineering works like the Aivaz, Baranovsky, Vulcan, New Lessner and the Phoenix, where the Bolsheviks were already entrenched.[25] Contracts of employment, rulebooks and black lists were torn up and police informers, bribe-takers and tyrannical managers expelled. At the Putilov the director and his aide were killed and their bodies flung in the Obvodny canal. Forty managers were thrown out in the first three days of freedom. In the engine-assembly shop, Puzanov, leader of the factory's Black Hundreds, was thrown into a wheelbarrow, red lead poured over his head, and dumped in the street. The workforce elected the Bolshevik Leonid Krasin as the plant's new director. He had just returned from exile in Germany where he worked as an engineer (a skill he had once used to boost party funds by robbing banks).

In a ferment of meetings, factories and offices elected delegates to the Soviet, chose factory committees, and discussed how to gain control of production. Ironically, it was the Mensheviks who began setting up the factory committees which later played such a role in the October Revolution. 'Defencism' dominated the huge state-run arms factories like the Pipe and Cartridge works, and the shop stewards who called for 'Workers' Control of Production' were mostly concerned with the war effort. The February Revolution made popular a war of 'just defence' which deserved sacrificial efforts and the postponing of reform. But 'defencism' was a tangle of contradictions in practice. The Mensheviks could scarcely deny the very real grievances felt by workers, but their priority was speeding up production in what were already militarised factories. Workers rejected this.

Early in April a conference of workers in naval enterprises discussed the factory committees, and a bitter row took place when a Menshevik member of the Soviet EC, G.E.Breido, opposed suggestions that the committees should take direct control of production.[26] The workers had other ideas: bosses should be elected, and supervised by the factory committee, which would keep the firm's accounts and decide pay and conditions. This decision was the beginning of their break with Menshevism and the whole 'bourgeois programme', although the notion of 'workers' control' was still hopelessly vague and presented no real alternative. How was it possible to have 'control' without actual responsibility for production, that is, without eliminating private ownership? The decline of Menshevism merely began the argument.

Bill Shatov, who returned from American exile (where he had won notoriety as organiser of the 'Wobblies'[27]), saw the factory committees fitting into his anarcho-syndicalist conception of factory and rural communes forming a society with no state or government, no central authorities, no plan and no political struggle. These beguiling prospects were none the less rejected by the mass of workers; nor was this only because anarchist fantasies were utopian in the circumstances. In practice it was impossible to envisage any future without capitalism which did not also mean more, not less, planning.

This became increasingly obvious as the economy spiralled to disaster in the spring and summer of 1917 and employers began to opt out (often simply disappearing with their assets and even factory machinery). The Central

Council of Factory Committees had to step in to coordinate production, the distribution of manufactured goods to the countryside, and the supply of raw materials and especially of food. Factory committee conferences called for centralised, planned control over the economy, and 'workers' control' was increasingly linked to the transfer of state power to the soviets, land to peasants, and nationalisation of the 'commanding heights' of the economy. Lenin would argue:

> the question of workers' control boils down to who controls whom, which class is controlling and which is being controlled ... we must resolutely and irrevocably move on to control over the landowners and capitalists by the workers and peasants ...[28]

While workers began to take the economy into their own hands, the bosses found support in, of all places, *Izvestia*, the newspaper published by the Soviet EC. It spoke of 'the wartime situation' which 'made caution necessary' in using 'the sharper weapons of class struggle such as strikes and lockouts'; 'open conflict' was to be avoided in preference for 'negotiation and agreement'.[29]

The Provisional Government, hamstrung in economic affairs, tried to win support with an apparently ambitious programme of reforms. It set up an industrial relations conciliation machinery, set new health and safety standards and established a social insurance scheme. At the instigation of the Soviet, it made other reforms too: the death penalty was abolished and on 17 March the corporal punishment of peasants was abolished. Decrees guaranteeing religious freedom and the rights of national minorities (of which there were more than 100 in the Russian Empire) were promulgated. The main purpose of this was to encourage the Poles to rise up against their German occupiers (they didn't). But Finland, also part of the Empire and still in Russian hands, was denied its freedom.

On 17 April the police force (which had disappeared anyway) was replaced by a militia. Like all its reforms, the Provisional Government's decree on the militia was ambiguous. It ratified one of the results of the revolution while trying to reverse it in practice. It was supposed to eliminate a duplication between the City Duma's own militia and the Red Guard detachments. Needless to say, the new 'regular' force made the volunteer militias unnecessary, and they were to disband.

Would the militia be given the traditional police role of protecting private property? Or would it be 'the people in arms'? A police force would empty the factories of strikers, but a militia would defend the workers, who many saw as the real source of social wealth. The militia suddenly came into the foreground as a focus of the struggle between workers and capital, between Provisional Government and the Soviet. The secretary of the Vasilievski Island Bolshevik committee, Vera Slutskaya (who had once been a medical student) threw herself into training the *sanitarki* and these young militiawomen in their red kerchiefs became a familiar sight in the slums and factories, visiting mothers and children and combining some elementary health education with a stark political lesson: only ending the war would end the hunger, disease and squalor of the Vyborg Side and Vasilievski.

These initiatives did not go down well with the Mensheviks, and Kerensky was more interested in organising middle-class women into 'Death's Head Battalions', intended to shame trench-soldiers into a new offensive spirit. By the end of March 10,000 out of 20,000 militiamen were workers, but the campaign by the government reduced their number to 2,000 two months later. But in factory after factory the officially disbanded militia came together again as a Red Guard, committed, as a resolution of the Vyborg District Soviet put it, to fight counter-revolution and defend 'weapons in hand, all the gains of the working class'. The Soviet EC dismissed this as the work of 'leninists' which 'directly threatened the unity of the revolutionary forces'.

In the aftermath of the February Revolution a patriotic euphoria swept the country. The regiments which had made the revolution marched in parades, bearing banners which read 'The 8-Hour Day!', 'Long Live Democracy, Land and Freedom!' but which also said 'Conquer or Die!' and 'Soldiers to the Trenches, Workers to their Benches!' or (from a cavalry detachment): 'Comrades, Forge the Weapons! Let's Bathe our Horses in German Blood!'

In the last two weeks of March the pro-war agitation reached a climax. 'Pacifists and 8-Hour Day Mongers' were denounced under the endlessly-repeated slogan 'War till Victory'. The gutter press began to vilify trade unions, *soldatki* self-help groups and the factory committees, which were all presented as not only unpatriotic in time of war, but unworthy of Russians anyway.

A constant stream of delegations from the front visited the capital, as the soldiery tried to make up its mind about the issues at stake. Shabby men stained with the mud of the trenches took their earnest simplicity and endless questions first to the Marian Palace, where they sipped tea with bourgeois ministers. Then they went to the Soviet and drank in its heady atmosphere.

The Soviet continued to grow, reflecting the steady emergence of those huge, subterranean forces which constantly confounded the expectations of liberal political and business circles. By the end of March there were more than 3,000 delegates. The plenum moved to the Naval Academy on Vasilievski Island, which boasted the biggest hall in the capital. The EC, which had kept its offices in the Tauride, travelled there in a column of cars. The Soviet's sessions were more extraordinary than ever. Sometimes visitors from the front spoke, hesitant at first but drawing strength from the meeting. These were always emotional occasions, as even that dry intellectual, Sukhanov, was moved to record. Peasants, he wrote:

> so ignorant and illiterate they could barely pronounce the word 'revolution', in a self-oblivious flood of words pouring out of their soul, seemed the voice of the people and its revolution. And all around ... the 'conscious' vanguard,

the marxist thinkers sat and listened in rapt silence, with burning eyes and set smiles ...

Sukhanov described what became a familiar event:

A peasant mounted the rostrum with (as was often the case) his sack on his back. In a soft, urgent voice, so that the silent multitude strained to hear, he spoke of his comrades in the trenches who sent him to salute the fighters at this, other, front – to thank them for the great deeds, for the freedom won. Not knowing how to repay this debt and help the cause of the nation, or how to show their devotion to the revolution and support of their kinsmen in the Soviet of Workers' and Soldiers' Deputies, the soldiers decided to send 'the most precious thing we've got. So in this sack are all the decorations we've won with our blood; no-one kept anything for himself. I've been sent to give them to you, together with our sacred, unbreakable vow to give our lives for the freedom that's been won and to serve the revolution and obey without question all the orders of the Soviet.'[30]

Support for the Provisional Government, but only if it sought an equitable peace and convoked a Constituent Assembly. No support for 'War till Victory'. On the other hand, the Soviet received unconditional loyalty from the soldier-masses freed by its 'Order No. 1'. The message was clear and (as the war dragged on) ominous for the Provisional Government.

The exiles were returning, seemingly from all quarters of the globe. Leon Trotsky arrived, the Menshevik leader Chernov arrived, and the founder of 'Scientific Anarchism', Peter Kropotkin. Almost every day military bands and honour guards were dispatched to the Finland Station and the other great terminals, to hail a returning grandee of the revolutionary diaspora. The less well known came in without fanfare, rolled up their sleeves without fuss, and went to work. The opening act was over; a new stage in the revolution was beginning, and the cast too had begun to change. The Menshevik leaders, Lieber and Dan, returned. Joseph Stalin came from Siberia on 13 March, together with Lev Kamenev, and at once joined the Soviet EC. Stalin, a member of the Bolshevik Central Committee since 1912, took over from Shlyapnikov as leader in Petrograd. Kamenev, who was no great thinker or writer (his main gift was oratory), was far more cautious, passive and conciliationist than Molotov, from whom he took over *Pravda*, at once swinging the paper sharply to the right. Thus when Kerensky told the world that Russia 'would proudly defend its freedom' and 'not retreat before the bayonets of the aggressors', Kamenev followed up with the first of an extraordinary series of articles which overnight began to drag the Bolsheviks into the 'conciliationist' camp.

When army faces army, [he wrote in *Pravda*] it would be the most inane policy to suggest to one of those armies that it lay down its arms and go home. This is not a policy of peace but of slavery, which a free people will reject with disgust.[31]

This about-face dismayed Bolshevik factory workers, and the paper was deluged with protests. It seemed that now even the Bolsheviks were falling into what Lenin called 'the profound and fatal error of revolutionary defencism'.

Georgy Plekhanov, the grand old man of Russian socialism, arrived on 31 March, to a triumphal welcome. At one time the teacher and collaborator in exile of the young Lenin, certainly the founder of Marxism in Russia, Plekhanov's name was hallowed in the ears of all revolutionaries, despite his support of the war and break with Bolshevism. But in fact, Plekhanov and his tiny *Yedinstvo* (Unity) group were to play no role in the Revolution, and he died of TB in 1918.

Exiles were not the only import from the outside world; the new religious freedom encouraged evangelical missions, and for a while the Salvation Army won the poster battle. Its placards crammed the walls, and huge congregations attended its services at the People's House (a temperance hall).

As the economy worsened, life in Russia's towns slid into a chaos of hunger and darkness and the countryside boiled with discontent. People began to call for the convening of an All-Russian Congress of Soviets and on 28 March a preliminary conference opened, with 400 delegates from around the country. When it closed six days later they had adopted the slogan 'Peace, Land and Bread!' The chauvinist campaign for 'war till victory' had won support for the idea of a new offensive, but had also triggered off a backlash. Spurred on by the Bolsheviks, whose numbers grew daily, the Menshevik and SR parties organised great mass meetings against continuing with the Tsar's war aims. The Provisional Government split, with Kerensky, Lvov and Nekrasov opposing Miliukov, who was determined to stick by the Tsar's annexationist demands. On 27 March Miliukov was forced to renounce annexations, a decision greeted with jubilation in the Soviet.

On the same day a national conference of the Bolsheviks opened in the palace belonging to Kshesinskaya, the Tsar's favourite ballerina. The conference was meant to prepare the party for Lenin's return from exile. It turned out to be a dispiriting affair. The leadership was trapped in a grey realism, seemingly the product of a weary seniority among the leadership, which blanketed the revolutionary *elan* of the young faithful. The party was moving towards unity with the Mensheviks. While the conference was still in session, a telegram arrived from Lenin, then travelling across Germany in a sealed train, along with 31 other exiles. Its terse urgency conflicted with the mood of resignation spreading through the conference. 'Our only guarantee – to arm the workers', it said. 'No agreement with the other parties. Last is *sine qua non*. We do not trust Chkheidze.'

Lenin was due to arrive on Easter Sunday. A party of Central Committee members, including Kamenev and Alexandra Kollontai, went ahead to meet his train at Belo-Ostrov on the Finnish border. Kamenev tried to brief Lenin on the situation in the capital and was brusquely cut short: 'What is this you are writing in *Pravda*?' Lenin asked. 'We saw some of your articles and roundly abused you.' ('We must answer bullet with bullet and shell with shell', Kamenev had said.)

At Petrograd's Finland Station, the party's Russian Bureau had organised a theatrical welcome for the émigrés. Sukhanov described the scene. Huge crowds had gathered in the station square and the adjoining streets. Hundreds of red flags fluttered overhead, lit by arc lights and dominated by a magnificent banner embroidered in gold with the legend: 'Central Committee of the RS-DWP (Bolsheviks)'. Armoured cars bearing Bolshevik agitators began to arrive, while a searchlight mounted on a lorry cut swaths of light through the startled crowd and slashed the cloudy sky. Drawn up near the station entrance were companies of troops and bands, which played the 'Marseillaise' as the train drew in.

Lenin's speeches to the waiting crowds – made standing on an armoured car – caused consternation among Bolshevik leaders present, and set the pattern for what was to come:

Dear comrades, soldiers, sailors and workers! I greet you, with joy, as the embodiment of the victorious Russian revolution, and I greet you as the vanguard of the worldwide proletarian army. The piratical imperialist war is the beginning of civil war throughout Europe. The hour is not far distant when at the call of our comrade, Karl Liebknecht, the German people will take up arms against their own capitalist exploiters ... The worldwide Socialist Revolution has already dawned![32]

This was the first time any party leader had used the word 'socialist' in connection with the Russian Revolution.

At the Kshesinskaya he spoke again, and as he spoke, there were cries from the audience. 'It seemed', Alexandra Kollontai was to say, 'that Vladimir Ilyich had lost his reason.' 'Delirium, the delirium of a madman', cried Bogdanov, a former Bolshevik. 'Lenin has proposed himself as candidate for a throne vacant for 30 years, the throne of Bakunin' (the anarchist leader), said another. Of the party leadership, only Kollontai spoke in his support; but among the ardent rank-and-file the reaction to Lenin's speech was much more enthusiastic.

'Vladimir Ilyich was a man who knew better than anyone else before him how to stop people leading their customary lives', Maxim Gorky was to say. According to Gorky, Lenin spoke in a matter-of-fact, direct way, without histrionics, but his eyes had 'the cold glitter of steel shavings'.[33] And never was Lenin more fiery, more determined or more irresistible than in the first days and weeks of his return from exile. These first speeches, published in millions of copies as the *April Theses*, affected the national mood and the eventual course of the revolution.

Lenin believed that removing Tsarism had served only to propel the country into the deeper international crisis of capitalism. Whichever alliance of capitalist powers was victorious on the battlefield, capitalism as a whole, as a world-system, stood to be defeated in the world war. In 1871, an earlier war between France and Prussia had led to the first socialist revolution. The Paris Commune, though drowned in blood, was a model for any future socialist government. In the age of imperialism – capitalism's 'highest, final stage' – inter-imperialist war would always end in social revolution – something lost sight of when the socialist parties of Europe rallied to their national flags in 1914 (despite the Second International).

The defeated countries (starting with Russia) would undergo a social revolution. In the period since 1871, world capitalism had undergone enormous growth and transformation. In 1917 its contradictions were more explosive than half a century earlier. The insurrectionary impulse spawned by the crisis of war must unleash a tidal wave of revolution, dwarfing the Commune in power and scope. Revolution in any one country would be the prelude to world revolution. Revolutionaries had to assume this and act accordingly. Even if the Russian socialist revolution, which now seemed inevitable, was annihilated like the Commune, there would be other revolutions, as world capitalism bred new and deeper crises, until the system was finally breached. But the difference in circumstances from 1871 meant the socialist revolution in Russia would not be destroyed.

Lenin's *April Theses* were true in the sense that Russia was already finished militarily. The longer hostilities continued, the more certain was the second, socialist revolution. But suppose the front collapsed overnight? Nearly one half of German and Austro-Hungarian forces were fighting in the East. Would not the prospect then be, not socialist revolution, but national annihilation? This argument for 'revolutionary defence' did not deter Lenin. A complex evolution of events was in train, both at the front and in the rear, and the timing of the second revolution depended on this. The Bolsheviks must also wait, confining themselves to patient explanation and agitation. Only when there were Bolshevik majorities on the Soviets would conditions finally be ready for insurrection. In the meantime, there was nothing to gain, and everything to lose, by embracing 'defencism'. Despite the clamour of treason, the Bolsheviks would continue to argue that the workers and peasants had no stake in this war and should 'vote with their feet' against it. Lenin did not believe that the Germans were socially or militarily capable of swallowing up Russia. When, if, the country was finally defeated, there would still be something more than the Muscovite rump left, and that something would be a socialist republic of workers and peasants.

Lenin's arguments gave people a licence to dream. The age-old hopes of socialists and populists began to seem not just feasible, but historically inevitable and even the only possible future for Russia. The *April Theses* pointed beyond Russia's wartime predicament into a different future. They called for unconditional opposition to the Provisional Government and to 'revolutionary defencism', proposing instead to organise mass fraternisation between Russian and German soldiers at the fronts. The Bolsheviks should resolutely oppose a parliamentary republic and organise the seizure of power by the proletariat and poor peasantry, the abolition of the standing army and the formation of workers' militias. Land must be nationalised, and the future Soviet Republic would rest upon the alliance of workers and peasants.

Lenin's *Theses* gained credence when they melded with a sudden turn of events which threatened to overwhelm the Provisional Government. On 18 April Miliukov informed the Allies that Russia would continue the war and fulfil all treaty obligations. The result was an explosion of public anger, and it became clear not only that Foreign Minister Miliukov and War Minister Guchkov would have to resign but that the whole bourgeois government might collapse, leaving the Soviet EC to carry the can for prolonging the war. The Menshevik *Rabochaya Gazeta* said on 20 April:

> Miliukov's Note, published yesterday, called forth great indignation on the streets ... Everywhere, at street meetings, in trams, passionate, heated disputes over the war take place. The caps and handkerchiefs stand for peace, the derbies and bonnets for war ... From time to time, counter-demonstrations ... small, disorderly crowds, among them officers and women, run along Nevsky Prospekt with placards and shout 'Long Live the Provisional Government!' and 'Down with Lenin!' ...

As fierce demonstrations erupted in the capital and throughout the provinces, the Soviet debated Miliukov's Note in an atmosphere governed by the opportunistic majority's fear of civil war and determination to coat-tail the Provisional Government.

It was decided to negotiate with the Provisional Government. Then, two days later, as the tide of popular anger grew, Lenin said 'The time has come to seize power.' Rallies both for and against the war grew in scale. Once again, gunfire could be heard around the city. On 21 April thousands of women textile workers paraded down the odd-numbered side of Nevsky; on the even-numbered side, crowds of well-dressed women, officers, merchants and lawyers walked in the same direction with placards reading 'Long Live the PG', 'Arrest Lenin' and the like. At the corner with Sadovaya they began shouting insults at the poor women: 'Trollops! Illiterate rabble! Filthy scum!' A textile worker shouted back 'The hats you're wearing are made from our blood!' and the women flew at each other, tearing and scratching. A detachment of sailors arrived, complete with the customary brass band, and the middle-class women beat a hasty retreat. As a consequence of the rioting, Miliukov and Guchkov were driven from the government, which was obliged publicly to repudiate Miliukov's Note. Only the support of the Soviet prevented the bourgeois government from collapsing.

In the *April Theses*, Lenin had called for the abolition of the armed forces, at a time when parts of the country were still under German occupation. The politicians and publicists of the capital were treated to the spectacle of a major public figure urging his supporters to visit the frontlines and to prevail upon the defenders of desperate trenches to abandon the struggle. Such a thing was unthinkable in any other combatant country.

Nor was this all. Lenin spurned the Constituent Assembly, urging people to take matters in their own hands. 'For us it is the revolutionary act which is important', he said, 'while the law should be its consequence.'[34] To the lawyers and politicians of the other parties this was an outrage against constitutional principle. It made political outlaws of the Bolsheviks. Telling the soldiers to 'vote with their feet', Lenin's encouragement to workers to take control of industry, to peasants to seize the land, and to the minority nations to decide their own futures, threatened the survival of the nation.

Fuelling the ferment, a tide of propaganda published by all the parties, according to John Reed, 'went out every day [by] tons, car-loads, train-loads, saturating the land'. Agitators fanned out from the capital, to 'lectures, debates, speeches – in theatres, circuses, school-houses, clubs, Soviet meeting-rooms, Union headquarters, barracks ... Meetings in the trenches at the front, in village-squares, in factories.' In words, cartoons for the illiterate, simple plays and music, in street-theatre, in the hundreds of newspapers and thousands of books, pamphlets and brochures, Russia explored its past and future. Not all was Bolshevik propaganda, of course, but neither, as Reed said, were Russians reading 'fables, falsified history, diluted religion and the cheap religion which corrupts – but social and economic theories, philosophy, the works of Tolstoy, Gogol and Gorky...'[35]

February had roused a hurricane of expectations, which seemed incompatible with the unity and survival of the nation in wartime. National self-determination implied the secession of the Ukraine, Finland and the Baltikum, a disaster that would ensure defeat. Yet the Soviet was hoist on the petard of its own commitment to a peace without annexations, a peace of self-determination. It had no moral authority to resist any minority nation's determination to secede. Attacking Lenin when the latter merely traced out the logic of this commitment was hypocrisy.

Jews, Armenians, Georgians, Ukrainians, all began to stir. Muslims representing the great Central Asian nations – the Uzbeks, Azerbaijanis, Tadjiks, Kazakhs, Turkmen and Kirghizes – called for an All-Russian Conference, which was held in Moscow on 1 May. A woman – Selima Yakubova – was elected president of the Congress, in a vote which outraged the clerics, who had tried to exclude women from even attending. Many of the participants were radicalised intellectuals living in the capital and for this reason the conference was not truly representative of feeling in the Central

Asian national minorities.[36] None the less its proceedings raised what were to become enduring themes in the modernising of Islamic societies during the twentieth century.

The conference tried to balance the conflict between demands for national autonomy, and for the rights of oppressed groups – women, workers and peasants – within the minority nations, which were generally backward, patriarchal-feudal societies. It debated a resolution opposing federal autonomy and arguing instead for unity within a Russian state, on the grounds that:

> In the so-called Muslim states, the workers would not know how to profit from All-Russian social legislation ... the immaturity and disorganisation of the working class will keep it in abominable conditions of exploitation. There will be many struggles before ... the 8-hour day, social security, disability and unemployment benefits [are won and federalism] will split Islam ... throttling the unity of Shi-ites and Sunni muslims, and lead to heresies.

Self-determination taken too far might also 'make the emancipation of women difficult in Turkestan and the Caucasus, because the legislators will still be men accustomed to treating women as slaves'. Despite these considerations, the balance of opinion came down in favour of seeking national autonomy within a future federal state. The reason was clear: the emancipation of oppressed social groups within the national minorities depended on the whole nation being first liberated from exploitation by a chauvinistic Russian Empire. The conference decided that Islam's 'two great tasks' – the rebirth of Asia's Muslim culture and the smashing of European tutelage – required national self-determination.

This was a recurrent refrain in the months after the February Revolution. But of all the parties, only the Bolsheviks enshrined the yearning for national liberation unreservedly into their programme, offering all nations the right to secede. Bolshevik nationalities policy combined principle with calculation. Lenin and Stalin, its authors, believed that, with the possible exceptions of Finland, Poland and the Ukraine, the national-chauvinist groupings (mostly bourgeois) in the minorities would be torn between fear of going it alone and the desire to quit the old Empire. The Bolsheviks tried to expose nationalist pretensions while emphasising the fundamental right of self-determination which alone could ensure working-class support among the national minorities for a 'Republic of Soviets'. Their propaganda resulted in the steady Bolshevisation of Soviets in the nationalities.

The revolution was gathering pace in the countryside, as the peasantry began expropriating the great estates. Somehow this vast upheaval was ignored by the politicians in the capital, for whom the war dominated everything. The price of Soviet support for continuing a war of defence (Tsarist dreams of conquest were abandoned after the April Days) was the pursuit of a peace of no annexations or indemnities and the democratisation of the army.

Resolutions calling for peace talks poured in, as the chaos in the army deepened. There was growing fraternisation across enemy lines. Units who disliked their orders arrested their own commanders, imprisoned, tried and sometimes executed them; were themselves threatened with arrest and were indeed imprisoned, denied property and civil rights and disbanded, resulting in many desertions but in not a few cases a new submission by the chastened troops to military discipline. The *Soldier-Citizen*, a Moscow Bolshevik paper, soliloquised about the insistent demands for more discipline and for a restoration of the military death penalty:

'Until the end', croaks the crow, picking clean the bones on the battlefield. What does he care about the old woman awaiting her son, or the eighty-year old forced to lead the plough with trembling hands? 'War to the End!' cries the student to thousands on the public square, assuring them that 'our' hardships are due to the Germans. Meanwhile his father, seller of oats at 16 roubles a pud, sits in a festive cabaret where he expounds the same theory.[37]

This propaganda had a devastating effect; the General Staff wrung its hands while Bolshevik agitators toured the fronts with impunity. General Cheglov telegraphed headquarters about a typical episode on the front:

An agitator from the Petrograd Soviet [it was the Bolshevik leader, Frunze], armed with authorisation dated 25 April, No.126, has arrived at our division. Among other things, he urges fraternisation with the Germans, and only today has organised fraternisations with the 220th Regt. They are spreading ... Does [Frunze] really have authority to do such things?[38]

In province after province, usurers, rack-renting landlords, gluttonous priests and the land-captains with their flogging-courts, began to disappear. The peasantry, in and out of uniform, was turning the Russian countryside, for the first and perhaps only time, into the vast rural commune dreamt of by an earlier generation of revolutionaries. Forced grain exactions, commodities, finally money itself began to disappear from the rural economy.

Meanwhile the politicians of all parties except the Bolsheviks consoled themselves with the thought that 'dual power' – supposedly fatal to the army and the nation – had now been ended by the coalition set up after the April Days. However, the coalition's peace policy soon began to flounder. The Central Powers were at their zenith, while the allies were in disarray after the disasters of the Somme, Verdun and the failed Nivelle offensive. There were mutinies in the British army and the French soldiery politely told their General Staff that there would be no more offensives. Germany's unexpected success in the submarine war played havoc with the Allied war effort; the US had yet to become involved (indeed, it only did so when the likelihood of German victory imperilled its vast war loans to Britain and France). During the summer of 1917 the Central Powers were able massively to reinforce their armies in the East.

The Germans had every reason to impose a punitive peace. To do otherwise would be seen as weakness by the Allies (as the Germans themselves saw Soviet talk of a peace without annexations and indemnities). Besides, Germany had too much at stake in Alsace-Lorraine and in the vast, ramshackle Habsburg empire, to offer a Wilsonian peace of self-determination. A generous peace would leave a stronger rather than weaker Russia poised at Germany's back door. Thus the Soviet's peace policy was no more credible than Miliukov's war policy had been. Only the fear of civil war sustained the remarkable self-deception of the Cadets and Soviet moderates, and the parliamentary charades that went with it.

At their conference in April, the Bolsheviks adopted the agrarian programme of the Socialist Revolutionaries, the traditional party of the peasantry, in whose hands, according to Lenin, agrarian reform would nevertheless be mere 'deception' of the peasantry. Under the Bolsheviks, this same programme would inaugurate 'the kingdom of socialism, the kingdom of peace, the kingdom of the toilers'. These were heady words. Many dismissed them as nonsense. Maxim Gorky was among the doubters:

When in the year 1917, on his arrival in Russia, Lenin published his 'thesis', I thought that the thesis sacrificed the small and heroic band of politically educated workers, as well as all the truly revolutionary intelligentsia, to the Russian peasantry. The only active force in Russia would be thrown, like a pinch of salt, into the flat bog of the village, and it would dissolve without a trace, without changing the spirit, the life, the history, of the Russian nation.[39]

This seemed but melancholy realism to anyone who, like Gorky himself, was acquainted with 'the beastly individualism of the peasants, and their almost complete lack of social emotions'. But the Bolsheviks were not disposed to pessimism. They were now the most dynamic and well-organised party in Russia. Their rank and file grew steadily while the other parties shrank. Bolshevik cells multiplied in the fleet and on the fronts. In the capital and in many other towns Bolshevik cells in working-class districts and workplaces organised their Red Guard detachments.

What fuelled their rising popularity was the endless crisis which deepened for workers and middle classes alike. Prices rose 2,300 per cent between February and October, and real wages fell by almost half. Strikes proved ineffective as bankruptcies and closures soared. Instead workers occupied factories and took control.

The failure of the coalition government's attempts to interest the other belligerents in peace talks left them with no alternative but to resume the war.

Kerensky's offensive, planned for June, loomed, a desperate gamble whose failure would precipitate the country into civil war.

As preparations for the offensive intensified, alarm grew at the chaos enveloping the country; the yellow press was filled with stories of mutiny, lynchings, arson, attacks on property by peasants in Bessarabia, Orel, Samara and many other places. Stories of fields left fallow while peasants burned out landowners led to fear of famine. There were reports that marauding bands of deserters were instituting their own 'governments' like the 'republic' founded by the 'pro-German Corporal Shilov' in the Caucasus, and 'run on Bolshevik lines'.

As the right-wing backlash developed, anti-semitic pogroms took place in Nizhni-Novgorod, Elisavetgrad, Kishnev and some Ukrainian cities; in Moscow a regiment refused to accept Jewish officers and turned away Soviet agitators because 'the Soviet was in Jewish hands'. Irredentism, obscurantism, chauvinism; the call of 'blood and soil' began to tell. The Soviet sent teams of agitators to Odessa where they fanned out through the south and west to combat the tide of anti-semitism being whipped up by the right. The officers' clubs, the Church, the Cossacks, were all involved, as were the shadowy remnants of the Black Hundreds, well funded by landlords.

'The time of the Anti-Christ has come! Do you not see that you should confess and not revolt against God!' cried a priest at Buguronslansky, brandishing a horsewhip at the mutinous soldiery. While the Old Society thus girded itself, elections were being held for the First All-Russian Congress of Soviets, which was convened on 3 June. A total of 20 million votes was cast, and the coalition parties, the Mensheviks and SRs, won a huge majority. The Bolsheviks were outnumbered. Lenin was undismayed, arguing that 'public opinion is more left than our left', and driving the Bolsheviks on their course to power. As the Congress opened, Lenin, Trotsky and Lunacharsky called again for a Soviet government. When Tsereteli, defending the coalition, said from the rostrum 'There is no political party in Russia which at the present time would say: Give us power', from his seat Lenin replied: 'There is such a party', adding 'No party has the right to refuse power and ours does not'; but the applause which greeted him was drowned out by laughter.

Kerensky began touring the fronts in preparation for his offensive, making the fervent speeches for which he became famous. 'What has happened now?' he asked one unit.

> Can't you suffer any longer? Or has free Russia become steadily a nation of revolted slaves? ... Ah! Comrades! It's too bad I didn't die two months ago – then I would have died with the sweetest dreams ... The country is in danger! Its destiny is in your hands![40]

Kerensky ordered the great summer offensive to begin on 18 June. It was a disaster. The Germans knew of every preparation. The half-starved, often diseased troops, short of every kind of war materiel, advanced briefly then fell back in disorder. The operation was not just a defeat, but the death-knell of the Tsarist military tradition. A new army and a new tradition would have to be created before Russians would take the field again.

The catastrophe at the front left the 'patriotic' gentry, the officers, general staff, Cadet leaders and the big capitalists and landowners, in a bitter and frightened mood. They blamed the disaster on the cowardice of the foot-soldiery, on the despised Soviet and most of all on the Bolsheviks. A common parlour topic became the need for an 'exemplary' German victory, to chasten the proletariat.

Then came a new upheaval in the capital itself. In the first days of July the High Command used Czech mercenaries to drive recalled veterans into the lines. Garrison regiments poured onto the streets of the capital to protest. They were joined by hundreds of thousands of workers. An angry mob invaded the Soviet; white with rage, a worker jumped on the platform and shook his fist at the SR Minister of Agriculture, Chernov, yelling 'take power, you son of a bitch, when it's given to you!'

Chernov escaped being lynched by sailors only because an electrifying speech by Trotsky, in which he called the Kronstadters 'the pride and beauty of the Revolution', persuaded them otherwise. Later that day Lenin told Bonch-Bruevich, his secretary, there must be an armed rising 'not later than the autumn'.

As insurgent soldiers, sailors and workers took control of the streets, the government bombarded the fronts with pleas for help. There was desperate confusion on all sides. In a typical incident, the 176th Regiment, based at Tsarskoye Selo, marched through the rain to Petrograd. A Bolshevik regiment, it had come only to demand 'All Power to the Soviets!' But at the Tauride, Tsereteli warmly greeted the troops, who without more ado agreed to mount guard on the palace to fend off 'counter-revolutionaries'. The Bolshevik troops kept the Bolshevik workers at bay until more reliable reinforcements arrived, and the government was able to restore order on the streets ...

Immediately after the July Days, the Ministry of Justice published allegations that Lenin was a German agent. The allegations had a dramatic effect. Regiments which had proclaimed their neutrality now came out against the Bolsheviks. The loyalists went on the offensive, clearing the city of anti-government demonstrators, smashing Bolshevik printing presses, arresting and killing those suspected of Bolshevik sympathies. A special squad was formed on Kerensky's orders, to hunt down Lenin and shoot him on sight. The July Days – a spontaneous rising of the insurgent population of the capital – had failed, and the lesson was clear to many. Lenin called the episode 'more than a demonstration and less than a revolution'. He told Ordzhonikidze 'now it is possible to take power only by means of an armed rising'.

But now a vicious reaction began as the government stepped up its drive against the Bolsheviks. Lenin went into hiding rather than submit to arrest, whatever openings for scurrility this gave his enemies. For 'there are no guarantees of a fair trial in Russia at present ...'

Lenin hid in Sestroretsk (20 miles from Petrograd) in a loft belonging to a Bolshevik worker, then moved with Zinoviev and a few followers to a *shagash* (an igloo-shaped hut made of straw) concealed in the deep forests overlooking the gulf of Finland. It was late summer; the sky was still pale at night. The next 26 days were a strange interlude in a time so saturated with event. The fugitives fished and swam in the steel-blue, mirror-flat waters of the Gulf. During this period Lenin worked on that extraordinary testament to the optimism of the period, *State and Revolution*, every day receiving a constant stream of messengers and party officials from the capital. Finally Lenin was smuggled over the administrative frontier with Finland, disguised as a locomotive fireman.

As the tide of reaction reached high water, Kamenev, Lunacharsky and many others were arrested. Incarcerated in the Peter-Paul, Alexandra Kollontai was subjected to brutal humiliation; her bourgeois breeding and looks seemed to provoke her captors. Perhaps characteristically, Trotsky asked the Provisional Government for the same treatment and was duly arrested. Bolshevised regiments like the Machine-gun Regiment were broken up. Factories were searched for arms caches. On 12 July the death penalty was reintroduced at the front: in fact, Kerensky, now Minister-President, had already authorised a policy of 'exemplary executions'. New decrees restricted press freedom. But the repression was not enough to destroy the Bolsheviks, with all their experience of underground work, and their popularity began to rise again as the war dragged on and the prospect loomed of another winter in the trenches.

The Bolsheviks had begun to eclipse their competitors. The Mensheviks had by now all but disappeared as an organised party, while the Socialist Revolutionaries were in the process of a split which would soon yield a major new ally for the Bolsheviks.

The whole country was splitting, as the slide towards civil war continued. Miliukov considered Kerensky to be 'too socialist', but he thought the Cadets must support the new government because 'not only does catastrophe threaten us; we are already in the vortex. If it turns out that we have to do not with a declining influence of the Soviets and of socialist utopianism, if ... the Bolsheviki again appear on the streets of Petrograd, then we shall talk in a different tone.'

At a Duma conference, deputy Maslennikov said:

The population is scrounging, thinking only of looting. Our valiant army has become a horde of cowards ... The revolution was made thanks to the Duma; but in that great, tragic moment of history, a handful of crazy fanatics, adventurers and traitors, calling themselves the Executive Committee of the Council of Workers' and Soldiers' Deputies, attached itself to the Revolution ...[41]

At a Congress of Industrialists on 3 August, stormy applause greeted a speaker who announced 'the need for the long bony hand of hunger and national immiseration to seize by the throat those false friends of the people ... the soviets', and there were open calls for a 'military dictatorship' or a 'strongman'. [42]

On the other hand, the clear and almost universal reaction of workers to the deepening crisis after the July Days was finally to turn away from conciliation and defencism. Skilled workers had already abandoned Menshevism, whose electoral support collapsed. The unskilled 'worker-peasant' stratum was beginning to desert its traditional SR affiliation as well. But the working class of the capital was still in retreat after the defeat of the July Days. Conscious of their political and social isolation, Petrograd's militant workers and soldiers had learnt their lesson; in future the insurgent population of the capital unswervingly accepted Bolshevik leadership, no matter how impatient it grew with Lenin's sometimes tortuous, painstaking tactics.

On 31 July General Kornilov was appointed Commander-in-Chief. A group of Moscow business leaders, headed by Rodzianko, sent him a telegram: 'In this threatening hour of heavy trial all thinking Russia looks to you with faith and hope.' The Cossacks' Council, the Knights of St George, and other 'Junker' bodies rallied around the new saviour. But none had mass support; even the Union of Cossack Troops was out of touch with rank and file Cossack opinion. Kornilov had already begun plotting to take power, placing his most reliable Cossack and mountain-Caucasian troops within striking distance of Petrograd and Moscow.

On 10 August he visited Kerensky, arriving at the Winter Palace with a spectacular bodyguard of Tekintsi and Turkmen warriors. Kerensky seemed a broken man; his moment had come and gone. Kornilov on the other hand had only recently felt the touch of destiny's wings. There was to be no meeting of the minds. Kornilov was a political primitive, unable to make a distinction between any of the socialist parties and regarding them all as no better than paid German spies. He saw himself as the Saviour of the Motherland, thought Kerensky was pathetic, temporising, and said to his Chief of Staff, General Lukomsky:

It's time to hang the German supporters and spies, with Lenin at their head. And to disperse the Soviet of Workers' and Soldiers' Deputies so that it would never reassemble ... I am bringing the Cavalry Corps to Petrograd by the end of August ... if necessary, [we'll] hang every member of the Soviet.[43]

Kornilov wanted 'nothing for myself. I only want to save Russia and I will obey unconditionally a cleaned-up, strong Provisional Government.' Before

Kornilov got his chance a 'State Conference' was convened by the government in Moscow between 12–15 August. It was to rally all the 'forces of revolutionary democracy'.

Moscow's workforce greeted the conference with a general strike. Delegates watched in dismay as the cooks, porters and cleaning staff walked out of the conference hall. The event had been staged away from the capital to avoid such scenes ('many are those who have sung the meekness and patriarchal spirit of Moscow', said Sukhanov).

The conference split into two opposed camps at its first session. On the right side of the auditorium sat representatives of the old propertied and military classes. Bemedalled generals and officers, some in picturesque Caucasian uniforms, mixed with businessmen, Duma politicians, lawyers and professors. On the left sat the 'democratic forces': journalists, radical lawyers, moderate socialists, trade union officials, and a sprinkling of junior officers and NCOs. The Bolsheviks were not invited. A sense of dread seems to have pervaded the proceedings, of disaster creeping and rushing up. Meanwhile Kornilov arrived in Moscow and was greeted by a huge guard of honour, with bands playing. Amidst deferential deputations and garlanded with flowers, he went first to the Chapel of the Iberian Virgin, there to pray as had the Tsars before their coronation.

The atmosphere of bathos and despair at the State Conference reached a climax with Kerensky's closing speech, a rambling affair during which he said: 'Let my heart become stone; let all the springs of faith in man perish, let all the flowers and wreaths of man dry up ... I shall throw far away the keys of my heart, which loves men; I will think only of the state.'[44]

Kerensky continued in this vein until the audience tried to applaud him into silence. Women cried as Kerensky, near collapse, wandered off the stage, only to be led back by his minders. The Minister-President had forgotten to close the conference.

On 28 August, Kornilov moved his Cossacks against the capital's insurgent garrison. Prices on the Petrograd Stock Exchange soared, as a jubilant bourgeoisie anticipated the crushing of the Soviet and the emergence of a 'strong man'. It was a false dawn. The previous night the factory hooters had sounded as the working class rallied to the defence of their revolution. The passivity and despair following the defeat of the July Days was dispelled, and the great arms factories worked feverishly to provide arms for the defence of the capital. Men and women streamed out of the Vyborg towards Kornilov's advancing Cossacks; as the railway workers shunted troop trains around the capital, frustrating the planned encirclement, agitators argued and pleaded with the confused soldiery, who soon melted away as had the Tsar's armies in February.

After this, the Menshevik-dominated Soviet lost its last shreds of popular legitimacy. Kerensky, though supposedly at one with the 'revolutionary democracy' in the crushing of Kornilov, maintained the fiction of a government of coalition in which Cadet ministers retained their posts. It could not last. Across the country towns and cities came out for an end to the Provisional Government and for all power to the Soviets. Now the capital began to lag behind the rest of the country as the revolution deepened and accelerated. In many towns the Soviet took power during the Kornilov Days and refused to relinquish it subsequently.

Meanwhile food shortages, industrial closures and hardships of every kind pressed harder and harder on the capital's population. The nights were growing cold; it seemed unthinkable that the troops would winter again in the trenches; yet the same immobility as before the Kornilov Days seemed once more to be glaciating over the surface of the revolution. Lenin was still in hiding. In the public prints, among the political parties, in all the teeming discourse of everyday life, there was scant sense of the momentous events to come.

The fatalism of bourgeois and right-wing politicians grew more pronounced after the Kornilov revolt. Suddenly the whole of political Russia, apart from the Bolsheviks, found itself staring into an abyss. The result was a kind of reckless indifference. 'Petrograd is in danger', Mikhail Rodzianko wrote in a Cadet newspaper, as the Germans pressed on from Riga. 'I say to myself: Let God take care of Petrograd.'[45] Contemplating the destruction of the capital with feelings akin to relish, the arbiter of revolutionary fortunes in February added: 'With the taking of Petrograd the Baltic Fleet will also be destroyed ... But there will be nothing to regret ...'

On 9 September, the Bolsheviks won a majority on the Petrograd Soviet. Trotsky was elected President – something which in 1905, he told the cheering delegates, had swiftly been followed by the bloody repression of the people and by his own imprisonment. 'We are stronger now than then!' he said. A few days later, the Moscow Soviet went Bolshevik; in Siberian Krasnoyarsk, in Ekaterinburg and throughout the industrial Urals, in the Ukraine, down the Volga, in the Donetz Basin, it was the same story. The Baltic Fleet urged 'the adventurer Kerensky' to be 'removed from the ranks': 'to you, betrayer of the Revolution, Bonaparte Kerensky, we send our curses.' Elections to the city councils in Moscow and other towns showed a dramatic rise in the Bolshevik vote, the sweeping aside of the Right SRs and Mensheviks – and the continuing solidarity of the Cadet bastions.

In the Petrosoviet, the Menshevik Lieber won a roar of half-ironic cheers when he angrily called on 'Trotsky, Kamenev, Zinoviev and Lenin to take power – they won't find it so easy.' The revolution was accelerating, blown before an economic hurricane, as fuel, raw material and food shortages worsened, factories closed or were occupied, and the class war deepened. At the Fourth Factory Committee Conference the Bolshevik Skrypnik could say: 'We are no longer standing in the antechamber of economic collapse; we have entered the zone of collapse itself.'

On 23 September the Soviet EC reluctantly agreed to convoke the long-postponed Second All-Russian Congress of Soviets on 20 October. It was under immense pressure from the rank and file; typical of the resolutions passed was one from workers of the Military Horseshoe Factory, who:

> look with scorn upon the pitiful conciliators, trying by means of detours and machinations to avoid the approaching new wave of revolution ... we will not be fooled by any 'democratic conferences', and 'pre-parliaments'. We believe only in our Soviets. For their power we will fight to the death ... Hail the last decisive battle and our victory![46]

In John Reed's phrase, the Congress 'loomed over Russia like a thunder-cloud'. It could not be rigged. It would represent the real wishes of the submerged masses on the issues of peace, bread and land. Many opposed it. According to Reed:

> Delegates were sent through the country, messages flashed by wire to committees in charge of local Soviets, to Army Committees, instructing them to halt or delay elections to the Congress. Solemn public resolutions against the Congress, declarations that the democracy was opposed to the meeting so near the date of the Constituent Assembly ... The Council of the Russian Republic was one chorus of disapproval. The entire machinery set up by the Russian Revolution of [February] functioned to block the Congress of Soviets ...[47]

On the other hand was the shapeless will of the proletariat – the workmen, common soldiers and poor peasants. Winter approached. Petrograd's workers were in a race against time; while the second revolution swept the country, the factory-owners sought to grind them down by unemployment, hunger and forced evacuations. But as October neared, the factories grew quiet. There were few demands for wage rises, and almost no demonstrations. An eerie calm settled on Petrograd, in stark contrast to the vast upheaval in the rest of Russia. Many have commented on this strange prelude to the second revolution. Trams ran to schedule, factory shifts were normal, the crowds so characteristic of February were by-and-large absent. But this did not mean that the revolutionary wave had receded, or that a Bolshevik rising would be a putsch organised by a minority. As Russia capsized, so did the logic of everyday life also seem inverted. In the midst of the first proletarian revolution, the working class clung for dear life to the routines of normal living and working. It was the employers who sabotaged; the workers meant to inherit a going concern.

The Bolshevik Central Committee received a letter from the 'state criminal, Ulyanov-Lenin', who was still in hiding ('we are searching for him', said Kerensky). 'Now the Bolsheviks have a majority in the Soviets of Workers' and Soldiers' Deputies in both capitals, they can and must take state power into their own hands.' The Bolsheviks were never more popular, he wrote, while the

Democratic Conference was completely unrepresentative. The need to take power was even more urgent because of the danger of Germany capturing Petrograd which 'will make our chances one hundred times worse ... We must remember and reflect on Marx's words ... insurrection is an art ... The patience of the Peter and Moscow workers is exhausted ... History will not forgive us if we do not take power now ...'[48]

The last 'Defencists' lost their places on the Soviet. In the Cartridge Works the Menshevik and SR delegates were voted out when they admitted voting against the land to the tiller and the publication of the secret treaties. A worker told the Bolshevik newspaper *Workers' Way* 'they advised us to leave these matters to the Constituent Assembly. And that was the final straw.' The same at the Obukhovsky Factory. 'Who could have conceived of this a month ago?' said *Workers' Way*. 'Thus fall the last bastions of defencism.'[49]

Lenin's letter to the Central Committee had called for immediate preparations for a rising. This was a step from which they still shrank. Would it not, Kamenev asked, be irresponsible to jeopardise everything in an act which by its very desperation seemed to imply that history, the working class, the people, were not ready? If socialism was already prepared in the womb of history, it would not need forcing upon events by an act of the will. But Lenin was prepared to be the midwife even if others still drew back, and according to him the moment was ripe. There was a revolutionary upsurge of the people, the backing of the vanguard class, and a vacillating enemy. Unlike July, when workers and soldiers were not ready to die for Petrograd, there was now 'such "savageness", such seething hatred' against the counter-revolutionaries, particularly among peasants who had become convinced that the SRs would never give them the land.

The Central Committee suppressed Lenin's inflammatory letters, voting to take no action. Lenin had them circulated anyway and according to Malakhovsky, the Red Guard Commander in the Vyborg, they created a feverish atmosphere. Lenin said the time had come to strike into the enemy's vitals:

> Without losing a moment, organise the command of insurgent detachments, distribute our forces, send loyal regiments to strongpoints, surround the Alexandrine Theatre [seat of the Council of the Republic], occupy the Peter-Paul, arrest the General Staff, arrest the government.[50]

The party should 'summon the armed workers to a desperate and final fight, occupy the telephone exchange and move our insurrection headquarters there ... all this ... illustrates that now it is impossible to stay true to Marxism, true to the revolution, without treating insurrection as an art.' Five days later the CC met again. Among those present were Trotsky, Bukharin, Dzerzhinsky, Sverdlov, Smilga, Kollontai, Ioffe, Rykov (not Stalin): the Bolshevik *creme de la creme*. Their response to Lenin's urgings showed why the October

Revolution would not have happened without him. His arguments passed them by. The CC was gripped by a reflexive routinism, seemingly incapable of registering the import of his words. Their agenda ignored the call for insurrection. Within days another meeting was held, and, astoundingly, the CC this time discussed etiquette, resolving that: 'After hearing a report that Comrade Ryazanov called Tsereteli "comrade" ... the CC suggests to comrades that people whose description as "comrades" might offend the revolutionary feelings of the workers should not be addressed this way in public.'

Lenin, in agonies of impatience, wrote:

> To wait is a crime. The Bolsheviks have no right to wait for the Congress of Soviets, they must take power at once ... To delay is a crime. To wait for the Congress of Soviets is an infantile formality, a shameful play at formality, treachery to the revolution ...[51]

And his pen flamed out at Gorky's *Novaya Zhizn* for daring to suggest that the Bolsheviks could not hold power:

> Since the 1905 revolution, Russia has been governed by 130,000 landowners, who have perpetrated endless violence against 150,000,000 people, heaped unconstrained abuse upon them, and condemned the vast majority to inhuman toil and semi-starvation.
>
> Yet we are told that the 240,000 members of the Bolshevik Party will not be able to govern Russia, govern her in the interests of the poor, and against the rich.[52]

On 24 September, a party conference called for the transfer of power to the soviets, but the CC continued, in its own words, to 'mark time' – while noting that the popular mood was now 'extremely tense' – that 'the masses are putting forward the demand for concrete measures of some kind.' They decided to 'suggest to Ilyich that he move to Petrograd', and Lenin returned illegally on 7 October.

The climax neared. A German squadron appeared in the Baltic and German forces broaching Finnish soil were fiercely resisted by the Baltic Fleet, whose Soviet told the proletarians of the world:

> The slandered fleet fulfils its duty before the great revolution. We vowed to hold the front firmly and to guard the approaches to Petrograd ... We send you a last flaming appeal, oppressed of the whole world!
>
> Lift the banner of insurrection! Long live the world revolution! Long live the just general peace! Long live socialism![53]

The Germans did not advance on the capital, and the revolution rushed on unimpeded. Lenin's letters appeared on the streets in pamphlet form: 'The Bolsheviks Must Take Power', 'Marxism and Insurrection', 'The Crisis is Ripe!'

On 10 October, three days after his return, Lenin attended his first Central Committee meeting. It was held in Nikolai Sukhanov's flat. His wife was a Bolshevik sympathiser, and she made sure that the future chronicler of the revolution was not present to record what turned out to be a historic meeting. Lenin and Zinoviev – both of whom were still being hunted down – arrived; the meeting went on till late, and Mme Sukhanov served a supper of tea and sausage sandwiches.

Scourging irony, exhortations to act, bitter denunciations of the Committee's prevarications: Lenin scolded them to the starting-line. Did they want 'All Power to the Soviets' or not? 'Since the beginning of September a certain indifference to the question of insurrection has been noticeable', Lenin said. 'Nothing has been done, considerable time' for preparation has been lost. Meanwhile, the enemy is closing on Petrograd, evidently with the government's connivance. 'The international situation is ripe; the majority is now behind us. The moment has arrived for the transfer of power. Yet we seem to regard insurrection as a political sin.'

There was as a violent debate – 'we have passed a mass of resolutions' said one speaker. 'But done nothing.' Kamenev and Zinoviev furiously opposed: 'We can and must confine ourselves to a defensive position.' Later they would circulate a statement through the Bolshevik organisations – and leak it to the press. They argued the Bolsheviks would be the strongest opposition party in the Constituent Assembly, and that things were still moving their way. 'We do not have the right before history, before the international proletariat, before the Russian Revolution and the Russian working class, to stake the whole future on the card of an armed insurrection now.' Powerful forces were arrayed against 'the proletarian party': shock troops, Cossacks, thousands of 'magnificently armed' junkers, and 'artillery deployed in a fan round Peter'. The Menshevik–SRs who had fought alongside the Bolsheviks against Kornilov would this time side with the government. Moreover, 'if everyone oppressed by poverty were always ready to support an armed rising of socialists, we should have won socialism long ago,' they said, claiming that the slogan 'All power to the Soviets' signified only 'the most determined resistance to the slightest encroachment by the authorities on their rights.' But the mood had begun to change; Lenin's passionate arguments overwhelmed all resistance, and the meeting voted that the party should prepare itself for an armed rising. The imperialist powers threatened a separate peace, the resolution argued, in order to turn on Russia and strangle the revolution instead. But the uprush of revolution in the countryside, the growing trust of the people in the party, coupled with the danger of a second Kornilov, together meant 'that armed insurrection is inevitable, and the time is ripe' ... Orders were given to begin preparations, and a Political Bureau was established; its members were: Lenin,

Stalin, Trotsky, Sokolnikov, Bubnov – and Zinoviev and Kamenev, the only dissenters in the vote for a rising.[54]

14 October. In the Menshevik paper *Rabochaya Gazeta*: 'As a great revolutionist said: "Let us hasten, friends, to terminate the Revolution. He who makes it last too long will not gather the fruits" ...' That same day the Moscow Bolsheviks resolved 'to proceed to the organisation of armed insurrection ...' Among the intelligentsia the joke was to call the Soviet *'Sobachikh Deputatov'* ('Dogs' Deputies') rather than *'Rabochikh* (Workers') *Deputatov'*. At the Troitsky Farce Theatre, acording to John Reed, monarchists attacked actors performing 'Sins of the Tsar', for 'insulting the Emperor'.[55]

15 October. Industrialist Stepan Lianozov told John Reed 'starvation and defeat may bring the Russian people to their senses'; the government should abandon the capital so that the military 'can deal with these gentlemen [the Bolsheviks] without any legal formalities' – a fate also reserved for the Constituent Assembly, should it 'manifest any Utopian tendencies'.[56] On the same day the Sestroretsk arms factory delivered 5,000 rifles intended for General Kaledin's Cossacks to the Military Revolutionary Committee (MRC). Colonel Polkovnikov, Petrograd Military Commander, warned against 'irresponsible armed outbreaks' and promised 'the most extreme measures' in defence of order – as had General Khabalov, the Tsar's garrison commander, seven months before. Then on 16 October came the decisive meeting of the Bolshevik Central Committee, when the decision to overthrow the Provisional Government was taken in earnest. Speaking in haste, under enormous pressure, the members of the Central Committee finally crossed the Rubicon. 'The spirit of the resolution is the need ... to use the first suitable opportunity to grab power', argued Ioffe, expressing the majority view as it emerged in the course of the meeting.

'There is bread for just one day', Lenin said. 'We cannot wait for the Constituent Assembly. I move the resolution be affirmed, and that we get a move on with preparations. Let the CC and the Soviet decide just when to do it.'

The Bolsheviks convened a Congress of Soviets of the Northern Region; Trotsky told it 'the hour has come' and the delegates voted 148-2 to smash the Provisional Government. A ring of towns and cities, of garrisons and fleets, had voted for insurrection within the capital city they encircled. The Lettish delegate, Peterson, promised '40,000 riflemen' to defend the All-Russian Congress of Soviets. Kerensky would have to bring reinforcements, if he had any, through an enfilade ...

As the storm of the Second Congress loomed over the capital, and rumours flew of the counter-revolution, in meetings in the factories and in great halls like the Cirque Moderne, workers would rise from their seats saying it would be better 'to die with honour than live with shame'. All 'to the last man' should 'fight for the power of the Soviets of Workers', Soldiers' and Peasants' Deputies'.

Wednesday, 18 October. Kamenev and Zinoviev published their opposition to insurrection in Gorky's *Novaya Zhizn*. Lenin fulminated against the dissident two, calling them 'strike-breaking, blacklegs, despicable, treacherous'. 'I do not regard either of them as comrades any more ...'

The leaders, the party, the insurrectionary working class, were poised on a cusp of fate. An air of terrible expectancy lurked beneath the capital's seeming normality. It was autumn, and pouring rain turned the streets into seas of mud, through which clanked the city's overloaded trams. The Nevsky's cafes were crowded as usual. Meyerhold's *Death of Ivan the Terrible* was on at the Alexandrinsky, and the great singer, Fyodor Chaliapin, performed in *Boris Godunov*. In the mills and factories the shifts clocked on and off; but the Red Guards drilled constantly.

Appeals and proclamations were plastered on every wall: from the government, the Soviet EC, the Mensheviks and SR parties, from Polkovnikov, the garrison commander – all exhorting and demanding soldiers and workers, the whole populace, to 'stay at their posts', to support the government, to ignore the 'cursed Bolsheviki', 'friends of the Dark Forces'. Kerensky paced his quarters in the Winter Palace, nervous and irascible and taking drugs to lift his mood, and announced he was planning a holiday on the Volga; he expected to be away 'for a long time'. Four days before the Bolshevik Revolution, he pacified a prominent Cadet by saying 'I could pray for such an uprising. I have more strength than I need. They will be irrevocably smashed.'

As preparations intensified, they indiscernibly merged into the rising itself. It had begun! But still the decisive moment had yet to arrive; the Congress was yet to meet, the Provisional Government was still at large, Lenin still waited in hiding, in agonies of impatient worry for the outcome. Early in the afternoon of 24 October, Kerensky went to the pre-parliament to arraign Lenin and the leaders of what was now clearly an assault on the state created by the February Revolution.[57] As he spoke, a minister, Konovalov, handed him a proclamation just issued by the MRC to the garrison:

> We order the regiments to be put in a state of military preparedness and to await new orders. Any delay or non-execution of the order will be regarded as treason to the Revolution; signed, For the President: Podvoisky; Secretary: Antonov.[58]

The pre-parliament had been set up on the initiative of the Petrosoviet and the Executive Committee elected by the First All-Russian Congress of Soviets. Now the Petrosoviet had voted for 'All Power to the Soviets'; the Second All-Russian Congress was about to convene, and was the only lawful body in Russia which could decide the future dispensation. The Provisional Government had no mandate, no support and had effectively ceased to exist. Something had to take its place, and that could only be a Soviet government.

On the day of the revolution, the factories worked normally. There were no great crowds in the streets as in February. *Rabochaya Gazeta*, reporting two days later, used this circumstance to denounce the Bolshevik insurrection:

> Look at the streets. They are empty in the working class districts. There are no triumphal processions, no delegations to meet the victors with red banners ... The Bolsheviks will hardly last a week.[59]

But this was to ignore the essential nature of the rising. It was a planned operation carried out by the military arms of the Soviets. As Lenin had said in July, demonstrations were a thing of the past.

Also on 24 October, Central Committee met and at the insistence of Kamenev (who had recanted and been reinstated), decided that none of its members should leave the Smolny while the issue of power was being decided ... Jobs were allocated: Bubnov, to the railway workers; Dzerzhinsky, the communications workers; Milyutin, food supply; Sverdlov, to monitor the last acts of the Provisional Government. Trotsky proposed to prepare Peter-Paul as a reserve base should Smolny be taken by government forces. The Kronstadt sailors and the boisterous Red Guards were to spearhead the final assault on the key government centres and the Winter Palace itself. Everything was in readiness. The Smolny burned like a fever; outside, the city fell silent, waiting and watching. From hiding Lenin addressed a last letter to the Central Committee, who were still hesitating, and to other party bodies: 'Comrades! ... the situation is critical in the extreme. In fact it is now absolutely clear that to delay the uprising would be fatal ... power must not be left in the hands of Kerensky & Co until the 25th ...' Later that same evening he left a note for his hostess: 'I am going where you did not want me to go. Good bye', and crossed the city on foot and by tram, with one companion, arriving at Smolny at 11 pm; from that moment the pace of events quickened.

That night Trotsky told an exultant Petrosoviet, 'the government awaits the broom of history'. At midnight the old Soviet Executive Committee, themselves about to be swept away, called a meeting of delegates to the new Congress and to the Petrosoviet. Dan, wearing the uniform of a military doctor, spoke of the 'counter-revolution', which 'was never so strong as now; the Black Hundred press is more widely read in the factories and barracks than is the Socialist press'; in the wake of a Bolshevik rising, the provinces would quarantine and starve the capital, but 'only over the corpse of the EC will the bayonets of the two sides clash.'

'That corpse has been stiff for a long time', a voice shouted back. Trotsky was on his feet, shouting to the mass of Soviet deputies which had invaded the EC meeting: 'Don't back down ... our enemies will immediately capitulate, and you will occupy the place that belongs to you by right – masters of the Russian land ...'

As John Reed left the meeting he bumped into Zorin, a Bolshevik former exile back from the US and now sporting a rifle: 'We're moving', he said. 'We've pinched the Minister of Justice and the Minister of Religions. They're in the cellar now. One regiment is on the march to capture the Telephone Exchange, another the Telegraph Agency, another the State Bank. The Red Guard is out ...'[60] Kerensky tried in vain to summon up support; his lonely figure could be seen from time to time crossing the huge windswept parade ground between the Winter Palace and the quarters of the General Staff. The Cossack cavalry told him they were 'preparing to saddle up', but soon they stopped answering his calls. The situation was hopeless; the government had for its defence no more than one or two thousand junkers and a few hundred women's battalion troops. Ministers swamped the telegraph lines with pleas and proclamations to the army, the fronts, the country, to no avail.

At ten in the morning of 25 October, Kerensky went to the American Embassy to borrow a car, and left for the front. As he slipped away, the MRC issued the following message:

To the Citizens of Russia

The Provisional Government is overthrown. State power has passed into the hands of the organ of the Petrograd Soviet of Workers' and Soldiers' Deputies – the Military Revolutionary Committee, which stands at the head of the Petrograd proletariat and garrison.

The cause for which the people fought – the immediate proposal of a democratic peace, abolition of landlords' property rights, workers' control of production, the creation of a Soviet government – all this is assured.

Long live the revolution of the workers, soldiers and peasants.[61]

While Kerensky was escaping under American colours, sailors from the MRC arrived at the Marian Palace and told the pre-parliament to 'run along home'. Many of the delegates went to the Duma building, which was already besieged by frantic middle-class citizens, as rumours spread of Bolshevik atrocities. During the night of 26 October the Petrograd City Duma set up a 'Committee for the Salvation of the Revolution', and under its banner gathered the remnants of the old Soviet EC, the old front Committees, the presidium of the pre-parliament, officials of the railway and other unions, and many others who had lost, or would soon lose, their positions, who had turned their backs on the risen people and would soon be swept into oblivion.

At 2.35 in the afternoon of the 25th Lenin, Trotsky and Zinoviev addressed the Petrosoviet at the Smolny. It was Lenin's first public appearance since July. Their reception was tumultuous. Trotsky told the Soviet that 'power had passed to the people', amid thunderous applause. Then Lenin and Zinoviev spoke. 'Each word burned the soul', according to Arsenev, a Menshevik-Internationalist delegate to the Soviet, who 'saw that many people were clenching their fists, that an unshakable determination was forming in them to struggle to the end.'

Lenin said:

We shall have a Soviet government, our own instrument of power, in which the bourgeoisie shall not share. The oppressed will create their own power. The old state will be shattered ... we shall be helped by the world's working class, already thrusting forward in Italy, Germany, Britain ... All the secret treaties will be published immediately, to strengthen the confidence of the proletariat ... A single decree annihilating landed property will win the peasants to us ... we have the power of mass organisation, it will overcome every obstacle and lead the proletariat to the world revolution.[62]

At 6.30 pm the Military Revolutionary Committee ordered the final assault on the Winter Palace. Blank shots were fired from the cruiser *Aurora* and sailors and Red Guards began to infiltrate the Palace. At 9.30 pm a final despairing appeal came over the last open line available to the ex-ministers holed up in the palace: 'Let the country and the people reply to the mad effort of the Bolsheviks to raise an uprising in the rear of the fighting army.' There was no reply.

About midnight the invaders penetrated the Palace as far as the Malachite Chamber, with its columns and ornaments of lustrous green stone, where the ministers were guarded by a thin line of junkers, who were soon entreated to surrender. The thin figure of Antonov-Ovseenko, wearing a broad-brimmed hat and pince-nez, burst in on the ministers and arrested them 'in the name of the Military Revolutionary Committee'. Narrowly rescuing them from being lynched, he had the ex-government escorted over the Neva to the dungeons of the Peter-Paul; they were soon released into house-arrest. Six people had died in the storming of the Winter Palace – five soldiers and one sailor. None of the defenders was killed. Others arrested in the hours after the fall of the Provisional Government included Mme Kerensky, who was found wandering the streets, tearing down Bolshevik posters; she was released when the guard found out who she was.

The Congress of Soviets of Workers' and Soldiers' Deputies was due to begin at 1 pm on 25 October. Of 670 delegates, 350 were Bolsheviks, 80 Mensheviks and 60 Right SRs; the remainder were Left SRs. The Mensheviks and SRs quit the Congress almost at once. Reduced as they were, they represented still less, coming for the most part from the gerrymandered rumps of old army and regional committees. They left for the city Duma, where the Committee for the Salvation of the Revolution was being set up. The deposed Soviet EC members wired to all Soviets and Army Committees saying that the

'Soviet EC considers the Second Congress of Soviets has not taken place, and regards it as a conference of Bolshevik delegates.' John Reed described the scene in the Smolny that night:

> Smolny was tenser than ever, if that were possible. The same running men in the dark corridors, squads of workers with rifles, leaders with bulging portfolios, arguing, explaining, giving orders as they hurried anxiously along, surrounded by friends and lieutenants Men literally out of themselves, living prodigies of sleeplessness and work ...[63]

The opening of the Congress was delayed while a fierce argument raged behind the scenes about the composition of the first Soviet government. The Left SRs and Menshevik-Internationalists – the main non-Bolshevik groups left – could not bring themselves to join. There was a strong current of opinion arguing for a new coalition, excluding only the Cadets. The Bolsheviks seemed isolated, and there were still few reports about the progress of the revolution in other parts of the country. Martov's Menshevik Internationalists strove to mediate between the various groups to form a new coalition. They were keenly supported by Kamenev and Zinoviev, who remained unconvinced that the Bolsheviks could go it alone.

Finally, according to John Reed, at 8.40 pm a

> thundering wave of cheers announced the entrance of the presidium, with Lenin – great Lenin – among them. A short stocky figure, with a big head set down on his shoulders, bald and bulging. Little eyes, a snubbish nose, wide generous mouth, and heavy chin; clean-shaven now but already beginning to bristle with the well-known beard of his past and future. Dressed in shabby clothes, his trousers much too long for him. Unimpressive, to be the idol of a mob, loved and revered as perhaps few leaders in history have been ...[64]

Kamenev reported on the progress of the insurrection, and a succession of speakers followed, some for, some against, the Bolshevik rising. Soldier delegates fresh from the front brought, Reed said, 'enthusiastic greetings'. Then Lenin:

> gripping the edge of the reading-stand, letting his little winking eyes travel over the crowd as he stood there waiting, apparently oblivious to the long-rolling ovation, which lasted several minutes. When it finished, he said simply, 'We shall now proceeed to construct the Socialist order!' Again that overwhelming human roar ...[65]

The first session of the Congress adjourned at 6 am on the morning of 26 October. During the night it heard many items of cheering news: the fall of the

Winter Palace, the pledges of loyalty of new divisions, fronts and units (even some, like the cyclists, who were thought to be Kerensky loyalists), the fleeing of Kerensky. And it had voted to take power, and to elect the first Soviet Government, a Council of People's Commissars, headed by Lenin.

On 26 October *Izvestia*, which a short time before was preparing to put itself and the whole soviet movement out of business, flamed out with a new message, hailing the victorious proletarian revolution and, in the words of the Petrosoviet resolution, emphasising 'particularly the solidarity, organisation, discipline and complete unanimity displayed by the masses in this unusually bloodless and unusually successful uprising ... The Soviet is convinced that the urban workers, allies of the poor peasants, will display strict, comradely discipline and establish the strictest revolutionary order, essential for the victory of socialism.' The resolution was drafted by Lenin.

He also drafted a proclamation passed by the Petrosoviet and delegates from the peasant Soviets and published in *Worker and Soldier*. 'The Congress takes power into its own hands', it began, announcing the arrest of the Provisional Government, and proposing an immediate armistice on all fronts and a democratic peace, the expropriation of landed, crown and church property, workers' control of industry, complete democracy in the army, the convocation 'at the time appointed' of the Constituent Assembly, and a guarantee of self-determination to all the nations inhabiting Russia. Lenin ended by appealing to soldiers, railwaymen and other workers to defend the revolution against Kerensky's troops.

The same day Lenin reported to the Second All-Russia Congress of Soviets on 'the burning question of peace'.

'Plenty has been said and written, and all of you, no doubt, have discussed it endlessly. Permit me, therefore, to read a declaration which a government you elect ought to publish.' 'Exhausted, tormented, racked by war', the decree read, 'working people in all the belligerent countries crave a just, democratic peace', without annexations or indemnities. Annexation was 'seizure and violence', the forcible incorporation of small, weak and backward nations, in Europe and overseas, into larger states.

'The government considers it the worst crime against humanity to continue the war for the division among strong and rich states of the weaker nations they have conquered, and solemnly announces its determination ... to stop this war on terms which are equally just for all nationalities without exception.' The secret treaties would be published and 'the government proclaims the immediate and unconditional annulment of everything they contain which, as is mostly the case, is intended to secure advantages and privileges for Russian landowners and capitalists.' Calling for 'negotiations conducted openly in the full view of the people', Lenin appealed to 'the class-conscious workers of the three most advanced nations of mankind, ... Great Britain, France and Germany', whose workers 'have made the greatest contribution to the cause of progress and socialism, including the great examples of the English Chartists, the revolutions of historic importance effected by the French working class, and the heroic struggle against the Anti-Socialist law in Germany.'[66]

The Decree on Peace was carefully presented not as an ultimatum to the imperialist powers 'for that would give our enemies the opportunity to say ... that it is useless to start negotiations with us ... We are willing to consider any peace terms and all proposals ... War cannot be ended by refusal, it cannot be ended by one side ... In the Manifesto of March 14 we called for the overthrow of the bankers, but we didn't smash our own bankers, we entered into alliance with them. But now we have cast down the government of the bankers. The governments and the bourgeoisie will make every effort to unite their forces and drown the workers' and peasants' revolution in blood. But ... the workers' movement will triumph, will pave the way to peace and socialism.'

Pravda and *Izvestia* blazoned the Decree on Land on their front pages on 28 October. 'The Menshevik and SR appeasers', they said, 'committed a crime when they kept putting off settlement of the land question ... Their talk of riots and anarchy in the countryside was lies, cowardice, deceit. Where and when has good government provoked riots and anarchy? If they had acted wisely, and their measures had met the needs of the poor peasants, there would have been no unrest ... Having provoked a revolt, ... they were going to crush it in blood and iron, but were themselves swept away.'

Lenin told the Congress that the Decree on Land 'can pacify and satisfy the vast masses of poor peasants': Lenin went on: 'Voices are being raised that the decree itself and the Mandate were the work of the Socialist-Revolutionaries. What of it? ... We cannot ignore the decision of the people, even if we disagree with it. In the furnace of experience, putting the decree into life, enacting it in their own localities, the peasants will realise where the truth lies. And even were the peasants to follow the Socialist-Revolutionaries, to the point of giving this party a majority in the Constituent – then we shall say: What of it? Life is the best teacher! Life will show who is right. Let the peasants solve this problem from one end and we shall solve it from the other ... they want to settle all land problems themselves: and we are opposed to any amending this draft law. We don't want any details in it, because this is a decree, not a programme of action ... the peasants must know that now there are no more landowners, and they must decide all questions for themselves, they must arrange their own lives ...'[67]

Gorky's *Novaya Zhizn* wrote:

At present, a purely Soviet government can only be Bolshevik. But with each day it becomes clearer that the Bolsheviks cannot govern – they issue decrees like hot cakes and cannot carry them into life. Why cannot a government supported by the broad masses of workers and soldiers rule? The Bolsheviks say: sabotage of the intelligentsia led by the defencist parties ... There is also the striking ignorance of the Bolsheviks in state affairs and legislation.

Decrees read more like newspaper editorials ... The proletariat cannot rule without the intelligentsia.[68]

The counter-revolution began. Kerensky tried to move on Petrograd from Pskov, where the headquarters of the Northern Front were situated. He could only mobilise some Cossacks from the Savage Division, who occupied Gatchina on 27 October and Tsarskoye Selo on the 28 October. During those few days Petrograd's workers organised to defend their revolution. On a snow-swept morning, 25 degrees below zero, thousands upon thousands of people, in thin, tattered clothes, with white pinched faces, women and men, even children, poured forth from the factories and working class quarters; with 'infinite courage, infinite faith', as eye-witness Louise Bryant recorded, they marched out 'untrained and unequipped to meet the traditional bullies of Russia, the paid fighters, the paid enemies of freedom.' No one knew where the advancing Cossacks were, so they followed the sound of gunfire rolling back from the battlefield. These were the same working-class women who on International Women's Day, eight long months before, had begun the revolution which overthrew Tsardom. Of their commitment, Angelica Balabanova said to Bryant: 'Women have to go through such a tremendous struggle before they are free in their own minds that freedom is more precious to them than to men.' On 30 October the workers and a large force of Kronstadt sailors destroyed the remnants of Kerensky's Savage Division. These were the first skirmishes in a civil war which was to rage across the territory of the former Russian Empire for a further four years, during which up to seven million would lose their lives, as armies from 14 different countries, including Japan, Germany, the USA, Great Britain and France, tested with fire and sword the Great October Socialist Revolution.

Notes

1 The Duma was the Tsar's consultative body set up after the 1905 revolution, and elected on a rigged franchise.
2 The Cadets (Constitutional-Democrats) were a centre-left liberal party.
3 Ferro (1972) contains a valuable non-Marxist discussion of the dynamics of crisis induced by the war.
4 Shlyapnikov (1983) p. 38.
5 David Elliott (1986) discusses the ferment in the arts during this period.
6 On Sunday, 9 January 1905 innocent, peaceful demonstrators led by Father Gapon (a Tsarist agent provocateur) were fired upon by troops in St Petersburg (as it was then called), an event which led to the 1905 revolution.
7 Until 1918 the Julian calendar was used; it was 13 days behind the Gregorian calendar used elsewhere.
8 Schapiro (1983) provides a sympathetic account of the attitude of the Duma men at this juncture.

9 Accounts vary of this episode, as of much else which took place during these hectic few days.

10 Sukhanov (1955) p. 61.

11 Sukhanov (1955) p. 66 ff.

12 Schapiro and others dismiss this episode, reported by Sukhanov, as probably apocryphal, but that such events occurred on a wide scale cannot be questioned.

13 *Soviet Weekly* (1987).

14 See Thompson (1966) pp. 41-5 for a discussion of Wilson's view of Russia.

15 Lenin (1974) vol. 23, p. 297.

16 See Krupskaya (1970) Chap. 15 for an account of this period.

17 Lenin (1974) vol. 23, p. 329.

18 Ibid., p. 330.

19 Ibid., p. 339.

20 Lenin (1974) vol. 24, p. 88.

21 Sukhanov has a vivd account of this period, when he himself played a leading role in the conduct of Soviet policy.

22 Sukhanov (1955) p. 12.

23 Ibid., p. 125.

24 Ibid., p. 183.

25 Smith (1985) p. 54 ff.

26 Ibid., p. 62.

27 The 'Wobblies' – the Industrial Workers of the World (IWW) – an American syndicalist trade union with revolutionary aspirations.

28 Lenin (1979) p. 27.

29 Smith (1985) p. 77.

30 Sukhanov (1955) p. 237.

31 Carr (1966) vol. 1, p. 86.

32 Sukhanov (1955) pp. 280-2.

33 Gorky (1967) p. 34.

34 See Liebman (1975) pp. 190-209 for a useful discussion of Lenin's attitude to mass spontaneity and the bearing it had on the meaning of 'socialist democracy'.

35 Reed (1966) p. 39.

36 Insufficient account is taken of this circumstance in Ferro's acount of the conference, in which its importance is somewhat over-inflated.

37 Ferro (1972) p. 189.

38 Ferro (1980) p. 82.

39 Gorky (1967) p. 30.

40 Ferro (1972) p. 210.

41 Mandel (1984) p. 211.

42 Mandel (1984) p. 212.

43 Ferro (1980) p. 51.

44 Chamberlin (1935) p. 342.

45 Reed (1966) p. 51.
46 Mandel (1984) p. 260.
47 Reed (1966) p. 51.
48 Lenin (1980) p. 9.
49 Mandel (1984) p. 253.
50 Lenin (1980) p. 15.
51 Lenin (1964) vol. 26, p. 84.
52 Lenin (1977) p. 377.
53 Knyazev and Konstantinov (1957) p. 375 (translation modified).
54 Bone (1974) pp. 85-9.
55 Reed (1966) p. 33.
56 Ibid., p. 34.
57 This is Kerensky's Speech before the Council of the Republic, included in this collection (see below p. 79)
58 Reed (1966) p. 80.
59 Rabochaya Gazeta in Mandel (1984) p. 320.
60 Reed (1966) p. 87.
61 Lenin (1984) p. 15.
62 Ibid., p. 16.
63 Reed (1966) p. 125.
64 Ibid., p. 128.
65 Ibid., p. 129.
66 Lenin (1984) pp. 22-6.
67 Ibid., pp. 27-31.
68 Mandel (1984) p. 326.

1

The Historical Limits
of Capitalism

KARL MARX

...The contradiction, to put it in a very general way, consists in that the capitalist mode of production involves a tendency towards the absolute development of the productive forces, regardless of the value and surplus-value it contains, and regardless of the social conditions under which capitalist production takes place; while, on the other hand, its aim is to preserve the value of the existing capital and promote its self-expansion to the highest limit (i.e. to promote an ever more rapid growth of this value). The specific feature about it is that it uses the existing value of capital as a means of increasing this value to the utmost. The methods by which it accomplishes this include the fall of the rate of profit, depreciation of existing capital, and development of the productive forces of labour at the expense of already-created productive forces.

The periodical depreciation of existing capital – one of the means immanent in capitalist production to check the fall of the rate of profit and hasten the accumulation of capital through the formation of new capital – disturbs the given conditions within which the process of circulation and reproduction of capital takes place, and is therefore accompanied by sudden stoppages and crises in the production process.

The decreasing proportion of labour to fixed capital, which goes hand in hand with the development of the productive forces, stimulates the growth of the working population, while continually creating an artificial over-population. The accumulation of capital in terms of value is slowed down by the falling rate of profit, to hasten still more the accumulation of use-values, while this, in turn, adds new momentum to accumulation in terms of value.

Capitalist production seeks continually to overcome these immanent barriers, but overcomes them only by means which again place these barriers in its way and on a more formidable scale.

The *real barrier* of capitalist production is *capital itself*. It is that capital and its self-expansion appear as the starting and the closing point, the motive and the purpose of production; that production is only production for *capital* and not vice versa, the means of production are not mere means

1

for a constant expansion of the living process of the society of producers. The limits within which the preservation and self-expansion of the value of capital resting on the expropriation and pauperisation of the great mass of producers can alone move — these limits come continually into conflict with the methods of production employed by capital for its purposes, which drive towards the unlimited extension of production, towards production as an end in itself, towards the unconditional development of the social productivity of labour. The means — unconditional development of the productive forces of society — comes continually into conflict with the limited purpose, the self-expansion of the existing capital. The capitalist mode of production is, for this reason, a historical means of developing the material forces of production and creating an appropriate world-market, and is, at the same time, a continual conflict between this its historical task and its own corresponding relations of social production.

2

The Historical Destiny
of the Doctrine of
Karl Marx

V. I. LENIN

The chief thing in the doctrine of Marx is that it brings out the historic role of the proletariat as the builder of socialist society. Has the course of events all over the world confirmed this doctrine since it was expounded by Marx?

Marx first advanced it in 1844. The *Communist Manifesto* of Marx and Engels, published in 1848, gave an integral and systematic exposition of this doctrine, an exposition which has remained the best to this day. Since then world history has clearly been divided into three main periods: (1) from the revolution of 1848 to the Paris Commune (1871) ; (2) from the Paris Commune to the Russian revolution (1905); (3) since the Russian revolution.

Let us see what has been the destiny of Marx's doctrine in each of these periods.

At the beginning of the first period Marx's doctrine by no means dominated. It was only one of the very numerous groups or trends of socialism. The forms of socialism that did dominate were in the main akin to our Narodism: incomprehension of the materialist basis of historical movement, inability to single out the role and significance of each class in capitalist society, concealment of the bourgeois nature of democratic reforms under diverse, quasi-socialist phrases about the 'people', 'justice', 'right' and so on.

The revolution of 1848 struck a deadly blow at all these vociferous, motley and ostentatious forms of *pre*-Marxian socialism. In all countries, the revolution revealed the various classes of society *in action*. The shooting of the workers by the republican bourgeoisie in Paris in the June days of 1848 finally revealed that the proletariat *alone* was socialist by nature. The liberal bourgeoisie dreaded the independence of this class a hundred times more than it did any kind of reaction. The craven liberals grovelled before reaction. The peasantry were content with the abolition of the survivals of feudalism and joined the supporters of order, wavering but occasionally

3

between *workers' democracy and bourgeois liberalism*. All doctrines of *non*-class socialism and *non*-class politics proved to be sheer nonsense.

The Paris Commune (1871) completed this development of bourgeois changes; the republic, i.e. the form of political organisation in which class relations appear in their most unconcealed form, owed its consolidation solely to the heroism of the proletariat.

In all the other European countries, a more tangled and less complete development led to the same result — a bourgeois society that had taken definite shape. Towards the end of the first period (1848-71), a period of storms and revolutions, pre-Marxian socialism was *dead*. Independent *proletarian* parties came into being as the First International (1864-72) and the German Social-Democratic Party.

The second period (1872-1904) was distinguished from the first by its 'peaceful' character, by the absence of revolutions. The West had finished with bourgeois revolutions. The East had not yet risen to them.

The West entered a phase of 'peaceful' preparations for the changes to come. Socialist parties, basically proletarian, were formed everywhere, and learned to use bourgeois parliamentarism and to found their own daily press, their educational institutions, their trade unions and their cooperative societies. Marx's doctrine gained a complete victory and *began to spread*. The selection and mustering of the forces of the proletariat and its preparation for the coming battles made slow but steady progress.

The dialectics of history were such that the theoretical victory of Marxism compelled its enemies to *disguise themselves* as Marxists. Liberalism, rotten within, tried to revive itself in the form of socialist *opportunism*. They interpreted the period of preparing the forces for great battles as renunciation of these battles. Improvement in the conditions of the slaves to fight against wage-slavery they took to mean the sale by the slaves of their right to liberty for a few pence. They cravenly preached 'social peace' (i.e. peace with the slave-owners), renunciation of the class struggle, etc. They had very many adherents among socialist members of parliament, various officials of the working-class movement, and the 'sympathising' intelligentsia.

However, the opportunists had scarcely congratulated themselves on 'social peace' and on the non-necessity of storms under 'democracy' when a new source of great world storms opened up in Asia. The Russian revolution was followed by revolutions in Turkey, Persia and China. It is in this era of storms and their 'repercussions' in Europe that we are now living. No matter what the fate of the great Chinese republic, against which various 'civilised' hyenas are now whetting their teeth, no power on earth can restore the old serfdom in Asia or wipe out the heroic democracy of the masses in the Asiatic and semi-Asiatic countries.

Certain people who were inattentive to the conditions for preparing and developing the mass struggle were driven to despair and to anarchism by the lengthy delays in the decisive struggle against capitalism in Europe. We can now see how short-sighted and faint-hearted this anarchist despair is.

The fact that Asia, with its population of 800 million, has been drawn into the struggle for these same European ideals should inspire us with optimism and not despair.

The Asiatic revolutions have again shown us the spinelessness and baseness of liberalism, the exceptional importance of the independence of the democratic masses, and the pronounced demarcation between the proletariat and the bourgeoisie of all kinds. After the experience both of Europe and Asia, anyone who speaks of *non*-class politics and *non*-class socialism, ought simply to be put in a cage and exhibited alongside the Australian kangaroo or something like that.

After Asia, Europe has also begun to stir, although not in the Asiatic way. The 'peaceful' period of 1872-1904 has passed, never to return. The high cost of living and the tyranny of the trusts are leading to an unprecedented sharpening of the economic struggle, which has set into movement even the British workers who have been most corrupted by liberalism. We see a political crisis brewing even in the most 'diehard', bourgeois-Junker country, Germany. The frenzied arming and the policy of imperialism are turning modern Europe into a 'social peace' which is more like a gunpowder barrel. Meanwhile the decay of *all* the bourgeois parties and the maturing of the proletariat are making steady progress.

Since the appearance of Marxism, each of the three great periods of world history has brought Marxism new confirmation and new triumphs. But a still greater triumph awaits Marxism, as the doctrine of the proletariat, in the coming period of history.

Pravda, 1 March 1913

3

In Exile, 1898-1901

NADEZHDA KRUPSKAYA

(Nadezhda Krupskaya (Lenin's wife) gives a vivid evocation of Siberian exile at the turn of the century.)

It was dusk when we arrived at Shushenskoye, where Vladimir Ilyich lived; Vladimir Ilyich was out hunting. We unloaded and were led into the *izba* (log-hut). In the Munusinsk regions of Siberia the peasants are particularly clean in their habits. The floors are covered with brightly coloured home-spun mats, the walls whitewashed and decorated with fir-branches. The room used by Vladimir Ilyich, though not large, was spotlessly clean. My mother and I were given the remaining part of the cottage. The owners of the *izba* and their neighbours all crowded in, eagerly looking us up and down and questioning us...

At last Vladimir Ilyich returned from the hunt. He was surprised to see a light in his room. The master of the house told him that it was Oscar Alexandrovich (an exiled Petersburg worker) who had come home drunk and scattered all his books about. Vladimir Ilyich quickly bounded up the steps. At that moment I emerged from the *izba*. We talked for hours and hours that night. Ilyich looked much fitter and fairly vibrated with health...

Vladimir Ilyich had a peasant friend, Zhuravlev, of whom he was very fond. A consumptive, thirty years of age, Zhuravlev had formely been a rural clerk. Vladimir Ilyich said of him that he was by nature a revolutionary, a protester. Zhuravlev courageously opposed the rich and would not countenance the slightest injustice. He went away somewhere, and before long died from consumption.

Another acquaintance of Ilyich's was a poor peasant with whom he frequently went hunting. He was a most thick-headed old *mujik*, and they called him Sosipatich. But he was on excellent terms with Vladimir Ilyich, and used to make him presents of all manner of strange things: one time it would be a crane, another time cedar cones.

It was through Sosipatich and through Zhuravlev that Vladimir Ilyich

6

studied the Siberian countryside. He told me once about a conversation of his with the wealthy peasant with whom he was lodging. A farm-labourer had stolen a skin from the latter. The rich peasant caught him red-handed, and finished him off there and then. Apropos of this, Ilyich spoke of the ruthless cruelty of the petty-proprietor, the ruthless way he exploited the farm-labourers. And truly, the Siberian farm-hands worked as if in servitude, only snatching a little rest at holiday time.

Ilyich had yet another method of studying the countryside. On Sundays he ran a juridical consultation. He enjoyed great popularity as a jurist, as he had helped one worker, who had been turned off the gold-mines, to win his case against the gold-field proprietor. News about the winning of this case quickly spread among the peasants. *Mujiks* and peasant women came and unburdened their woes. Vladimir Ilyich listened attentively and probed into everything, afterwards giving his advice. Once a peasant came twenty *versts* for advice as to how he could get judgement against his brother-in-law for not having invited him to his wedding, where there had been a fine drinking-bout. 'But if I go to see him now, will my brother-in-law offer any drinks?' 'Of course he will, if you go now.' And it took Vladimir Ilyich the best part of an hour before he could persuade the *mujik* to make peace with his brother-in-law. Sometimes it was quite impossible to make head or tail of the case from the stories they narrated, and therefore Vladimir Ilyich always asked them to bring him a copy of the relevant documents. Once a bull owned by some wealthy farmer gored a cow belonging to a poor peasant woman. The Volost court ordered the proprietor to pay the woman ten roubles. She contested this decision and demanded a 'copy' of the case. 'What d'you want, a copy of the white cow, eh?' mockingly asked the assessor. The enraged peasant brought her complaint to Vladimir Ilyich. It was often sufficient for the offended person to threaten to complain to Ulyanov and the offender would desist. Vladimir Ilyich studied the Siberian village very closely — just as he had formerly acquired a thorough knowledge of the Volga countryside. Ilyich told me once: 'My mother wanted me to take up farming. I was going to start when I saw that it was not possible. My relations with the *mujiks* would have become abnormal.'

Strictly speaking, Vladimir Ilyich, as an exile, had not the right to occupy himself with juridical affairs. But these were liberal times in the Minusinsk region, and there was practically no surveillance.

The 'assessor' — a wealthy local peasant — was more concerned with selling us his veal than in seeing that 'his' exiles did not escape. Things were astonishingly cheap at Shushenskoye. For example, Vladimir Ilyich, on his 'salary' — a subvention of eight roubles — had a clean room, food and his laundry and mending done. And this was considered dear! It is true, dinner and supper were rather plain. One week they would kill a sheep and feed Vladimir Ilyich with it from day to day until it was all eaten up. When it was all gone they would buy the meat for another week, and the farm-girl chopped up this supply in the trough where the cattle fodder was prepared. This mincemeat was used for cutlets for Vladimir Ilyich — also for a whole week. But there was plenty of milk for both Vladimir Ilyich and his dog — a fine Gordon setter named Zhenka, whom he taught to fetch and carry, to retrieve and to perform other canine manoeuvres.

As the Zyryanovs often held peasant drinking-bouts at their place, and as family life was uncomfortable there in many respects, we soon moved to other quarters. We hired half a house with yard and kitchen-garden attached, for four roubles. We lived as one family. In the summer it was impossible to find anyone to help with the housework. I and another together fought with the Russian stove. At first I knocked over with the oven-hook the soup and dumplings, which were scattered over the hearth. But afterwards I got used to it. All sorts of things grew in our kitchen-garden — cucumbers, carrots, beetroots, pumpkins; I was very proud of our kitchen-garden. We also turned the yard into a garden, getting hops from the woods to plant in it.

In October a girl-help appeared on the scene. This was thirteen-year-old Pasha, scraggy, with pointed elbows. She soon picked up the whole gamut of household duties. I taught her to read and write, and she adorned the walls with my mother's instructions: 'never, never, spill the tea'. She also kept a diary, where such entries were inscribed as: 'Oscar Alexandrovich and Prominsky called. They sang a "sing". I also sang.'

Then the infantile element put in an appearance. Across the way lived a settler, a Lettish felt-bootmaker. He had had fourteen children, but only one was still living. This was Minka. Minka was six years old, and had a transparent, pale little face. His father was a confirmed drunkard. Minka had clear eyes and a serious way of talking. He began to come every day. We would only just be up when the door would bang, and a little figure appear, clad in a big fur cap and warm jacket wound round in a scarf, joyfully exclaiming: 'And here I am!' He knew that my mother was infatuated with him, and that Vladimir Ilyich was always willing for a joke or a game. Minka's mother would run across, shouting:

'Minichka, have you seen a rouble?'

'Yes, but I saw that it was lying about on the table, so I put it in the box.'

When we went away Minka fell ill with grief. Now he is no longer living, and the bootmaker has written asking for a piece of land over by the Yenisei — 'for I don't want to go hungry in my old age'.

Our household grew still larger. We were joined by a kitten.

In the mornings Vladimir Ilyich and I set to and translated the Webbs, which Struve had obtained for us. After dinner we spent an hour or two jointly rewriting *The Development of Capitalism in Russia*. Then there was other work of all kinds. I think it was Potresov sent us for two weeks only Kautsky's book against Bernstein. We put aside all other jobs and translated it in the appointed period — just two weeks. The work ended, we went walking. Vladimir Ilyich was passionately fond of hunting. He procured himself some leather breeches, and got into any number of bogs. 'Well, there was game there', was his excuse. When I arrived it was spring and I had been perplexed. Prominsky would come in, and with a joyful smile, exclaim: 'I've seen them — the ducks have flown over.' Then Oscar would enter — also full of ducks. They talked for hours on the subject, but by the following spring I had also become capable of conversing about ducks — who had seen them, and where, and when. After the winter frosts, Nature burst forth tempestuously into the spring. Her power became mighty. Sunset. In the great spring-time pools in the fields wild swans were swimming. Or we stood at the edge of a wood and listened to a rivulet burbling, or wood-cocks clucking. Vladimir Ilyich went into the wood while I held back Zhenka. As I held her the dog trembled with excitement and one felt how overwhelming was this tumultuous awakening of nature. Vladimir Ilyich was an ardent huntsman, but too apt to become heated over it. In the autumn we went to far-off forest clearances. Vladimir Ilyich said: 'If we meet any hares, I won't fire as I didn't bring any straps, and it won't be convenient to carry them.' Yet immediately a hare darted out Vladimir Ilyich fired.

Late in the autumn, when small ice was already drifting down the Yenisei, we went after hares on the islands. The hares were already turning white. They could not get away from the islands, and were jumping around like goats. Our hunters would sometimes shoot whole boat-loads.

When we lived in Moscow Vladimir Ilyich also hunted at times in latter years, but by that time the huntsman's ardour had considerably ebbed. Once we organised a fox-hunt. Vladimir Ilyich was greatly interested in the whole enterprise. 'Very skilfully thought out', he said. We placed the hunters in such a way that the fox ran straight at Vladimir Ilyich. He grasped his gun and the fox, after standing and looking at him for a moment, turned and made off to the wood. 'Why on earth didn't you fire?' came our perplexed inquiry. 'Well, he was so beautiful, you know', said Vladimir Ilyich.

Late in the autumn, when the snow had not yet begun to fall, but the rivers were already freezing, we went far up the streams. Every pebble, every little fish, was visible beneath the ice, just like some magic kingdom. And winter-time, when the mercury froze in the thermometers, when the rivers were frozen to the bottom, when the water, flowing over the ice, quickly froze into a thin upper ice-layer — one could skate two *versts* or so with the upper layer of ice crunching beneath one's feet. Vladimir Ilyich was tremendously fond of all this...

In the evenings he usually read either books on philosophy — Hegel, Kant and the French naturalists — or, when very tired, Pushkin, Lermontov or Nekrasov...

The post came twice a week. There was extensive correspondence. Anna Ilyinichna (Lenin's sister:trans.) wrote about everything, and comrades wrote from Petersburg. Among other matters, Nina Alexandrovna Struve wrote me about her little son: 'he can already hold his head up and every day we take him up to the portraits of Darwin and Marx, and say: nod to Uncle Darwin, nod to Uncle Marx, and he nods in such a funny way'. We also received letters from distant places of exile, from Martov in Turukhansk, from Orlov in the Vyatka Gubernia, and from Potresov. But most of all were letters from comrades scattered throughout neighbouring villages. From Minusinsk which was fifty *versts* from Shushenskoye came letters from the Krzhizhanovskys and Starkov; thirty *versts* away, at Yermakovsk, lived Lepeshinsky, Vaneyev, Silvin and Panin – a comrade of Oscar's. Seventy *versts* away, at Tess, were Lengnik, Shapoval, and Baramzin, while Kurnatovsky lived at a sugar-mill. We corresponded on every conceivable subject. On Russian news, on plans for the future, on books, on new tendencies, on philosophy. We even wrote about chess matters, especially to Lepeshinsky. Games were played by correspondence. Vladimir Ilyich used to set up the chessmen, and sit for hours working out problems. At one time he was so taken up by chess that he even cried out in his sleep: 'If he puts his knight here, I'll stick my rook there!'

Both Vladimir Ilyich and Alexander Ilyich were great chess enthusiasts from childhood. Their father also played. 'At first father used to win', Vladimir Ilyich related to me. 'Then my brother and I got hold of a chess manual and began to beat father. Once — when our room was upstairs — we met father coming out of the room with a candle in his hand, and the manual under his arm. Then he went and studied it.'

On his return to Russia, Vladimir Ilyich abandoned chess-playing. 'Chess gets hold of you too much, and hinders work.' And as he did not like to do anything by halves, but devoted his entire energy to whatever he undertook, he sat down unwillingly to a game of chess even for recreation or while in exile.

From his early youth Vladimir Ilyich was capable of giving up whatever activity hindered his main work...

In the new year, we went to Minusinsk, where all the exiled Social Democrats had gathered. At Minusinsk there were also 'Narodnaya Volya' exiles. These old chaps bore an attitude of mistrust towards the social-democratic youth. They did not believe them to be real revolutionaries. On these grounds, an 'exile scandal' had taken place in the Minusinsk district just prior to my arrival at Shusenskoye. At Minusinsk there had been a social-democratic exile named Raichin, who came from the border-lands and was connected with the Emancipation of Labour group. He decided to make his escape. They provided him with money for the flight, but the day of the flight had not yet been decided on. But Raichin, on receiving the money, got into such a state of nerves that he made his escape without informing any of the comrades. The old men of the 'Narodnaya Volya' accused the Social Democrats of having known of Raichin's escape without warning them about it, and that there might be police searches before they had time to 'clean up'. The 'scandal' grew like a snowball. When I arrived, Vladimir Ilyich talked to me about it. 'There is nothing worse than these exile scandals', he said. 'They pull us back terribly. These old men have got bad nerves. Just look what they've been through, the penal sentences they have undergone. But we cannot let ourselves be drawn away by such scandals — all our work lies ahead, we must not waste ourselves on these affairs.' And Vladimir Ilyich insisted that we should break with these old people. I remember the meeting at which the rupture took place. The decision as to the break had been made beforehand. It was now a question of carrying it out as painlessly as possible. We made the break because a break was necessary. But we did it without malice, indeed with regret. And so we lived afterwards in separation.

Generally speaking, exile did not pass by so badly. Those were years of serious study. The nearer we approached the end of the period of exile, Vladimir Ilyich gave more and more thought to future work. News from Russia was very scant. Economism there had grown and become stronger. For all practical purposes there was no Party, and no printing press. The attempt to arrange publishing activity through the *Bund* had failed. Meanwhile to restrict ourselves to writing popular pamphlets without expressing ourselves on the fundamental questions of our work was no longer possible. The most complete dispersion prevailed in our work; repeated arrests made all continuity impossible. People went as far as talking about the *'Credo'*, and even to the lengths of *The Workers' Thought*, which printed a letter from a worker evidently taken in by the propaganda of the Economists. This correspondent wrote: 'We workers don't need your Marx or Engels...'

L. Tolstoy wrote somewhere that travelling the first part of a journey one usually thinks about what is left behind, and on the second half about what is waiting ahead. It is the same thing in exile. On the first period we spent more time summing up the results of the past. On the second half we thought more about what lay ahead. Vladimir Ilyich concentrated his thoughts more and more on what was to be done in order to bring the Party out of its present state, what was to be done to direct the work along the right course, to assure a correct social democratic leadership of the Party. How were we to start? In the last year of his exile Vladimir Ilyich conceived the organisational plan which he subsequently developed in *Iskra*, in the pamphlet *What is to be done?* and in the *Letter to a Comrade*. It was necessary to begin with the organisation of an all-Russian newspaper, to establish it abroad, to connect it up as closely as possible with activities in Russia, and to arrange transport in the best way possible. Vladimir Ilyich began to spend sleepless nights. He became terribly thin. It was these nights that he thought out his plan in every detail, discussed it with Krzhizhanovsky, with me, corresponded about it with Martov and Potresov, conferred with them about the journey abroad. The more time went on, the more Vladimir Ilyich was overcome with impatience, the more eager he was to get to work. And here again we were surprised by a police search. They had taken from somebody a receipt for a letter sent to Vladimir Ilyich. The letter contained reference to a monument to Fedoseev and the gendarmes made this an excuse for an official search. They found the letter, and it proved to be very innocent. They looked over our correspondence and also found nothing interesting. In accordance with an old Petersburg custom we kept all illegal literature or correspondence separate. It was true, however, that this lay in the bottom shelf of the cupboard. Vladimir Ilyich gave the gendarmes a bench to stand on so that they could start the search from the upper shelves, which were filled with various books of statistics — and they got so tired that they did not even look at the bottom shelf, being satisfied with my statement that it only contained my teaching text-books. The search ended without any complications, though we feared they might make this an occasion for adding a few years to our term of exile. In those days escapes were still not such common occurrences as in later times. In any case it would have complicated matters had we tried that course. For, prior to going abroad, it was necessary to undertake extensive organisational work in Russia. All went well, however, and our term was not increased.

In February 1900, when Vladimir Ilyich's exile came to an end, we left for Russia. Pasha, who in those two years had become a real beauty, shed torrents of tears that night. Minka was fidgety and carried home all the paper, pencils and other stationery we left behind. Oscar Alexandrovich, who came and sat on the edge of a chair, was evidently deeply moved. He brought me a present, a hand-made brooch in the form of a book, inscribed 'Karl Marx', in memory of our joint studies of *Capital*. The housewife and neighbours kept looking into the room to see what was going on. Our dog wondered what was meant by all this hubbub, and kept opening all the doors with her nose to see that everything was still in its place. Mother busied herself with the packing, coughing from the dust, while Vladimir Ilyich tied up his books in a business-like manner.

We reached Minusinsk, where we had to pick up Starkov and Olga Alexandrovna Silvina. All our brothers in exile were gathered there. We were in the mood that usually prevailed when any of the exiles went back to Russia: everybody was thinking about when and whether he himself would go, and how he would work. Vladimir Ilyich had already previously discussed the matter of collaboration with all those who were also about to return to Russia. He arranged with those remaining as to future correspondence. Everybody was thinking about Russia — yet we talked about all kinds of trivialities.

Baramzin was giving sandwiches to Zhenka, who had been left him as a heritage. But the dog took no notice of him. She lay at mother's feet, not taking her eyes off her and following her every movement.

At last, equipped in felt boots, elk-skin coats, and the rest, we started on our journey. We went on horseback 300 *versts* along the Yenisei day and night — thanks to the moonlight, which lit up everything. Vladimir Ilyich carefully wrapped us up at every stopping-place, looking round to see whether we had forgotten anything. He joked with Olga Alexandrovna, who felt the cold intensely. We kept hurrying on the whole of the journey, and Vladimir Ilyich — who travelled without elk-skin cloak, as he assured us he was hot in them — stuck his hands into a muff borrowed from mother, and let his thoughts wander to Russia, where it would be possible to work at will.

On the day of our arrival at Ufa we were met by the local people — A.D. Tsyurupa, Svidersky, Krokhmal. 'We have been to six hotels, ...' said Krokhmal, all out of breath, 'and at last have found you.'

Vladimir Ilyich stayed a couple of days at Ufa, and after having talked with our people and entrusted me and mother to comrades, moved on farther — nearer to Petersburg. Of these two days there only remains in my memory, a visit to the old Narodnaya Volya member, Chetvergova, whom Vladimir Ilyich had known in Kazan. She had a bookshop in Ufa. On the first day Vladimir Ilyich went to see her, and his voice and face seemed to become particularly gentle as he talked with her. When later I read what Vladimir Ilyich wrote at the end of *What is to be done?* I remembered that visit.

'Many of them' — (referring to the young Social Democrat leaders of the Labour movement), wrote Vladimir Ilyich in *What is to be done?* — 'commenced their revolutionary thinking as Narodovolists. Nearly all of them in their early youth enthusiastically worshipped the terrorist heroes. It was a great wrench to abandon the captivating impressions of these heroic traditions and it was accompanied by the breaking off of personal relationships with people who were determined to remain loyal to *Narodnaya Volya* and for whom the young Social Democrats had profound respect.' This paragraph is a piece of the biography of Vladimir Ilyich.

It was a great pity to have to part, just at a time when 'real' work was commencing. But it did not even enter Vladimir Ilyich's head to remain in Ufa when there was a possibility of getting nearer to Petersburg.

Vladimir Ilyich went to stay at Pskov, where Potresov and L.N. Radchenko and his children subsequently lived. Vladimir Ilyich once laughingly related how Radchenko's little daughters Zhenyurka and Lyuda used to tease him and Potresov. Placing their hands behind their backs they paced solemnly up and down the room side by side, one saying 'Bernstein' and the other replying 'Kautsky'. There, at Pskov, Vladimir Ilyich was busily engaged weaving the network of the organisation which was to assure a close contact between the future Russian newspaper to be published abroad and activities in the homeland. He had interviews with Babushkin and a great many others ...

I could hardly wait for the end of my exile, and what is more, there did not seem to have been any letters from Vladimir Ilyich for a long time. I wanted to go to Astrakhan to see 'the little uncle' (L.M. Knippovich), and was in a great hurry.

Mother and I called at Moscow to see Maria Alexandrovna, Vladimir Ilyich's mother. She was then alone in Moscow. His sister Maria Ilyinichna was in prison, and his other sister Anna Ilyinichna was abroad.

I was very fond of Maria Alexandrovna. She was always so thoughtful and attentive. Afterwards, when we lived abroad and she wrote letters, she always wrote to us jointly, never to Vladimir Ilyich alone. This was only a trifle, but what thoughtfulness there was in that trifle. Vladimir Ilyich had great affection for his mother. 'She has tremendous will-power', he once said to me, 'if that had happened to my brother when father was still alive, Lord knows what she might not have done.'

It was from his mother that Vladimir Ilyich inherited his strength of will, as also he inherited her kindness and her attention for people.

While we lived abroad, I endeavoured to describe to her our life in as realistic a way as possible, so that she could at least feel a little nearer to her son. When Vladimir Ilyich was in exile in 1897, the papers contained the obituary notice of Maria Alexandrovna Ulyanova, who had died in Moscow. Oscar told me: 'I went to Vladimir Ilyich and he was as white as a sheet — "my mother is dead", he said.' But that proved to be the obituary of some other M. A. Ulyanova.

A great deal of sorrow fell to the lot of Maria Alexandrovna — the execution of her eldest son, death of her daughter Olga, and the continual arrests of the other children. When Vladimir Ilyich fell ill in 1895, she immediately went to nurse him, and herself cooked his food. When he was arrested, she was again at her post. She sat for hours in the dimly lit waiting-room at the Preliminary Detention House; took parcels on visiting days; and her lips trembled but slightly.

I promised her I would look after Vladimir Ilyich, but I did not succeed ...

From Moscow I accompanied my mother to Petersburg, where I arranged things for her and then made my way across the frontier. I travelled on this journey looking purposely like an innocent provincial going abroad for the first time. I went to Prague, thinking that Vladimir Ilyich lived there under the name of Modraczek.

I sent a telegram and arrived in Prague. But no one came to meet me. I waited and waited. Greatly disconcerted I hailed a top-hatted cabby, piled him up with my baskets and started off. Arriving in the working-class district, we took a narrow turning and stopped at a large tenement building, the windows of which revealed a multitude of mattresses put out for airing...

I climbed to the fourth floor. A little white-haired Czech woman opened the door. 'Modraczek', I repeated, 'Herr Modraczek.' A worker came out and said: 'I am Modraczek.' Flabbergasted, I stammered: 'No, my husband is!' Modraczek finally tumbled to what had happened. 'Ah, you are probably the wife of Herr Rittmeyer. He lives at Munich, but sent books and letters to you at Ufa through me.' Modraczek ran around with me the whole of that day. I told him about the Russian movement, and he told me of the Austrian. His wife showed me some lace she had made, and they fed with with Czech 'klossc' (rissoles).

Arrived in Munich — I travelled in a fur coat, and at that time in Munich people were already going about in dresses only — having learned by experience, I left my baggage in the station cloak-room and went by tram to find Rittmeyer. I found the house, and Apartment No. 1 turned out to be a beershop. I went to the counter, behind which was a plump German, and timidly asked for Herr Rittmeyer, having a presentiment that again something was wrong. 'That's me', he said. 'No, it's my husband', I faltered, completely baffled.

And we stood staring at one another like a couple of idiots, until Rittmeyer's wife walked in and, looking at me, guessed what was the matter: 'Ach, you must be the wife of Herr Meyer. He is expecting his wife from Siberia. I'll take you to him.'

I followed Frau Rittmeyer out through the backyard of a big house into a kind of uninhabited apartment. The door opened, and there at a table sat Vladimir Ilyich, his sister Anna Ilyinichna and Martov. Forgetting to thank the landlady I cried: 'Why the devil didn't you write and tell me where I could find you?'

'Didn't write to you!' exclaimed Vladimir Ilyich. 'Why, I've been going three times a day to meet you. Where have you sprung from?' We afterwards ascertained that the friend, to whom had been sent a book containing the Munich address, kept the book to read!

Many of us Russians went on a wild-goose chase in a similar fashion. Shlyapnikov at first went to Genoa instead of Geneva; Babushkin, instead of going to London, had been about to start off for America.

4
Correspondence

Letter from Empress Alexandra to Tsar Nicholas II, February 1917:

Riots occurred yesterday in Vasilievsky Ostrov and in the Nevsky, and the poor stormed the bakeries. They smashed Fillipov's to pieces and Cossacks were called out to subdue them.

I hope Kedrinsky (Kerensky) from the Duma will be hanged for his horrible speech — this is necessary (military law, wartime) and it would set an example. Everybody thirsts for and entreats you to be firm.

A rowdy movement is afoot — young kids are running about, shouting that they haven't got bread — just to create excitement. And workers, too, who hinder others at work. If the weather was cold, they probably would have stayed at home.

But this will all pass and become quiet, if only the Duma would behave itself. The worst speeches are not printed, but I think people should be punished immediately and very severely for making anti-dynastic speeches, the more so that it is now wartime.

Extract from a telegram from Prime Minister Rodzianko to C-in-C, Northern Front, 27 February 1917:

The riots which have started in Petrograd are acquiring a spontaneous nature and alarming proportions. Their basis is the scarcity of baked bread and poor deliveries of flour, which cause panic; but mainly it is a complete lack of confidence in a government which is incapable of lifting the country out of its present difficulties.

No doubt these events will continue to develop, although they can be held temporarily in check at the price of shedding some civilian blood; but this cannot continue.

The movement may spread to the railways and the country's life would come to a standstill at the most difficult moment. Petrograd's war industries are coming to a halt for lack of fuel and raw materials, the workforce is idle, and the hungry, unemployed mob are plunging towards irresistible anarchy. Railway communications are in total disorder throughout Russia.

From the diary of Nicholas II :

March 2. Sunday. The situation in Petrograd is such that the State Duma ministers are powerless to act because the Social Democratic Party, through the workers' committee, is waging a struggle against it.

For the salvation of Russia, and to keep the army at the Front, I decided on this step. I agreed, and the draft manifesto was sent from GHQ. In the evening Guchkov and Shulgin arrived from Petrograd and after a discussion I gave them the amended manifesto, signed by me.

The Tsar's manifesto:

At a time of great struggle against the external foe, who strove for nearly three years to enslave the motherland, it was the Lord Almighty's will to visit a heavy new trial upon Russia.

The internal upheaval of the people which has started, threatens the further conduct of this lingering war.

The fate of Russia, the honour of our heroic army and our dear fatherland's whole future, demand the waging of the war to a victorious end no matter what.

The cruel enemy is straining his last efforts, and the hour is near when our gallant army, jointly with our glorious allies, will crush the foe.

At this decisive moment in the life of Russia, we deemed it the duty of conscience to further the closest unity of the whole people and the consolidation of popular forces for the achievement of a speedy victory and, in agreement with the State Duma, we deemed it necessary to abdicate the crown of the Russian State and to shed our sovereign power. Let the Lord Almighty help Russia.

Nicholas
Pskov, 3 pm, 2 March 1917

5

New York

LEON TROTSKY

(Trotsky — who also spent time in Siberia — here recalls another period of exile, in the United States. He was evidently deeply impressed by what he called 'the foundry in which the fate of man is to be forged'.

The revolutionary diaspora played an important and little-understood role in shaping 1917 (like Trotsky, most prominent political personalities, Bolshevik and non-Bolshevik, had returned from abroad). Gathered in Paris, London, Geneva and Berlin (as well as New York), the exiles came for the first time into contact with Western philosophers like James and Bergson, with the enlightened sexual psychology of Freud, or with the semi-mystical 'God-building' doctrines which seemed designed for the consolation of demoralised revolutionaries (such currents as Mach's empirio-monist critiques of Marxism acquired adherents among the Bolsheviks, and Lenin railed against them in *Materialism and Empirio-criticism*).

The revolutionaries abroad were teachers as well as students, and the Russian community which Trotsky describes played an important role in the American labour and trade union movement of the day.

If the cross-fertilisation of ideas was important, so was the fascination and sometimes obsession with all things American which some of the exiles acquired, and which was later to influence notions of 'building socialism' which seemed to centre on 'catching up and overtaking the Americans'.)

Here I was in New York, city of prose and fantasy, of capitalist automatism, its streets a triumph of cubism, its moral philosophy that of the dollar. New York impressed me tremendously because, more than any other city in the world, it is the fullest expression of our modern age.

Of the legends that have sprung up about me, the greater number have to do with my life in New York. In Norway, which I only touched in passing, the resourceful journalists had me working as a codfish cleaner. In New York, where I stayed for two months, the newspapers had me engaged in any number of occupations, each more fantastic than the one before. If all the adventures that the newspapers ascribed to me were banded together in a book, they would make a far more entertaining biography than the one I am writing here.

But I must disappoint my American readers. My only profession in New York was that of a revolutionary socialist. This was before the war for 'liberty' and 'democracy', and in those days mine was a profession no more reprehensible than that of a bootlegger. I wrote articles, edited a newspaper, and addressed labour meetings. I was up to my neck in work, and consequently I did not feel at all like a stranger. In one of the New York libraries I studied the economic history of the United States assiduously. The figures showing the growth of American exports during the war astounded me; they were, in fact, a complete revelation. And it was those same figures that not only predetermined America's intervention in the war, but the decisive part that the United States would play in the world after the war as well. I wrote several articles about this at the time, and gave several lectures. Since that time the problem of 'America versus Europe' has been one of my chief interests. And even now I am studying the question with the utmost care, hoping to devote a separate book to it. If one is to understand the future destiny of humanity, this is the most important of all subjects.

The day after I arrived in New York I wrote in the Russian paper, the *Novy Mir* (*The New World*): 'I left a Europe wallowing in blood, but I left with a profound faith in a coming revolution. And it was with no democratic "illusions" that I stepped on the soil of this old-enough New World.' Ten days later I addressed the international meeting of welcome as follows:

> It is a fact of supreme importance that the economic life of Europe is being blasted to its very foundations, whereas America is increasing in wealth. As I look enviously at New York — I who still think of myself as a European — I ask myself: 'Will Europe be able to stand it? Will it not sink into nothing but a cemetery? And will the economic and cultural centres of gravity not shift to America?'

And despite the success of what is called 'European stabilisation', this question is just as pertinent today.

I lectured in Russian and German in various sections of New York, Philadelphia and other near-by cities. My English was even worse than it is today, so that I never even thought of making public addresses in English. And yet I have often come across references to my speeches in English in New York. Only the other day an editor of a Constantinople paper described one of those mythical public appearances which he witnessed as a student in America. I confess that I didn't have the courage to tell him that he was the dupe of his own imagination. But alas! with even greater assurance, he repeated these same recollections of his in his paper.

We rented an apartment in a workers' district, and furnished it on the instalment plan. That apartment, at eighteen dollars a month, was equipped with all sorts of conveniences that we Europeans were quite unused to: electric lights, gas cooking-range, bath, telephone, automatic service-elevator, and even a chute for the garbage. These things completely won the boys over to New York. For a time the telephone was their main interest; we had not had this mysterious instrument either in Vienna or Paris.

The janitor of the house was a Negro. My wife paid him three months' rent in advance, but he gave her no receipt because the landlord had taken the receipt-book away the day before, to verify the accounts. When we moved into the house two days later, we discovered that the Negro had absconded with the rent of several of the tenants. Besides the money, we had entrusted to him the storage of some of our belongings. The whole incident upset us; it was such a bad beginning. But we found our property after all, and when we opened the wooden box that contained our crockery, we were surprised to find our money hidden away in it, carefully wrapped up in paper. The janitor had taken the money of the tenants who had already received their receipts; he did not mind robbing the landlord, but he was considerate enough not to rob the tenants. A delicate fellow, indeed. My wife and I were deeply touched by his consideration, and we always think of him gratefully. This little incident took on a symptomatic significance for me — it seemed as if a corner of the veil that concealed the 'black' problem in the United States had lifted.

During those months America was busily getting ready for war. As ever, the greatest help came from the pacifists. Their vulgar speeches about the advantages of peace as opposed to war invariably ended in a promise to support war if it became 'necessary'. This was the spirit of the Bryan campaign. The socialists sang in tune with the pacifists. It is a well-known axiom that pacifists think of war as an enemy only in time of peace. After the Germans came out for unrestricted submarine warfare, mountains of military supplies blocked the railways and filled all the eastern stations and ports. Prices instantly soared, and I saw thousands of women — mothers, in the wealthiest city of the world — come out into the streets, upset the stalls, and break into shops. What will it be like in the rest of the world after the war? I asked myself.

On 3 February came the long-awaited break in diplomatic relations with Germany. The volume of the chauvinistic music was increasing daily. The tenor of the pacifists and the falsetto of the socialists did not disrupt the general harmony. But I had seen the same thing in Europe, and the mobilisation of American patriotism was simply a repetition of what I had seen before. I noted the stages of the process in my Russian paper, and meditated on the stupidity of men who were so slow to learn their lessons.

I once saw, through the window of my newspaper office, an old man with suppurating eyes and a straggling grey beard stop before a garbage-can and fish out a crust of bread. He tried the crust with his hands, then he touched the petrified thing with his teeth, and finally he struck it several times against the can. But the bread did not yield. Finally he looked about him as if he were afraid or embarrassed, thrust his find under his faded coat, and shambled along down St Mark's Place. This little episode took place on 2 March 1917. But it did not in any way interfere with the plans of the ruling class. War was inevitable, and the pacifists had to support it.

Bukharin was one of the first people I met in New York; he had been deported from Scandinavia only a short time before. He had known us in the Vienna days, and welcomed us with the childish exuberance characteristic of him. Although it was late, and we were very tired, Bukharin insisted on dragging us off to the Public Library the very first day. That was the beginning of a close association that warmed — on Bukharin's part — into an attachment for me that grew steadily more intense until 1923, when it suddenly changed to an opposite sentiment.

Bukharin's nature is such that he must always attach himself to someone. He becomes, in such circumstances, nothing more than a medium for someone else's actions and speeches. You must always keep your eyes on him, or else he will succumb quite imperceptibly to the influence of someone directly opposed to you, as other people fall under an automobile. And then he will deride his former idol with that same boundless enthusiasm with which he has just been lauding him to the skies. I never took Bukharin too seriously and I left him to himself, which really means, to others. After the death of Lenin he became Zinoviev's medium, and then Stalin's. At the very moment that these lines are being written Bukharin is passing through still another crisis, and other fluids, as yet not known to me, are filtering through him.

Madame Kollontai was in America at that time, but she travelled a great deal and I did not meet her very often. During the war, she veered sharply to the left, without transition abandoning the ranks of the Mensheviks for the extreme left wing of the Bolsheviks. Her knowledge of foreign languages and her temperament made her a valuable agitator. Her theoretical views have always been somewhat confused, however. In her New York period nothing was revolutionary enough for her. She was in correspondence with Lenin and kept him informed of what was happening in America, my own activities included, seeing all facts and ideas through the prism of her ultra-radicalism. Lenin's replies to her reflected this utterly worthless information. Later, in their fight against me, the epigones have not hesitated to make use of mistaken utterances by Lenin, utterances that he himself recanted both by word and by deed. In Russia Kollontai took from the very first an ultra-left stand, not only towards me but towards Lenin as well. She waged many a battle against the 'Lenin-Trotsky' regime, only to bow most movingly later on to the Stalin regime.

In ideas the Socialist party of the United States lagged far behind even

European patriotic Socialism. But the superior airs of the American press
— still neutral at the time — towards an 'insensate' Europe, were reflected
also in the opinions of American socialists. Men like Hillquit welcomed the
chance to play the socialist American 'uncle' who would appear in Europe
at the crucial moment and make peace between the warring factions of the
Second International. To this day I smile as I recall the leaders of American
Socialism. Immigrants who had played some role in Europe in their youth,
they very quickly lost the theoretical premise they had brought with them
in the confusion of their struggle for success. In the United States there is
a large class of successful and semi-successful doctors, lawyers, dentists,
engineers and the like who divide their precious hours of rest between
concerts by European celebrities and the American Socialist party. Their
attitude towards life is composed of shreds and fragments of the wisdom
they absorbed in their student days. Since they all have automobiles, they
are invariably elected to the important committees, commissions and
delegations of the party. It is this vain public that impresses the stamp of
its mentality on American Socialism. They think that Wilson was infinitely
more authoritative than Marx. And, properly speaking, they are simply
variants of 'Babbitt', who supplements his commercial activities with dull
Sunday meditations on the future of humanity. These people live in small
national clans, in which the solidarity of ideas usually serves as a screen for
business connections. Each clan has its own leader, usually the most
prosperous of the Babbitts. They tolerate all ideas, provided they do not
undermine their traditional authority, and do not threaten — God forbid!
— their personal comfort. A Babbitt of Babbitts is Hillquit, the ideal
Socialist leader for successful dentists.

My first contact with these men was enough to call forth their candid
hatred of me. My feelings towards them, though probably less intense,
were likewise not especially sympathetic. We belonged to different worlds.
To me they seemed the rottenest part of that world with which I was and
still am at war.

Old Eugene Debs stood out prominently among the older generation
because of the quenchless inner flame of his socialist idealism. Although
he was a romantic and a preacher, and not at all a politician or a leader,
he was a sincere revolutionary; yet he succumbed to the influence of people
who were in every respect his inferiors. Hillquit's art lay in keeping Debs
on his left flank while he maintained a business friendship with Gompers.
Debs had a captivating personality. Whenever we met, he embraced and
kissed me; the old man did not belong to the 'drys'. When the Babbitts
proclaimed a blockade against me, Debs took no part in it; he simply drew
aside, sorrowfully.

I joined the editorial board of the *Novy Mir* at the very outset. The staff
included, besides Bukharin and myself, Volodarsky, who later was killed
by the Socialist-Revolutionists in Petrograd, and Chudnovsky, who later

was wounded outside Petrograd, and eventually was killed in the Ukraine. The paper was the headquarters for internationalist revolutionary propaganda. In all of the national federations of the Socialist party there were members who spoke Russian, and many of the Russian federation spoke English. In this way the ideas of the *Novy Mir* found their way out into the wider circles of American workers. The mandarins of official Socialism grew alarmed. Intrigues waxed hot against the European immigrant who, it was said, had set foot on American soil only the day before, did not understand the psychology of the American, and was trying to foist his fantastic methods on American workers. The struggle grew bitter. In the Russian federation the 'tried and trusted' Babbitts were promptly shouldered aside. In the German federation old Schlueter, the editor-in-chief of the *Volkszeitung*, and a comrade in arms of Hillquit's, was more and more yielding his influence to the young editor Lore, who shared our views. The Letts were with us to a man. The Finnish federation gravitated towards us. We were penetrating by degrees into the powerful Jewish federation, with its fourteen-storey palace from which two hundred thousand copies of the *Forward* were daily disgorged — a newspaper with the stale odour of sentimentally philistine socialism, always ready for the most perfidious betrayals.

Among the American workers the connections and influence of the Socialist party as a whole, and of our revolutionary wing in particular, were less effective. The English organ of the party, *The Call*, was edited in a spirit of innocuous pacifist neutrality. We decided to begin by establishing a militant Marxist weekly. The preparations for it were in full swing — when the Russian revolution intervened!

After the mysterious silence of the cables for two or three days came the first confused reports of the uprising in Petrograd. The cosmopolitan working class in New York was all excited. Men hoped and were afraid to hope. The American press was in a state of utter bewilderment. Journalists, interviewers, reporters, came from all sides to the offices of the *Novy Mir*. For a time our paper was the centre of interest of the New York press. Telephone calls from the Socialist newspaper offices and organisations never stopped.

'A cablegram has arrived saying that Petrograd has appointed a Guchkov-Miliukov ministry. What does it mean?'

'That tomorrow there will be a ministry of Miliukov and Kerensky.'

'Is that so? And what next?'

'Next? We shall be the next.'

'Oho!'

This sort of thing was repeated dozens of times. Almost everyone I talked with took my words as a joke. At a special meeting of 'worthy and most worthy' Russian Social Democrats I read a paper in which I argued that the proletariat party inevitably would assume power in the second stage of the Russian revolution. This produced about the same sort of impression as a stone thrown into a puddle alive with pompous and phlegmatic frogs. Dr Ingermann did not hesitate to explain that I was ignorant of the four first rules of political arithmetic and that it was not worth while wasting five minutes to refute my nonsensical dreams.

The working masses took the prospects of revolution quite differently. Meetings, extraordinary for their size and enthusiasm, were held all over New York. Everywhere, the news that the red flag was flying over the Winter Palace brought an excited cheer. Not only the Russian immigrants, but their children, who knew hardly any Russian, came to these meetings to breathe in the reflected joy of the revolution.

At home they saw me only in abrupt flashes. They had a complex life of their own there. My wife was building a nest and the children had new friends. The closest was the chauffeur of Dr M. The doctor's wife took my wife and the boys out driving and was very kind to them. But she was a mere mortal, whereas the chauffeur was a magician, a titan, a superman! With a wave of his hand, he made the machine obey his slightest command. To sit beside him was the supreme delight. When they went into a tea-room, the boys would anxiously demand of their mother, 'Why doesn't the chauffeur come in?'

Children have an amazing capacity for adapting themselves to new surroundings. In Vienna we had lived for the most part in the workers' districts, and my boys mastered the Viennese dialect to perfection, besides speaking Russian and German. Dr Alfred Adler observed with great satisfaction that they spoke the dialect like the good old Viennese cabmen. In the school in Zurich the boys had to switch to the Zurich dialect, which was the language in use in the lower grades, German being studied as a foreign language. In Paris the boys changed abruptly to French, and within a few months had mastered it. Many times I envied them their ease in French conversation. Although they spent, in all, less than a month in Spain and on the Spanish boat, it was long enough for them to pick up the most useful words and expressions. And then in New York they went to an American school for two months and acquired a rough-and-ready command of English. After the February revolution they went to school in Petrograd. But school life there was disorganised, and foreign languages vanished from their memory even more quickly than they had been acquired. But they spoke Russian like foreigners. We were often surprised to notice that they would build up a Russian sentence as if it were an exact translation from the French — and yet they could not form the sentence in French. Thus the story of our foreign wanderings was written on the brains of the children as indelibly as if they were palimpsests.

When I telephoned my wife from the newspaper office that Petrograd was in the midst of revolution, the younger boy was in bed with diphtheria. He was nine years old, but he realised definitely — and had for a long time —

that revolution meant an amnesty, a return to Russia and a thousand other blessings. He jumped to his feet and danced on the bed in honour of the revolution. It was a sign of his recovery.

We were anxious to leave by the first boat. I rushed from consulate to consulate for papers and visas. On the eve of our departure the doctor allowed the convalescent boy to go out for a walk. My wife let him go for half an hour, and began to pack. How many times she had gone through that same operation! But there was no sign of the boy. I was at the office. Three anxious hours; then came a telephone call to my wife. First, an unfamiliar masculine voice, and then Seryozha's voice: 'I am here.' 'Here' meant a police station at the other end of New York. The boy had taken advantage of his first walk to settle a question that had been worrying him for a long time: Was there really a First Street? (We lived on 164th Street, if I am not mistaken.) But he had lost his way, had begun to make inquiries, and was taken to the police station. Fortunately he remembered our telephone number.

When my wife arrived at the station an hour later with our older son, she was greeted gaily, like a long-awaited guest. Seryozha was playing chequers with the policemen, and his face was quite red. To hide his embarrassment over an excess of official attention he was diligently chewing some black American cud with his new friends. He still remembers the telephone number of our New York apartment.

It would be a gross exaggeration to say that I learned much about New York. I plunged into the affairs of American Socialism too quickly and I was straight away up to my neck in work for it. The Russian revolution came so soon that I only managed to catch the general life-rhythm of the monster known as New York. I was leaving for Europe with the feeling of a man who has had only a peep into the foundry in which the fate of man is to be forged. My only consolation was the thought that I might return. Even now I have not given up that hope.

6

In the First All-Russian
Congress of Soviets

M. PHILIPS PRICE

(Philips Price was the *Manchester Guardian* correspondent in Russia; his reports provided some of the most objective and detailed descriptions of the revolution. Here he describes a famous clash between Lenin and Kerensky at the Congress, which opened in Petrograd in June 1917.)

There now arose from an obscure corner of the room a thick-set little man with a round bald head and small Tartar eyes. He was leading a small group of delegates who had set themselves down on the extreme left and at the back of the hall. Nobody seemed to pay much attention to the corner where they sat, for there was a general impression that here had congregated the extremists, irreconcilables and faddists of all types, who were forming a little 'cave of Adullam'. But as soon as this short, thick-set little man rose and strode with firm step, and even firmer look upon his countenance, up the gangway, where sat the serried ranks of the 'Revolutionary Democracy', a hush came upon the whole assembly. For it was Lenin, the leader of that small, insignificant Bolshevik minority at this First All-Russian Soviet Congress. No uncertain words came from his lips. Straight to the point he went from the first moment of his speech and pursued his opponents with merciless logic. 'Where are we?' he began, stretching out his short arms and looking questioningly at his audience. 'What is this Council of Workers' and Soldiers' Delegates? Is there anything like it in the world? No, of course not, because nothing so absurd as this exists in any country today except in Russia. Then let us have either one of two things: either a bourgeois government with its plans of so-called social reforms on paper, such as exists in every country now, or let us have that government which you (pointing to Tsereteli) seemed to long for, but which you apparently have not the courage to bring into existence, a government of the proletariat which had its historic parallel in 1792 in France.

'Look at this anarchy, which we now have in Russia', he went on. 'What does it mean? Do you really think you can create a socialist form of society with the assistance of the capitalists? Can Tsereteli's fine plan for

26

persuading the bourgeois governments of Western Europe to come to our point of view on the peace settlement ever succeed? No, it will fail ignominiously, as long as power is not in the hands of the Russian proletariat. Look at what you are doing', he cried, pointing a scornful finger at the Socialist ministers: 'Capitalists with 800 per cent war profits are walking about the country just as if they were under Tsarism. Why don't you publish figures of their profits, arrest some of them and keep them locked up for a bit, even though you may keep them under the same luxurious conditions as you keep Nicholas Romanov. You talk about peace without annexations. Put that principle into practice here in Finland and in the Ukraine. You talk to us of an offensive on the front against the Germans. We are not against war on principle. We are only against a capitalist war fought for capitalist ends, and until you take the government entirely into your hands and oust the bourgeois you are only the tools of those who have brought this disaster upon the world.' And so saying he returned to his obscure corner amidst yells of delight from his followers and derisive laughter from the delegates of the 'Revolutionary Democracy'.

There was then another hush in the hall, as there rose up a short man with a square face and close-cropped hair. He wore a brown jacket and gaiters, his face was pale with nervous tension and his eyes blazed like fiery beads.

It was Kerensky, the popular hero of the moment who was believed to be about to lead the Russian Revolution to the successful realisation of its ideals, who was expected to bring land to the hungry peasants, land and peace to the weary soldiers without annexations or indemnities. Standing bolt upright with his right arm clasping the button of his breast pocket, he began his speech in quiet measured tones. 'We have just been given some historical parallels', he said. 'We have been referred to 1792 as an example of how we should carry out the Revolution of 1917. But how did the French Republic of 1792 end? It turned into a base Imperialism, which set back the progress of democracy for many a long year. Our duty is to prevent this very thing from happening so that our comrades who have just come back from exile in Siberia shall not have to go back there, and so that that comrade', he said, pointing a scornful finger at Lenin, ' who has been living all this time in safety in Switzerland, shall not have to fly back there. He proposes a new and wonderful recipe for our Revolution: we are to arrest a handful of Russian capitalists. Comrades! I am not a Marxist, but I think I understand Socialism better than Comrade Lenin, and I know that Karl Marx never proposed such methods of Oriental despotism. I am accused of opposing national aspirations in Finland and the Ukraine and of reducing the principle of peace without annexations to ridicule by my action in the Coalition government. But in the first Duma it was he', he said, turning savagely on Lenin, ' who attacked me when I stood up for a federal republic and national autonomy; it was he who called the Socialist Revolutionaries and Trudoviks (*the party led by Kerensky in the Duma*) dreamers and Utopianists.'

Turning to the point about fraternising on the front, he evoked a storm of laughter by referring to the naive people who imagined that by friendly meetings between a few parties of German and Russian soldiers it is possible to usher in the dawn of Socialism throughout the world. 'They will have to be careful', he added, 'or else they will find out one day that they are fraternising with the mailed fist of William Hohenzollern.' His face flushed, and his voice became harsher with excitement, as he braced himself up for his peroration. 'You will tell us that you fear reaction', he almost screamed, 'and yet you propose to lead us the way of France in 1792. Instead of appealing for reconstruction, you clamour for destruction. Out of the fiery chaos that you wish to make will arise, like a Phoenix, a dictator.' He paused and walked slowly across the platform till he was opposite the corner where the group surrounding Lenin was seated. Not a sound was heard in the hall, as we waited breathlessly for the next sentence. 'I will not be the dictator that you are trying to create', and so saying he turned his back upon Lenin. The latter was calmly stroking his chin, apparently wondering whether the words of Kerensky would come true, and on whose shoulders the cloak of dictatorship, if it came, would rest.

The debate was continued by the leader of the Socialist Revolutionaries, Victor Chernov. 'Comrades', he began, 'the tragedy of the Russian Revolution is the insufferable circumstances in which it was born. It is surrounded by the fiery ring of war. It has established its political position at home. Can it secure its international position abroad? For we see that the longer the war goes on the greater becomes its economic difficulties. The war is a great pump which sucks out the strength of the country. Here is the danger, and one all the greater because no one knows if the Revolution can live through it.'

He then proceeded to dissect the argument of Lenin and to show that his idea of social revolution throughout the world was too feeble a reed for the Russian Revolution to lean upon. There was reason to think that in the lands where capitalism was firmly established the revolutionary movement was hanging fire, while in economically underdeveloped countries it had gone furiously ahead. 'We cannot remove these circumstances by a single appeal to the world', he continued, ' nor ought we to look upon capitalism as a purely economic phenomenon. The history of recent years shows that capitalism has a very strong national character, and that its influence has penetrated the proletariat of many countries. If this be so, does not a serious question arise? Will the Russian Revolution spread outside the narrow limits of its national existence? or will it spend its energy and expire? or can it, by strengthening itself at home, wait till the time is ripe in the rest of the world? Can it, in other words, give an object lesson to the comrades in other lands? The world has been astonished by our Revolution in the midst of the war. Let us astonish the world still further by the later stages of its growth. The Russian Revolution is acting as a lever which is slowly moving the forces of Socialism throughout the world, and by its summons to the International it will lay the foundations of a peace, freed from all traces of Imperialism. It will destroy the old methods of secret diplomacy and secret treaties and make it no longer possible for millions to be slaughtered for the benefit of the few. Our hope is no longer in diplomatic embassies but in the democracy of the Allied countries. The next task which the Russian Revolutionary Democracy will accomplish is the meeting of the Socialist International of all countries.' And with these words the whole audience, with the exception of the little irreconcilable group in the obscure corner of the hall, rose to their feet and cheered the Socialist Revolutionary leader for several minutes. The President rang his bell, and the assembled Soviet delegates filed out for the division. The resolution of confidence in the Coalition government was passed by a majority of 543 to 126. The Block of the 'Revolutionary' Democracy in the Soviet was thus secured.

7

State and Revolution

V. I. LENIN

(Democracy, proletarian dictatorship, the building of communism and the withering away of the state, are the themes addressed in *State and Revolution*. Lenin's starting point is the thesis that 'the state is a special organisation of force: it is an organisation of violence for the suppression of some class'. Parliamentary democracy is a charade, 'curtailed, wretched, false, a democracy only for the rich', in which 'the oppressed are allowed once every few years to decide which particular representatives of the oppressing class shall represent and repress them in parliament'. Socialist democracy must be something qualitatively different.)

This pamphlet was written in August and September 1917. I had already drawn up the plan for the next, the seventh, chapter, 'The Experience of the Russian Revolutions of 1905 and 1917'. Apart from the title, however, I had no time to write a single line of the chapter; I was 'interrupted' by a political crisis — the eve of the October Revolution of 1917. Such an 'interruption' can only be welcomed; but the writing of the second part of the pamphlet ('The Experience of the Russian Revolutions of 1905 and 1917') will probably have to be put off for a long time. It is more pleasant and useful to go through the experience of the revolution than to write about it.

The Author
Petrograd
November 30, 1917

... In 1907, Mehring, in the magazine *Neue Zeit* (vol. XXV, 2, p.164), published extracts from Marx's letter to Weydemeyer dated March 5, 1852. This letter, among other things, contains the following remarkable observation:

> And now as to myself, no credit is due to me for discovering the existence of classes in modern society or the struggle between them. Long before me bourgeois historians had described the historical development of this class struggle and bourgeois economists, the economic anatomy of the

classes. What I did that was new was to prove: (1) that the *existence of classes* is only bound up with *particular, historical phases in the development of production* (historische Entwicklungsphasen der Produktion), (2) that the class struggle necessarily leads to the *dictatorship of the proletariat*, (3) that this dictatorship itself only constitutes the transition to the *abolition of all classes* and to a *classless society...*

In these words, Marx succeeded in expressing with striking clarity, first, the chief and radical difference between his theory and that of the foremost and most profound thinkers of the bourgeoisie; and, secondly, the essence of his theory of the state.

It is often said and written that the main point in Marx's theory is the class struggle. But this is wrong. And this wrong notion very often results in an opportunist distortion of Marxism and its falsification in a spirit acceptable to the bourgeoisie. For the theory of the class struggle was created *not* by Marx, *but* by the bourgeoisie *before* Marx, and, generally speaking, it is *acceptable* to the bourgeoisie. Those who recognise *only* the class struggle are not yet Marxists; they may be found to be still within the bounds of bourgeois thinking and bourgeois politics. To confine Marxism to the theory of the class struggle means curtailing Marxism, distorting it, reducing it to something acceptable to the bourgeoisie. Only he is a Marxist who *extends* the recognition of the class struggle to the recognition of the *dictatorship of the proletariat*. This is what constitutes the most profound distinction between the Marxist and the ordinary petty (as well as big) bourgeois. This is the touchstone on which the *real* understanding and recognition of Marxism should be tested. And it is not surprising that when the history of Europe brought the working class face to face with this question as a *practical* issue, not only all the opportunists and reformists, but all the Kautskyites (people who vacillate between reformism and Marxism) proved to be miserable philistines and petty-bourgeois democrats *repudiating* the dictatorship of the proletariat. Kautsky's pamphlet, *The Dictatorship of the Proletariat,* published in August 1918, i.e. long after the first edition of the present book, is a perfect example of petty-bourgeois distortion of Marxism and base renunciation of it *in deeds,* while hypocritically recognising it *in words* (see my pamphlet, *The Proletarian Revolution and the Renegade Kautsky,* Petrograd and Moscow, 1918).

Opportunism today, as represented by its principal spokesman, the ex-Marxist Karl Kautsky, fits in completely with Marx's characterisation of the *bourgeois* position quoted above, for this opportunism limits recognition of the class struggle to the sphere of bourgeois relations. (Within this sphere, within its framework, not a single educated liberal will refuse to recognise the class struggle 'in principle'!) Opportunism *does not extend* recognition of the class struggle to the cardinal point, to the period of *transition* from capitalism to communism, of the *overthrow* and the complete *abolition* of the bourgeoisie. In reality, this period inevitably is a period of an unprecedentedly violent class struggle in unprecedentedly acute forms, and, consequently, during this period the state must inevitably be a state that is democratic *in a new way* (for the proletariat and the propertyless in general) and dictatorial *in a new way* (against the bourgeoisie).

Further. The essence of Marx's theory of the state has been mastered only by those who realise that the dictatorship of a *single* class is necessary not only for every class society in general, not only for the *proletariat* which has overthrown the bourgeoisie, but also for the entire *historical period* which separates capitalism from 'classless society', from communism. Bourgeois states are most varied in form, but their essence is the same: all these states, whatever their form, in the final analysis are inevitably the *dictatorship of the bourgeoisie*. The transition from capitalism to communism is certainly bound to yield a tremendous abundance and variety of political forms, but the essence will inevitably be the same: *the dictatorship of the proletariat*.

Experience of the Paris Commune of 1871. Marx's Analysis

What Made the Communards' Attempt Heroic?
It is well known that in the autumn of 1870, a few months before the Commune, Marx warned the Paris workers that any attempt to overthrow the government would be the folly of despair. But when, in March 1871, a decisive battle was *forced* upon the workers and they accepted it, when the uprising had become a fact, Marx greeted the proletarian revolution with the greatest enthusiasm, in spite of unfavourable auguries. Marx did not persist in the pedantic attitude of condemning an 'untimely' movement as did the ill-famed Russian renegade from Marxism, Plekhanov, who in November 1905 wrote encouragingly about the workers' and peasants' struggle, but after December 1905 cried, liberal fashion: 'They should not have taken up arms.'

Marx, however, was not only enthusiastic about the heroism of the Communards, who, as he expressed it, 'stormed heaven'. Although the mass revolutionary movement did not achieve its aim, he regarded it as a historic experience of enormous importance, as a certain advance of the world proletarian revolution, as a practical step that was more important than hundreds of programmes and arguments. Marx endeavoured to analyse this experiment, to draw tactical lessons from it and re-examine his theory in the light of it.

The only 'correction' Marx thought it necessary to make to the *Communist Manifesto* he made on the basis of the revolutionary experience of the Paris Communards.

The last preface to the new German edition of the *Communist Manifesto*, signed by both its authors, is dated 24 June 1872. In this preface the authors, Karl Marx and Frederick Engels, say that the programme of the *Communist Manifesto* 'has in some details become out-of-date', and they go on to say: '... *One thing especially was proved by the Commune, viz., that "the working class cannot simply lay hold of the ready-made state machinery and wield it for its own purposes"...*'

The authors took the words that are in double quotation marks in this passage from Marx's book, *The Civil War in France*.

Thus, Marx and Engels regarded one principal and fundamental lesson of the Paris Commune as being of such enormous importance that they introduced it as an important correction into the *Communist Manifesto*.

Most characteristically, it is this important correction that has been distorted by the opportunists, and its meaning probably is not known to nine-tenths, if not ninety-nine hundredths, of the readers of the *Communist Manifesto*. We shall deal with this distortion more fully further on, in a chapter devoted specially to distortions. Here it will be sufficient to note that the current, vulgar 'interpretation' of Marx's famous statement just quoted is that Marx here allegedly emphasises the idea of slow development in contradistinction to the seizure of power, and so on.

As a matter of fact, *the exact opposite is the case*. Marx's idea is that the working class must *break up*, *smash* the 'ready-made state machinery', and not confine itself merely to laying hold of it.

On April 12, 1871, i.e, just at the time of the Commune, Marx wrote to Kugelmann:

If you look up the last chapter of my *Eighteenth Brumaire*, you will find that I declare that the next attempt of the French Revolution will be no longer, as before, to transfer the bureaucratic-military machine from one hand to another, but to *smash* it (Marx's italics — the original is *zerbrechen*), and this is the precondition for every real people's revolution on the Continent. And this is what our heroic Party comrades in Paris are attempting. (*Neue Zeit*, vol. XX, 1, 1901-2, p.709.)

The words, 'to smash the bureaucratic-military machine', briefly express the principal lesson of Marxism regarding the tasks of the proletariat during a revolution in relation to the state. And it is this lesson that has been not only completely ignored, but positively distorted by the prevailing, Kautskyite, 'interpretation' of Marxism!

As for Marx's reference to *The Eighteenth Brumaire*, we have quoted the relevant passage in full above.

It is interesting to note, in particular, two points in the above-quoted argument of Marx. First, he restricts his conclusion to the Continent. This was understandable in 1871, when Britain was still the model of a purely capitalist country, but without a militarist clique and, to a considerable degree, without a bureaucracy. Marx therefore excluded Britain, where a revolution, even a people's revolution, then seemed possible, and indeed was possible, *without* the precondition of destroying the 'ready-made state machinery'.

Today, in 1917, at the time of the first great imperialist war, this restriction made by Marx is no longer valid. Both Britain and America, the biggest and the last representatives — in the whole world – of Anglo-Saxon 'liberty', in the sense that they had no militarist cliques and bureaucracy, have completely sunk into the all-European filthy, bloody morass of bureaucratic-military institutions which subordinate everything to themselves, and suppress everything. Today, in Britain and America, too, 'the precondition for every real people's revolution' is the *smashing*, the *destruction* of the 'ready-made state machinery' (made and brought up to 'European', general imperialist, perfection in those countries in the year 1914-17).

Secondly, particular attention should be paid to Marx's extremely profound remark that the destruction of the bureaucratic-military state machine is 'the precondition for every real *people's* revolution'. This idea of a 'people's' revolution seems strange coming from Marx, so that the Russian Plekhanovites and Mensheviks, those followers of Struve who wish to be regarded as Marxists, might possibly declare such an expression to be a 'slip of the pen' on Marx's part. They have reduced Marxism to such a state of wretchedly liberal distortion that nothing exists for them beyond the antithesis between bourgeois revolution and proletarian revolution, and even this antithesis they interpret in an utterly lifeless way.

If we take the revolutions of the twentieth century as examples we shall, of course, have to admit that the Portuguese and the Turkish revolutions are both bourgeois revolutions. Neither of them, however, is a 'people's' revolution, since in neither does the mass of the people, their vast majority, come out actively, independently, with their own economic and political demands to any noticeable degree. By contrast, although the Russian bourgeois revolution of 1905-7 displayed no such 'brilliant' successes as at times fell to the Portuguese and Turkish revolutions, it was undoubtedly a 'real people's' revolution, since the mass of the people, their majority, the very lowest social groups, crushed by oppression and exploitation, rose independently and stamped on the entire course of the revolution the imprint of *their* own demands, *their* attempts to build in their own way a new society in place of the old society that was being destroyed.

In Europe, in 1871, the proletariat did not constitute the majority of the people in any country on the Continent. A 'people's' revolution, one actually sweeping the majority into its stream, could be such only if it embraced both the proletariat and the peasants. These two classes then constituted the 'people'. These two classes are united by the fact that the 'bureaucratic-military state machine' oppresses, crushes, exploits them.

To *smash* this machine, *to break it up*, is truly in the interest of the 'people', of their majority, of the workers and most of the peasants, is 'the precondition' for a free alliance of the poor peasants and the proletarians, whereas without such an alliance democracy is unstable and socialist transformation is impossible.

As is well known, the Paris Commune was actually working its way toward such an alliance, although it did not reach its goal owing to a number of circumstances, internal and external.

Consequently, in speaking of a 'real people's revolution', Marx, without in the least discounting the special features of the petty bourgeoisie (he spoke a great deal about them and often), took strict account of the actual balance of class forces in most of the continental countries of Europe in 1871. On the other hand, he stated that the 'smashing' of the state machine was required by the interests of both the workers and the peasants, that it united them, that it placed before them the common task of removing the 'parasite' and of replacing it by something new.

By what exactly?

What is to Replace the Smashed State Machine?

In 1847, in the *Communist Manifesto*, Marx's answer to this question was as yet a purely abstract one; to be exact, it was an answer that indicated the tasks, but not the ways of accomplishing them. The answer given in the *Communist Manifesto* was that this machine was to be replaced by 'the proletariat organised as the ruling class', by the 'winning of the battle of democracy'.

Marx did not indulge in utopias; he expected the *experience* of the mass movement to provide the reply to the question as to the specific forms this organisation of the proletariat as the ruling class would assume and as to the exact manner in which this organisation would be combined with the most complete, most consistent 'winning of the battle of democracy'.

Marx subjected the experience of the Commune, meagre as it was, to the most careful analysis in *The Civil War in France*. Let us quote the most important passages of this work.

Originating from the Middle Ages, there developed in the nineteenth century 'the centralised state power, with its ubiquitous organs of standing army, police, bureaucracy, clergy, and judicature'. With the development of class antagonisms between capital and labour, 'state power assumed more and more the character of a public force for the suppression of the working class, of a machine of class rule. After every revolution, which marks an advance in the class struggle, the purely coercive character of the state power stands out in bolder and bolder relief'. After the revolution of 1848-9, state power became 'the national war instrument of capital against labour'. The Second Empire consolidated this.

'The direct antithesis to the empire was the Commune.' It was the 'specific form' of 'a republic that was not only to remove the monarchical form of class rule, but class rule itself...'

What was this 'specific' form of the proletarian, socialist republic? What was the state it began to create? '...The first decree of the Commune ... was the suppression of the standing army, and its replacement by the armed people...'

This demand now figures in the programme of every party calling itself socialist. The real worth of their programmes, however, is best shown by the behaviour of our Socialist-Revolutionaries and Mensheviks, who, right after the revolution of February 27, actually refused to carry out   this demand!

The Commune was formed of the municipal councillors, chosen by universal suffrage in the various wards of Paris, responsible and revocable at any time. The majority of its members were naturally working men, or acknowledged representatives of the working class ...

The police, which until then had been the instrument of the Government, was at once stripped of its political attributes, and turned into the responsible and at all times revocable instrument of the Commune. So were the officials of all other branches of the administration. From the members of the Commune downwards, public service had to be done at *workmen's wages*. The privileges and the representation allowances of the high dignitaries of state disappeared along with the dignitaries themselves ... Having once got rid of the standing army and the police, the instruments of the physical force of the old Government, the Commune proceeded at once to break the instrument of spiritual suppression, the power of the priests ... The judicial functionaries lost that sham independence ... they were thenceforward to be elective, responsible, and revocable ...

The Commune, therefore, appears to have replaced the smashed state machine 'only' by fuller democracy: abolition of the standing army; all officials to be elected and subject to recall. But as a matter of fact this 'only' signifies a gigantic replacement of certain institutions by other institutions of a fundamentally different type. This is exactly a case of 'quantity being transformed into quality': democracy, introduced as fully and consistently as is at all conceivable, is transformed from bourgeois into proletarian democracy; from the state (=a special force for the suppression of a particular class) into something which is no longer the state proper.

It is still necessary to suppress the bourgeoisie and crush their resistance. This was particularly necessary for the Commune; and one of the reasons for its defeat was that it did not do this with sufficient determination. The organ of suppression, however, is here the majority of the population, and not a minority, as was always the case under slavery, serfdom and wage slavery. And since the majority of the people *itself* suppresses its oppressors, a 'special force' for suppression *is no longer necessary!* In this sense, the state *begins to wither away.* Instead of the special institutions of a privileged minority (privileged officialdom, the chiefs of the standing army), the majority itself can directly fulfil all these functions, and the more the functions of state power are performed by the people as a whole, the less need there is for the existence of this power.

In this connection, the following measures of the Commune, emphasised by Marx, are particularly noteworthy: the abolition of all representation allowances, and of all monetary privileges to officials, the reduction of the remuneration of *all* servants of the state to the level of *'workmen's wages'*. This shows more clearly than anything else the *turn* from bourgeois to proletarian democracy, from the democracy of the oppressors to that of the oppressed classes, from the state as a *'special force'* for the suppression of a particular class to the suppression of the oppressors by the *general force* of the majority of the people — the workers and the peasants. And it is on this particularly striking point, perhaps the most important as far as the problem of the state is concerned, that the ideas of Marx have been most completely ignored! In popular commentaries, the number of which is legion, this is not mentioned. The thing done is to keep silent about it as if it were a piece of old-fashioned 'naiveté', just as Christians, after their religion had been given the status of a state religion, 'forgot' the 'naiveté' of primitive Christianity with its democratic revolutionary spirit.

The reduction of the remuneration of high state officials seems to be 'simply' a demand of naive, primitive democracy. One of the 'founders' of modern opportunism, the ex-Social-Democrat Eduard Bernstein, has more than once repeated the vulgar bourgeois jeers at 'primitive' democracy. Like all opportunists, and like the present Kautskyites, he did not understand at all that, first of all, the transition from capitalism to socialism is *impossible* without a certain 'reversion' to 'primitive' democracy (for how else can the majority, and then the whole population without exception, proceed to discharge state functions?); and that, secondly, 'primitive democracy' based on capitalism and capitalist culture is not the same as primitive democracy in prehistoric or pre-capitalist times. Capitalist culture has *created* large-scale production, factories, railways, the postal service, telephones, etc., and *on this basis* the great majority of the functions of the old 'state power' have become so simplified and can be reduced to such exceedingly simple operations of registration, filing and checking that they can be easily performed by every literate person, can quite easily be performed for ordinary 'workmen's wages', and that these functions can (and must) be stripped of every shadow of privilege, of every semblance of 'official grandeur'.

All officials, without exception, elected and subject to recall *at any time*, their salaries reduced to the level of ordinary 'workmen's wages'— these simple and 'self-evident' democratic measures, while completely uniting the interests of the workers and the majority of the peasants, at the same time serve as a bridge leading from capitalism to socialism. These measures concern the reorganisation of the state, the purely political reorganisation of society; but, of course, they acquire their full meaning and significance only in connection with the 'expropriation of the expropriators' either being accomplished or in preparation, i.e. with the transformation of capitalist private ownership of the means of production into social ownership.

'The Commune', Marx wrote, 'made that catchword of all bourgeois revolutions, cheap government, a reality, by abolishing the two greatest sources of expenditure — the army and the officialdom.'

From the peasants, as from other sections of the petty bourgeoisie, only an insignificant few 'rise to the top', 'get on in the world' in the bourgeois sense, i.e. become either well-to-do, bourgeois or officials in secure and privileged positions. In every capitalist country where there are peasants (as there are in most capitalist countries), the vast majority of them are oppressed by the government and long for its overthrow, long for 'cheap' government. This can be achieved *only* by the proletariat; and by achieving it, the proletariat at the same time takes a step towards the socialist reorganisation of the state.

Abolition of Parliamentarism

'The Commune', Marx wrote, 'was to be a working, not a parliamentary, body, executive and legislative at the same time ...

'Instead of deciding once in three or six years which member of the ruling class was to represent and repress (*ver-und zertreten*) the people in parliament, universal suffrage was to serve the people constituted in communes, as individual suffrage serves every other employer in the search for workers, foremen and accountants for his business.'

Owing to the prevalence of social-chauvinism and opportunism, this remarkable criticism of parliamentarism, made in 1871, also belongs now to the 'forgotten words' of Marxism. The professional Cabinet Ministers and parliamentarians, the traitors to the proletariat and the 'practical' socialists of our day, have left all criticism of parliamentarism to the anarchists, and, on this wonderfully reasonable ground, they denounce *all* criticism of parliamentarism as 'anarchism'!! It is not surprising that the proletariat of the 'advanced' parliamentary countries, disgusted with such 'socialists' as the Scheidemanns, Davids, Legiens, Sembats, Renaudels, Hendersons, Vanderveldes, Staunings, Brantings, Bissolatis and Co., has been with increasing frequency giving its sympathies to anarcho-syndicalism, in spite of the fact that the latter is merely the twin brother of opportunism.

For Marx, however, revolutionary dialectics was never the empty fashionable phrase, the toy rattle, which Plekhanov, Kautsky and others have made of it. Marx knew how to break with anarchism ruthlessly for its inability to make use even of the 'pigsty' of bourgeois parliamentarism, especially when the situation was obviously not revolutionary: but at the same time he knew how to subject parliamentarism to genuinely revolutionary proletarian criticism.

To decide once every few years which member of the ruling class is to repress and crush the people through parliament — this is the real essence of bourgeois parliamentarism, not only in parliamentary-constitutional monarchies, but also in the most democratic republics.

But if we deal with the question of the state, and if we consider parliamentarism as one of the institutions of the state, from the point of view of the tasks of the proletariat in *this* field, what is the way out of parliamentarism? How can it be dispensed with?

Once again we must say: the lessons of Marx, based on the study of the Commune, have been so completely forgotten that the present-day 'Social-Democrat' (i.e. present-day traitor to socialism) really cannot understand any criticism of parliamentarism other than anarchist or reactionary criticism.

The way out of parliamentarism is not, of course, the abolition of representative institutions and the elective principle, but the conversion of the representative institutions from talking shops into 'working' bodies. 'The Commune was to be a working, not a parliamentary, body, executive and legislative at the same time.'

'A working, not a parliamentary, body'— this is a blow straight from the shoulder at the present-day parliamentarians and parliamentary 'lap dogs' of Social-Democracy! Take any parliamentary country, from America to Switzerland, from France to Britain, Norway and so forth — in these countries the real business of 'state' is performed behind the scenes and is carried on by the departments, chancelleries and General Staffs. Parliament is given up to talk for the special purpose of fooling the 'common people'. This is so true that even in the Russian republic, a bourgeois-democratic republic, all these sins of parliamentarism came out at once, even before it managed to set up a real parliament. The heroes of rotten philistinism, such as the Skobelevs and Tseretelis, the Chernovs and Avksentyevs, have even succeeded in polluting the Soviets after the fashion of the most disgusting bourgeois parliamentarism, in converting them into mere talking shops. In the Soviets, the 'socialist' Ministers are fooling the credulous rustics with phrase-mongering and resolutions. In the government itself a sort of permanent shuffle is going on in order that, on the one hand, as many Socialist-Revolutionaries and Mensheviks as possible may in turn get near the 'pie', the lucrative and honourable posts, and that, on the other hand, the 'attention' of the people may be 'engaged'. Meanwhile the chancelleries and army staffs 'do' the business of 'state'.

Dyelo Naroda, the organ of the ruling Socialist-Revolutionary Party, recently admitted in a leading article — with the matchless frankness of people of 'good society', in which 'all' are engaged in political prostitution — that even in the ministries headed by the 'socialists' (save the mark!), the whole bureaucratic apparatus is in fact unchanged, is working in the old way and quite 'freely' sabotaging revolutionary measures! Even without this admission, does not the actual history of the participation of the Socialist-Revolutionaries and Mensheviks in the government prove this? It is noteworthy, however, that in the ministerial company of the Cadets, the Chernovs, Rusanovs, Zenzinovs and the other editors of *Dyelo Naroda* have so completely lost all sense of shame as to brazenly assert, as if it were a mere bagatelle, that in 'their' ministries everything is unchanged!! Revolutionary-democratic phrases to gull the rural Simple Simons, and bureaucracy and red tape to 'gladden the hearts' of the capitalists — that is the *essence* of the 'honest' coalition.

The Commune substitutes for the venal and rotten parliamentarism of bourgeois society institutions in which freedom of opinion and discussion does not degenerate into deception, for the parliamentarians themselves have to work, have to execute their own laws, have themselves to test the results achieved in reality, and to account directly to their constituents. Representative institutions remain, but there is *no* parliamentarism here as a special system, as the division of labour between the legislative and the executive, as a privileged position for the deputies. We cannot imagine democracy, even proletarian democracy, without representative institutions, but we can and *must* imagine democracy without parliamentarism, if criticism of bourgeois society is not mere words for us, if the desire to overthrow the rule of the bourgeoisie is our earnest and sincere desire, and not a mere 'election' cry for catching workers' votes, as it is with the Mensheviks and Socialist-Revolutionaries, and also the Scheidemanns and Legiens, the Sembats and Vanderveldes.

It is extremely instructive to note that, in speaking of the functions of *those* officials who are necessary for the Commune and for proletarian democracy, Marx compares them to the workers of 'every other employer', that is, of the ordinary capitalist enterprise, with its 'workers, foremen and accountants'.

There is no trace of utopianism in Marx, in the sense that he made up or invented a 'new' society. No, he studied the *birth* of the new society *out* of the old, and the forms of transition from the latter to the former, as a natural-historical process. He examined the actual experience of a mass proletarian movement and tried to draw practical lessons from it. He 'learned' from the Commune, just as all the great revolutionary thinkers learned unhesitatingly from the experience of great movements of the oppressed classes, and never addressed them with pedantic 'homilies' (such as Plekhanov's: 'They should not have taken up arms' or Tsereteli's: 'A class must limit itself').

Abolishing the bureaucracy at once, everywhere and completely, is out of the question. It is a utopia. But to *smash* the old bureaucratic machine at once and to begin immediately to construct a new one that will make possible the gradual abolition of all bureaucracy — this is *not* a utopia, it is the experience of the Commune, the direct and immediate task of the revolutionary proletariat.

Capitalism simplifies the functions of 'state' administration; it makes it possible to cast 'bossing' aside and to confine the whole matter to the organisation of the proletarians (as the ruling class), which will hire 'workers, foreman and accountants' in the name of the whole of society.

We are not utopians, we do not 'dream' of dispensing *at once* with all administration, with all subordination. These anarchist dreams, based upon incomprehension of the tasks of the proletarian dictatorship, are totally alien to Marxism, and, as a matter of fact, serve only to postpone the socialist revolution until people are different. No, we want the socialist revolution with people as they are now, with people who cannot dispense with subordination, control and 'foremen and accountants'.

The subordination, however, must be to the armed vanguard of all the exploited and working people, i.e. to the proletariat. A beginning can and must be made at once, overnight, to replace the specific 'bossing' of state officials by the simple functions of 'foremen and accountants', functions which are already fully within the ability of the average town dweller and can well be performed for 'workmen's wages'.

We, the workers, shall organise large-scale production on the basis of what capitalism has already created, relying on our own experience as workers, establishing strict, iron discipline backed up by the state power of the armed workers. We shall reduce the role of state officials to that of simply carrying out our instructions as responsible, revocable, modestly paid 'foremen and accountants'(of course, with the aid of technicians of all sorts, types and degrees). This is *our* proletarian task, this is what we can and must *start* with in accomplishing the proletarian revolution. Such a beginning, on the basis of large-scale production, will of itself lead to the gradual 'withering away' of all bureaucracy, to the gradual creation of an order — an order without inverted commas, an order bearing no similarity to wage slavery — an order under which the functions of control and accounting, becoming more and more simple, will be performed by each in turn, will then become a habit and will finally die out as the *special* functions of a special section of the population.

A witty German Social-Democrat of the seventies of the last century called the *postal service* an example of the socialist economic system. This is very true. At present the postal service is a business organised on the lines of a state-*capitalist* monopoly. Imperialism is gradually transforming all trusts into organisations of a similar type, in which, standing over the 'common' people, who are overworked and starved, one has the same bourgeois bureaucracy. But the mechanism of social management is here already to hand. Once we have overthrown the capitalists, crushed the resistance of these exploiters with the iron hand of the armed workers, and smashed the bureaucratic machine of the modern state, we shall have a splendidly equipped mechanism, freed from the 'parasite', a mechanism which can very well be set going by the united workers themselves, who will hire technicians, foremen and accountants, and pay them *all*, as indeed *all* 'state' officials in general, workmen's wages. Here is a concrete, practical task which can immediately be fulfilled in relation to all trusts, a task whose fulfilment will rid the working people of exploitation, a task which takes account of what the Commune had already begun to practise (particularly in building up the state).

To organise the *whole* economy on the lines of the postal service so that the technicians, foremen and accountants, as well as *all* officials, shall receive salaries no higher than 'a workman's wage', all under the control and leadership of the armed proletariat — this is our immediate aim. This is the state and this is the economic foundation we need. This is what will bring about the abolition of parliamentarism and the preservation of representative institutions. This is what will rid the labouring classes of the bourgeoisie's prostitution of these institutions.

Organisation of National Unity

In a brief sketch of national organisation which the Commune had no time to develop, it states explicitly that the Commune was to be the political form of even the smallest village... The communes were to elect the 'National Delegation' in Paris.

...The few but important functions which would still remain for a central government were not to be suppressed, as has been deliberately mis-stated, but were to be transferred to communal, i.e. strictly responsible, officials.

...National unity was not to be broken, but, on the contrary, organised by the communal constitution; it was to become a reality by the destruction of state power which posed as the embodiment of that unity yet wanted to be independent of, and superior to, the nation, on whose body it was but a parasitic excrescence. While the merely repressive organs of the old governmental power were to be amputated, its legitimate functions were to be wrested from an authority claiming the right to stand above society, and restored to the responsible servants of society.

The extent to which the opportunists of present-day Social Democracy have failed — perhaps it would be more true to say, have refused – to understand these observations of Marx is best shown by that book of Herostratean fame of the renegade Bernstein, *The Premises of Socialism and the Tasks of the Social-Democrats*. It is in connection with the above passage from Marx that Bernstein wrote that 'as far as its political content is concerned', this programme 'displays, in all its essential features, the greatest similarity to the federalism of Proudhon ... In spite of all the other points of difference between Marx and the "petty-bourgeois" Proudhon (Bernstein places the word "petty-bourgeois" in inverted commas to make it sound ironical) on these points, their lines of reasoning run as close as could be.' Of course, Bernstein continues, the importance of the municipalities is growing, but 'it seems doubtful to me whether the first job of democracy would be such a dissolution (*Auflösung*) of the modern states and such a complete transformation (*Umwandlung*) of their organisation as is visualised by Marx and Proudhon (the formation of a National Assembly from delegates of the provincial or district assemblies, which, in their turn, would consist of delegates from the communes), so that consequently the previous mode of national representation would disappear' (Bernstein, *Premises*, German edition, 1899, pp.134 and 136).

To confuse Marx's views on the 'destruction of state power, a parasitic excrescence', with Proudhon's federalism is positively monstrous! But it is no accident, for it never occurs to the opportunist that Marx does not speak here at all about federalism as opposed to centralism, but about smashing the old, bourgeois state machine which exists in all bourgeois countries.

The only thing that does occur to the opportunist is what he sees around him, in an environment of petty-bourgeois philistinism and 'reformist' stagnation, namely, only 'municipalities'! The opportunist has even grown out of the habit of thinking about proletarian revolution.

It is ridiculous. But the remarkable thing is that nobody argued with Bernstein on this point. Bernstein has been refuted by many, especially by Plekhanov in Russian literature and by Kautsky in European literature, but neither of them has said *anything* about *this* distortion of Marx by Bernstein.

The opportunist has so much forgotten how to think in a revolutionary way and to dwell on revolution that he attributes 'federalism' to Marx, whom he confuses with the founder of anarchism, Proudhon. As for Kautsky and Plekhanov, who claim to be orthodox Marxists and defenders of the theory of revolutionary Marxism, they are silent on this point! Here is one of the roots of the extreme vulgarisation of the views on the difference between Marxism and anarchism, which is characteristic of both the Kautskyites and the opportunists, and which we shall discuss later.

There is not a trace of federalism in Marx's above-quoted observations on the experience of the Commune. Marx agreed with Proudhon on the very point that the opportunist Bernstein did not see. Marx disagreed with Proudhon on the very point on which Bernstein found a similarity between them.

Marx agreed with Proudhon in that they both stood for the 'smashing' of the modern state machine. Neither the opportunists nor the Kautskyites wish to see the similarity of views on this point between Marxism and anarchism (both Proudhon and Bakunin) because this is where they have departed from Marxism.

Marx disagreed both with Proudhon and Bakunin precisely on the question of federalism (not to mention the dictatorship of the proletariat). Federalism as a principle follows logically from the petty-bourgeois views of anarchism. Marx was a centralist. There is no departure whatever from centralism in his observations just quoted. Only those who are imbued with the philistine 'superstitious belief' in the state can mistake the destruction of the bourgeois state machine for the destruction of centralism!

Now if the proletariat and the poor peasants take state power into their own hands, organise themselves quite freely in communes, and *unite* the action of all the communes in striking at capital, in crushing the resistance of the capitalists, and in transferring the privately-owned railways, factories, land and so on to the *entire* nation, to the whole of society, won't that be centralism! Won't that be the most consistent democratic centralism and, moreover, proletarian centralism?

Bernstein simply cannot conceive of the possibility of voluntary centralism, of the voluntary amalgamation of the communes into a nation, of the voluntary fusion of the proletarian communes, for the purpose of destroying bourgeois rule and the bourgeois state machine. Like all philistines, Bernstein pictures centralism as something which can be imposed and maintained solely from above, and solely by the bureaucracy and the military clique.

As though foreseeing that his views might be distorted, Marx expressly emphasised that the charge that the Commune had wanted to destroy national unity, to abolish the central authority, was a deliberate fraud. Marx purposely used the words: 'National unity was ... to be organised', so as to oppose conscious, democratic, proletarian centralism to bourgeois, military, bureaucratic centralism.

But there are none so deaf as those who will not hear. And the very thing the opportunists of present-day Social-Democracy do not want to hear about is the destruction of state power, the amputation of the parasitic excrescence.

Abolition of the Parasite State

We have already quoted Marx's words on this subject, and we must now supplement them.

> ...It is generally the fate of new historical creations (he wrote) to be mistaken for the counterpart of older and even defunct forms of social life, to which they may bear a certain likeness. Thus, this new Commune, which breaks (*bricht*, smashes) the modern state power, has been regarded as a revival of the medieval communes ... as a federation of small states (as Montesquieu and the Girondists visualised it) ... as an exaggerated form of the old struggle against over-centralisation...
>
> The Communal Constitution would have restored to the social body all the forces hitherto absorbed by that parasitic excrescence, the 'state', feeding upon and hampering the free movement of society. By this one act it would have initiated the regeneration of France...
>
> The Communal Constitution would have brought the rural producers under the intellectual lead of the central towns of their districts, and there secured to them, in the town working men, the natural trustees of their interests. The very existence of the Commune involved, as a matter of course, local self-government, but no longer as a counterpoise to state power, now become superfluous.

'Breaking state power', which was a 'parasitic excrescence'; its 'amputation', its 'smashing'; 'state power, now become superfluous' — these are the expressions Marx used in regard to the state when appraising and analysing the experience of the Commune.

All this was written a little less than half a century ago; and now one has to engage in excavations, as it were, in order to bring undistorted Marxism to the knowledge of the mass of the people. The conclusions drawn from the observation of the last great revolution which Marx lived through were forgotten just when the time for the next great proletarian revolutions had arrived.

> The multiplicity of interpretations to which the Commune has been subjected, and the multiplicity of interests which expressed themselves in it show that it was a thoroughly flexible political form, while all previous forms of government had been essentially repressive. Its true secret was this: it was essentially *a working-class government*, the result of the struggle of the producing against the appropriating class, the political form at last discovered under which the economic emancipation of labour could be accomplished...
>
> Except on this last condition, the Communal Constitution would have been an impossibility and a delusion...

The utopians busied themselves with 'discovering' political forms under which the socialist transformation of society was to take place.The anarchists dismissed the question of political forms altogether. The opportunists of present-day Social-Democracy accepted the bourgeois political forms of the parliamentary democratic state as the limit which should not be overstepped; they battered their foreheads praying before this 'model', and denounced as anarchism every desire to *break* these forms.

Marx deduced from the whole history of socialism and the political struggle that the state was bound to disappear, and that the transitional form of its disappearance (the transition from state to non-state) would be the 'proletariat organised as the ruling class'. Marx, however, did not set out to *discover* the political *forms* of this future stage. He limited himself to carefully observing French history, to analysing it, and to drawing the conclusion to which the year 1851 had led, namely, that matters were moving towards the *destruction* of the bourgeois state machine.

And when the mass revolutionary movement of the proletariat burst forth, Marx, in spite of its failure, in spite of its short life and patent weakness, began to study the forms it had *discovered*.

The Commune is the form 'at last discovered' by the proletarian revolution, under which the economic emancipation of labour can take place.

The Commune is the first attempt by a proletarian revolution to *smash* the bourgeois state machine; and it is the political form 'at last discovered', by which the smashed state machine can and must be *replaced*...

Engels on the Overcoming of Democracy

Engels came to express his views on this subject when establishing that the term 'Social-Democrat' was *scientifically* wrong.

In a preface to an edition of his articles of the seventies on various subjects, mostly on 'international' questions (*Internationales aus dem Volksstaat*), dated 3 January 1894, i.e. written a year and a half before his death, Engels wrote that in all his articles he used the word 'Communist', and *not* 'Social-Democrat', because at that time Proudhonists in France and the Lassalleans in Germany called themselves Social-Democrats.

For Marx and myself, it was therefore absolutely impossible to use such a loose term to characterise our special point of view. Today things are different, and the word ('Social-Democrat') may perhaps pass muster (*mag passieren*), inexact (*unpassend*, unsuitable) though it still is for a party whose economic programme is not merely socialist in general, but downright communist, and whose ultimate political aim is to overcome the whole state and, consequently, democracy as well. The names of *real*

(Engels's italics) political parties, however, are never wholly appropriate; the party develops while the name stays.

The dialectician Engels remained true to dialectics to the end of his days. Marx and I, he said, had a splendid, scientifically exact name for the party, but there was no real party, i.e. no mass proletarian party. Now (at the end of the nineteenth century) there was a real party, but its name was scientifically wrong. Never mind, it would 'pass muster', so long as the party *developed*, so long as the scientific inaccuracy of its name was not hidden from it and did not hinder its development in the right direction!

Perhaps some wit would console us Bolsheviks in the manner of Engels: we have a real party, it is developing splendidly; even such a meaningless and ugly term as 'Bolshevik' will 'pass muster', although it expresses nothing whatever but the purely accidental fact that at the Brussels-London Congress of 1903 we were in the majority. Perhaps now that the persecution of our Party by republicans and 'revolutionary' petty-bourgeois democrats in July and August has earned the name 'Bolshevik' such universal respect, now that, in addition, this persecution marks the tremendous historical progress our Party has made in its *real* development — perhaps now even I might hesitate to insist on the suggestion made in April to change the name of our Party. Perhaps I would propose a 'compromise' to my comrades, namely, to call ourselves the Communist Party, but to retain the word 'Bolsheviks' in brackets.

But the question of the name of the Party is incomparably less important than the question of the attitude of the revolutionary proletariat to the state.

In the usual arguments about the state, the mistake is constantly made against which Engels warned and which we have in passing indicated above, namely, it is constantly forgotten that the abolition of the state means also the abolition of democracy: that the withering away of the state means the withering away of democracy.

At first sight this assertion seems exceedingly strange and incomprehensible: indeed, someone may even suspect us of expecting the advent of a system of society in which the principle of subordination of the minority to the majority will not be observed — for democracy means the recognition of this very principle.

No, democracy is *not* identical with the subordination of the minority to the majority. Democracy is a *state* which recognises the subordination of the minority to the majority, i.e. an organisation for the systematic use of *force* by one class against another, by one section of the population against another.

We set ourselves the ultimate aim of abolishing the state, i.e. all organised and systematic violence, all use of violence against people in general. We do not expect the advent of a system of society in which the principle of subordination of the minority to the majority will not be observed. In striving for socialism, however, we are convinced that it will develop into communism and, therefore, that the need for violence against people in general, for the *subordination* of one man to another, and of one section of the population to another, will vanish altogether since people will *become accustomed* to observing the elementary conditions of social life *without violence* and *without subordination*.

In order to emphasise this element of habit, Engels speaks of a new *generation*, 'reared in new, free social conditions', which will 'be able to discard the entire lumber of the state' — of any state, including the democratic-republican state.

In order to explain this, it is necessary to analyse the economic basis of the withering away of the state.

The Economic Basis of the Withering Away of the State

Marx explains this question most thoroughly in his *Critique of the Gotha Programme* (letter to Bracke, 5 May 1875, which was not published until 1891 when it was printed in *Neue Zeit*, vol. IX, 1, and which has appeared in Russian in a special edition). The polemical part of this remarkable work, which contains a criticism of Lassalleanism, has, so to speak, overshadowed its positive part, namely, the analysis of the connection between the development of communism and the withering away of the state.

Presentation of the Question by Marx

From a superficial comparison of Marx's letter to Bracke of 5 May 1875, with Engels's letter to Bebel of 28 March 1875, which we examined above, it might appear that Marx was much more of a 'champion of the state' than Engels, and that the difference of opinion between the two writers on the question of the state was very considerable.

Engels suggested to Bebel that all chatter about the state be dropped altogether, that the word 'state' be eliminated from the programme altogether and the word 'community' substituted for it. Engels even declared that the Commune was no longer a state in the proper sense of the word. Yet Marx even spoke of the 'future state in communist society', i.e. he would seem to recognise the need for the state even under communism.

But such a view would be fundamentally wrong. A closer examination shows that Marx's and Engels's views on the state and its withering away were completely identical, and that Marx's expression quoted above refers to the state in the process of *withering away*.

Clearly there can be no question of specifying the moment of the *future* 'withering away', the more so since it will obviously be a lengthy process. The apparent difference between Marx and Engels is due to the fact that they dealt with different subjects and pursued different aims. Engels set out to show Bebel graphically, sharply and in broad outline the utter absurdity of the current prejudices concerning the state (shared to no small degree by Lassalle). Marx only touched upon *this* question in passing, being interested in another subject, namely, the *development* of communist society.

The whole theory of Marx is the application of the theory of development — in its most consistent, complete, considered and pithy form — to modern capitalism. Naturally, Marx was faced with the problem of applying this theory both to the *forthcoming* collapse of capitalism and to the *future* development of *future* communism.

On the basis of what *facts*, then, can the question of the future development of future communism be dealt with?

On the basis of the fact that it *has its origin* in capitalism, that it develops historically from capitalism, that it is the result of the action of a social force to which capitalism *gave birth*. There is no trace of an attempt on Marx's part to make up a utopia, to indulge in idle guess-work about what cannot be known. Marx treated the question of communism in the same way as a naturalist would treat the question of the development of, say, a new biological variety, once he knew that it had originated in such and such a way and was changing in such and such a definite direction.

To begin with, Marx brushed aside the confusion the Gotha Programme brought into the question of the relationship between state and society. He wrote:

'Present-day society' is capitalist society, which exists in all civilised countries, being more or less free from medieval admixture, more or less modified by the particular historical development of each country, more or less developed. On the other hand, the 'present-day state' changes with a country's frontier. It is different in the Prusso-German Empire from what it is in Switzerland, and different in England from what it is in the United States. '*The* present-day state' is, therefore, a fiction.

Nevertheless, the different states of the different civilised countries, in spite of their motley diversity of form, all have this in common, that they are based on modern bourgeois society, only one more or less capitalistically developed. They have, therefore, also certain essential characteristics in common. In this sense it is possible to speak of the 'present-day state', in contrast with the future, in which its present root, bourgeois society, will have died off.

The question then arises: what transformation will the state undergo in communist society? In other words, what social functions will remain in existence there that are analogous to present state functions? This question can only be answered scientifically, and one does not get a flea-hop nearer to the problem by a thousandfold combination of the work people with the word state.

After thus ridiculing all talk about a 'people's state', Marx formulated the question and gave warning, as it were, that those seeking a scientific answer to it should use only firmly-established scientific data.

The first fact that has been established most accurately by the whole theory of development, by science as a whole — a fact that was ignored by the utopians, and is ignored by the present-day opportunists, who are afraid of the socialist revolution — is that, historically, there must undoubtedly be a special stage, or a special phase, of *transition* from capitalism to communism.

The Transition from Capitalism to Communism
Marx continued:

> Between capitalist and communist society lies the period of the revolutionary transformation of the one into the other. Corresponding to this is also a political transition period in which the state can be nothing but *the revolutionary dictatorship of the proletariat.*

Marx bases this conclusion on an analysis of the role played by the proletariat in modern capitalist society, on the data concerning the development of this society, and on the irreconcilability of the antagonistic interests of the proletariat and the bourgeoisie.

Previously the question was put as follows: to achieve its emancipation, the proletariat must overthrow the bourgeoisie, win political power and establish its revolutionary dictatorship.

Now the question is put somewhat differently: the transition from capitalist society — which is developing towards communism — to communist society is impossible without a 'political transition period', and the state in this period can only be the revolutionary dictatorship of the proletariat.

What, then, is the relation of this dictatorship to democracy?

We have seen that the *Communist Manifesto* simply places side by side the two concepts: 'to raise the proletariat to the position of the ruling class' and 'to win the battle of democracy'. On the basis of all that has been said above, it is possible to determine more precisely how democracy changes in the transition from capitalism to communism.

In capitalist society, providing it develops under the most favourable conditions, we have a more or less complete democracy in the democratic republic. But this democracy is always hemmed in by the narrow limits set by capitalist exploitation, and consequently always remains, in effect, a democracy for the minority, only for the propertied classes, only for the rich. Freedom in capitalist society always remains about the same as it was in the ancient Greek republics: freedom for the slave-owners. Owing to the conditions of capitalist exploitation, the modern wage slaves are so crushed by want and poverty that 'they cannot be bothered with democracy', 'cannot be bothered with politics'; in the ordinary, peaceful course of events, the majority of the population is debarred from participation in public and political life.

The correctness of this statement is perhaps most clearly confirmed by Germany, because constitutional legality steadily endured there for a remarkably long time — nearly half a century (1871-1914) — and during this period the Social-Democrats were able to achieve far more than in other countries in the way of 'utilising legality', and organised a larger proportion of the workers into a political party than anywhere else in the world.

What is this largest proportion of politically conscious and active wage slaves that has so far been recorded in capitalist society? One million members of the Social-Democratic Party — out of fifteen million wage-workers! Three million organised in trade unions — out of fifteen million!

Democracy for an insignificant minority, democracy for the rich — that is the democracy of capitalist society. If we look more closely into the machinery of capitalist democracy, we see everywhere, in the 'petty' — supposedly petty — details of the suffrage (residential qualification, exclusion of women, etc.), in the technique of the representative institutions, in the actual obstacles to the right of assembly (public buildings are not for 'paupers'!), in the purely capitalist organisation of the daily press, etc. — we see restriction after restriction upon democracy. These restrictions, exceptions, exclusions, obstacles for the poor seem slight, especially in the eyes of one who has never known want himself and has never been in close contact with the oppressed classes in their mass life (and nine out of ten, if not ninety-nine out of a hundred bourgeois publicists and politicians come under this category); but in their sum total these restrictions exclude and squeeze out the poor from politics, from active participation in democracy.

Marx grasped this *essence* of capitalist democracy splendidly when, in analysing the experience of the Commune, he said that the oppressed are allowed once every few years to decide which particular representatives of the oppressing class shall represent and repress them in parliament!

But from this capitalist democracy — that is inevitably narrow and stealthily pushes aside the poor, and is therefore hypocritical and false through and through — forward development does not proceed simply, directly and smoothly, towards 'greater and greater democracy', as the liberal professors and petty-bourgeois opportunists would have us believe. No, forward development, i.e. development towards communism, proceeds through the dictatorship of the proletariat, and cannot do otherwise, for the *resistance* of the capitalist exploiters cannot be *broken* by anyone else or in any other way.

And the dictatorship of the proletariat, i.e. the organisation of the vanguard of the oppressed as the ruling class for the purpose of suppressing the oppressors, cannot result merely in an expansion of democracy. *Simultaneously* with an immense expansion of democracy, which *for the first time* becomes democracy for the poor, democracy for the people, and not democracy for the moneybags, the dictatorship of the proletariat imposes a series of restrictions on the freedom of the oppressors, the exploiters, the capitalists. We must suppress them in order to free humanity from wage slavery, their resistance must be crushed by force; it is clear that there is no freedom and no democracy where there is suppression and where there is violence.

Engels expressed this splendidly in his letter to Bebel when he said, as the reader will remember, that 'the proletariat needs the state, not in the interests of freedom but in order to hold down its adversaries, and as soon as it becomes possible to speak of freedom the state as such ceases to exist'.

Democracy for the vast majority of the people, and suppression by force, i.e. exclusion from democracy, of the exploiters and oppressors of the people — this is the change democracy undergoes during the *transition* from capitalism to communism.

Only in communist society, when the resistance of the capitalists has been completely crushed, when the capitalists have disappeared, when there are no classes (i.e. when there is no distinctions between the members of society as regards their relation to the social means of production), *only* then 'the state ... ceases to exist', and '*it becomes possible to speak of freedom*'. Only then will a truly complete democracy become possible and be realised, a democracy without any exceptions whatever. And only then will democracy begin to *wither away*, owing to the simple fact that, freed from capitalist slavery, from the untold horrors, savagery, absurdities and infamies of capitalist exploitation, people will gradually *become accustomed* to observing the elementary rules of social intercourse that have been known for centuries and repeated for thousands of years in all copy-book maxims. They will become accustomed to observing them without force, without coercion, without subordination, *without the special apparatus* for coercion called the state.

The expression 'the state *withers away*' is very well chosen, for it indicates both the gradual and the spontaneous nature of the process. Only habit can, and undoubtedly will, have such an effect; for we see around us on millions of occasions how readily people become accustomed to observing the necessary rules of social intercourse when there is no exploitation, when there is nothing that arouses indignation, evokes protest and revolt, and creates the need for *suppression*.

And so in capitalist society we have a democracy that is curtailed, wretched, false, a democracy only for the rich, for the minority. The dictatorship of the proletariat, the period of transition to communism, will for the first time create democracy for the people, for the majority, along with the necessary suppression of the exploiters, of the minority. Communism alone is capable of providing really complete democracy, and the more complete it is, the sooner it will become unnecessary and wither away of its own accord.

In other words, under capitalism we have the state in the proper sense of the word, that is, a special machine for the suppression of one class by another, and, what is more, of the majority by the minority. Naturally, to be successful, such an undertaking as the systematic suppression of the exploited majority by the exploiting minority calls for the utmost ferocity and savagery in the matter of suppressing, it calls for seas of blood, through which mankind is actually wading its way in slavery, serfdom and wage labour.

Furthermore, during the *transition* from capitalism to communism suppression is *still* necessary, but it is now the suppression of the exploiting minority by the exploited majority. A special apparatus, a special machine for suppression, the 'state', is *still* necessary, but this is now a transitional state. It is no longer a state in the proper sense of the word; for the suppression of the minority of exploiters by the majority of the wage slaves of *yesterday* is comparatively so easy, simple and natural a task that it will entail far less bloodshed than the suppression of the risings of slaves, serfs or wage-labourers, and it will cost mankind far less. And it is compatible with the extension of democracy to such an overwhelming majority of the population that the need for a *special machine* of suppression will begin to disappear. Naturally, the exploiters are unable to suppress the people without a highly complex machine for performing this task, but *the people* can suppress the exploiters even with a very simple 'machine', almost without a 'machine', without a special apparatus, by the simple *organisation of the armed people* (such as the Soviets of Workers' and Soldiers' Deputies, we would remark, running ahead).

Lastly, only communism makes the state absolutely unnecessary, for there is *nobody* to be suppressed — 'nobody' in the sense of a *class*, of a systematic struggle against a definite section of the population. We are not utopians, and do not in the least deny the possibility and inevitability of excesses on the part of *individual persons*, or the need to stop *such* excesses. In the first place, however, no special machine, no special apparatus of suppression, is needed for this; this will be done by the armed people themselves, as simply and as readily as any crowd of civilised people, even in modern society, interferes to put a stop to a scuffle or to prevent a woman from being assaulted. And, secondly, we know that the fundamental social cause of excesses, which consist in the violation of the rules of social intercourse, is the exploitation of the people, their want and their poverty. With the removal of this chief cause, excesses will inevitably begin to *'wither away'*. We do not know how quickly and in what succession, but we do know they will wither away. With their withering away the state will also *wither away*.

Without building utopias, Marx defined more fully what can be defined *now* regarding this future, namely, the difference between the lower and higher phases (levels, stages) of communist society.

The First Phase of Communist Society
In the *Critique of the Gotha Programme*, Marx goes into detail to disprove Lassalle's idea that under socialism the worker will receive the 'undiminished' or 'full product of his labour'. Marx shows that from the whole of the social labour of society there must be deducted a reserve fund, a fund for the expansion of production, a fund for the replacement of the 'wear and tear' of machinery, and so on. Then, from the means of consumption must be deducted a fund for administrative expenses, for schools, hospitals, old people's homes, and so on.

Instead of Lassalle's hazy, obscure, general phrase ('the full product of his labour to the worker'), Marx makes a sober estimate of exactly how socialist society will have to manage its affairs. Marx proceeds to make a *concrete* analysis of the conditions of life of a society in which there will be no capitalism, and says:

> What we have to deal with here (in analysing the programme of the workers' party) is a communist society, not as it has *developed* on its own foundations, but, on the contrary, just as it *emerges* from capitalist society; which is, therefore, in every respect, economically, morally and intellectually, still stamped with the birthmarks of the old society from whose womb it comes.

It is this communist society, which has just emerged into the light of day out of the womb of capitalism and which is in every respect stamped with the birthmarks of the old society, that Marx terms the 'first', or lower, phase of communist society.

The means of production are no longer the private property of individuals. The means of production belong to the whole of society. Every member of society, performing a certain part of the socially necessary work, receives a certificate from society to the effect that he has done a certain amount of work. And with this certificate he receives from the public store of consumer goods a corresponding quantity of products. After a deduction is made of the amount of labour which goes to the public fund, every worker, therefore, receives from society as much as he has given to it.

'Equality' apparently reigns supreme.

But when Lassalle, having in view such a social order (usually called socialism, but termed by Marx the first phase of communism), says that this is 'equitable distribution', that this is 'the equal right of all to an equal product of labour', Lassalle is mistaken and Marx exposes the mistake.

'Equal right', says Marx, we certainly do have here; but it is *still* a 'bourgeois right', which, like every right, *implies inequality*. Every right is an application of an *equal* measure to *different* people who in fact are not alike, are not equal to one another. That is why 'equal right' is a violation of equality and an injustice. In fact, everyone, having performed as much social labour as another, receives an equal share of the social product (after the above-mentioned deductions).

But people are not alike: one is strong, another is weak; one is married, another is not; one has more children, another has less, and so on. And the conclusion Marx draws is:

> With an equal performance of labour, and hence an equal share in the social consumption fund, one will in fact receive more than another, one will be richer than another, and so on. To avoid all these defects, right would have to be unequal rather than equal.

The first phase of communism, therefore, cannot yet provide justice and equality: differences, and unjust differences, in wealth will still persist, but the *exploitation* of man by man will have become impossible because it will be impossible to seize the *means of production* — the factories, machines, land, etc. — and make them private property. In smashing Lassalle's petty-bourgeois, vague phrases about 'equality' and 'justice' *in general*, Marx shows the *course of development* of communist society, which is *compelled* to abolish at first *only* the 'injustice' of the means of production seized by individuals, and which is *unable* at once to eliminate the other injustice, which consists in the distribution of consumer goods 'according to the amount of labour performed' (and not according to needs).

The vulgar economists, including the bourgeois professors and 'our' Tugan, constantly reproach the socialists with forgetting the inequality of people and with 'dreaming' of eliminating this inequality. Such a reproach, as we see, only proves the extreme ignorance of the bourgeois ideologists.

Marx not only most scrupulously takes account of the inevitable inequality of men, but he also takes into account the fact that the mere conversion of the means of production into the common property of the whole of society (commonly called 'socialism') *does not remove* the defects of distribution and the inequality of 'bourgeois right', which *continues to prevail* so long as products are divided 'according to the amount of labour performed'. Continuing, Marx says:

> But these defects are inevitable in the first phase of communist society as it is when it has just emerged, after prolonged birth pangs, from

capitalist society. Right can never be higher than the economic structure of society and its cultural development conditioned thereby.

And so, in the first phase of communist society (usually called socialism) 'bourgeois right' is *not* abolished in its entirety, but only in part, only in proportion to the economic revolution so far attained, i.e. only in respect of the means of production. 'Bourgeois right' recognises them as the private property of individuals. Socialism converts them into *common* property. *To that extent* — and to that extent alone — 'bourgeois right' disappears.

However, it persists as far as its other part is concerned; it persists in the capacity of regulator (determining factor) in the distribution of products and the allotment of labour among the members of society. The socialist principle, 'He who does not work shall not eat', is *already* realised; the other socialist principle, 'An equal amount of products for an equal amount of labour', is also *already* realised. But this is not yet communism, and it does not yet abolish 'bourgeois right', which gives unequal individuals, in return for unequal (really unequal) amounts of labour, equal amounts of products.

This is a 'defect', says Marx, but it is unavoidable in the first phase of communism; for if we are not to indulge in utopianism, we must not think that having overthrown capitalism people will at once learn to work for society *without any standard of right*. Besides, the abolition of capitalism *does not immediately create* the economic prerequisites for *such* a change.

Now, there is no other standard than that of 'bourgeois right'. To this extent, therefore, there still remains the need for a state, which, while safeguarding the common ownership of the means of production, would safeguard equality in labour and in the distribution of products.

The state withers away insofar as there are no longer any capitalists, any classes, and, consequently, no *class* can be *suppressed*.

But the state has not yet completely withered away, since there still remains the safeguarding of 'bourgeois right', which sanctifies actual inequality. For the state to wither away completely, complete communism is necessary.

The Higher Phase of Communist Society
Marx continues:

> In a higher phase of communist society, after the enslaving subordination of the individual to the division of labour and with it also the antithesis between mental and physical labour has vanished, after labour has become not only a livelihood but life's prime want, after the productive forces have increased with the all-round development of the individual, and all the springs of co-operative wealth flow more

abundantly — only then can the narrow horizon of bourgeois right be crossed in its entirety and society inscribe on its banners: From each according to his ability, to each according to his needs!

Only now can we fully appreciate the correctness of Engels's remarks mercilessly ridiculing the absurdity of combining the words 'freedom' and 'state'. So long as the state exists there is no freedom. When there is freedom, there will be no state.

The economic basis for the complete withering away of the state is such a high stage of development of communism at which the antithesis between mental and physical labour disappears, at which there consequently disappears one of the principal sources of modern *social* inequality — a source, moreover, which cannot on any account be removed immediately by the mere conversion of the means of production into public property, by the mere expropriation of the capitalists.

This expropriation will make it *possible* for the productive forces to develop to a tremendous extent. And when we see how incredibly capitalism is already *retarding* this development, when we see how much progress could be achieved on the basis of the level of technique already attained, we are entitled to say with the fullest confidence that the expropriation of the capitalists will inevitably result in an enormous development of the productive forces of human society. But how rapidly this development will proceed, how soon it will reach the point of breaking away from the division of labour, of doing away with the antithesis between mental and physical labour, of transforming labour into 'life's prime want' — we do not and *cannot* know.

That is why we are entitled to speak only of the inevitable withering away of the state, emphasising the protracted nature of this process and its dependence upon the rapidity of development of the *higher phase* of communism, and leaving the question of the time required for, or the concrete forms of, the withering away quite open, because there is *no* material for answering these questions.

The state will be able to wither away completely when society adopts the rule: 'From each according to his ability, to each according to his needs', i.e. when people have become so accustomed to observing the fundamental rules of social intercourse and when their labour has become so productive that they will voluntarily work *according to their ability*. 'The narrow horizon of bourgeois right', which compels one to calculate with the heartlessness of a Shylock whether one has not worked half an hour more than somebody else, whether one is not getting less pay than somebody else – this narrow horizon will then be crossed. There will then be no need for society, in distributing products, to regulate the quantity to be received by each; each will take freely 'according to his needs'.

From the bourgeois point of view, it is easy to declare that such a social order is 'sheer utopia' and to sneer at the socialists for promising everyone the right to receive from society, without any control over the labour of the individual citizen, any quantity of truffles, cars, pianos, etc. Even to this day, most bourgeois 'savants' confine themselves to sneering in this way, thereby betraying both their ignorance and their selfish defence of capitalism.

Ignorance — for it has never entered the head of any socialist to 'promise' that the higher phase of the development of communism will arrive; as for the great socialists' *forecast* that it will arrive, it presupposes not the present productivity of labour and *not the present* ordinary run of people, who, like the seminary students in Pomyalovsky's stories, are capable of damaging the stocks of public wealth 'just for fun', and of demanding the impossible.

Until the 'higher' phase of communism arrives, the socialists demand the *strictest* control by society *and by the state* over the measure of labour and the measure of consumption; but this control must *start* with the expropriation of the capitalists, with the establishment of workers' control over the capitalists, and must be exercised not by a state of bureaucrats, but by a state of *armed workers*.

The selfish defence of capitalism by the bourgeois ideologists (and their hangers-on, like the Tseretelis, Chernovs and Co.) consists in that they *substitute* arguing and talk about the distant future for the vital and burning question of *present-day* politics, namely, the expropriation of the capitalists, the conversion of *all* citizens into workers and other employees of *one* huge 'syndicate' — the whole state — and the complete subordination of the entire work of the syndicate of a genuinely democratic state, *the state of the Soviets of Workers' and Soldiers' Deputies.*

In fact, when a learned professor, followed by the philistine, followed in turn by the Tseretelis and Chernovs, talks of wild utopias, of the demagogic promises of the Bolsheviks, of the impossibility of 'introducing' socialism, it is the higher stage, or phase, of communism he has in mind, which no one has ever promised or even thought to 'introduce', because, generally speaking, it cannot be 'introduced'.

And this brings us to the question of the scientific distinction between socialism and communism which Engels touches on in his above-quoted argument about the incorrectness of the name 'Social-Democrat'. Politically, the distinction between the first, or lower, and the higher phase of communism will in time, probably, be tremendous. But it would be ridiculous to recognise this distinction now, under capitalism, and only individual anarchists, perhaps, could invest it with primary importance (if there still are people among the anarchists who have learned nothing from the 'Plekhanov' conversion of the Kropotkins, of Grave, Cornelissen and other 'stars' of anarchism into social-chauvinists or 'anarcho-trenchists', as Ghe, one of the few anarchists who have still preserved a sense of honour and a conscience, has put it).

But the scientific distinction between socialism and communism is clear. What is usually called socialism was termed by Marx the 'first', or lower, phase of communist society. Insofar as the means of production become *common* property, the word 'communism' is also applicable here, providing we do not forget that this is *not* complete communism. The great significance of Marx's explanations is that here, too, he consistently applies materialist dialectics, the theory of development, and regards communism as something which develops *out of* capitalism. Instead of scholastically invented, 'concocted' definitions and fruitless disputes over words (What is socialism? What is communism?), Marx gives an analysis of what might be called the stages of the economic maturity of communism.

In its first phase, or first stage, communism *cannot* as yet be fully mature economically and entirely free from traditions or vestiges of capitalism. Hence the interesting phenomenon that communism in its first phase retains 'the narrow horizon of *bourgeois* right'. Of course, bourgeois right in regard to the distribution of *consumer* goods inevitably presupposes the existence of the *bourgeois* state, for right is nothing without an apparatus capable of *enforcing* the observance of the standards of right.

It follows that under communism there remains for a time not only bourgeois right, but even the bourgeois state, without the bourgeoisie!

This may sound like a paradox or simply a dialectical conundrum, of which Marxism is often accused by people who have not taken the slightest trouble to study its extraordinarily profound content.

But in fact, remnants of the old, surviving in the new, confront us in life at every step, both in nature and in society. And Marx did not arbitrarily insert a scrap of 'bourgeois' right into communism, but indicated what is economically and politically inevitable in a society emerging *out of the womb* of capitalism.

Democracy is of enormous importance to the working class in its struggle against the capitalists for its emancipation. But democracy is by no means a boundary not to be overstepped; it is only one of the stages on the road from feudalism to capitalism, and from capitalism to communism.

Democracy means equality. The great significance of the proletariat's struggle for equality and of equality as a slogan will be clear if we correctly interpret it as meaning the abolition of *classes*. But democracy means only *formal* equality. And as soon as equality is achieved for all members of society *in relation* to ownership of the means of production, that is, equality of labour and wages, humanity will inevitably be confronted with the question of advancing farther, from formal equality to actual equality, i.e. to the operation of the rule 'from each according to his ability, to each according to his needs'. By what stages, by means of what practical measures humanity will proceed to this supreme aim we do not and cannot know. But it is important to realise how infinitely mendacious is the ordinary bourgeois conception of socialism as something, lifeless, rigid, fixed once and for all, whereas in reality *only* socialism will be the beginning of a rapid, genuine, truly mass forward movement, embracing first the *majority* and then the whole of the population, in all spheres of public and private life.

Democracy is a form of the state, one of its varieties. Consequently, it, like every state, represents, on the one hand, the organised, systematic use of force against persons; but, on the other hand, it signifies the formal recognition of equality of citizens, the equal right of all to determine the structure of, and to administer, the state. This, in turn, results in the fact that, at a certain stage in the development of democracy, it first welds together the class that wages a revolutionary struggle against capitalism — the proletariat, and enables it to crush, smash to atoms, wipe off the face of the earth the bourgeois, even the republican-bourgeois, state machine, the standing army, the police and the bureaucracy and to substitute for them a *more* democratic state machine, but a state machine nevertheless, in the shape of armed workers who proceed to form a militia involving the entire population.

Here 'quantity turns into quality': *such* a degree of democracy implies overstepping the boundaries of bourgeois society and beginning its socialist reorganisation. If really *all* take part in the administration of the state, capitalism cannot retain its hold. The development of capitalism, in turn, creates the *preconditions* that *enable* really 'all' to take part in the administration of the state. Some of these preconditions are: universal literacy, which has already been achieved in a number of the most advanced capitalist countries, then the 'training and disciplining' of millions of workers by the huge, complex, socialised apparatus of the postal service, railways, big factories, large-scale commerce, banking, etc.

Given these *economic* preconditions, it is quite possible, after the overthrow of the capitalists and the bureaucrats, to proceed immediately, overnight, to replace them in the *control* over production and distribution, in the work of *keeping account* of labour and products, by the armed workers, by the whole of the armed population. (The question of control and accounting should not be confused with the question of the scientifically trained staff of engineers, agronomists and so on. These gentlemen are working today in obedience to the wishes of the capitalists, and will work even better tomorrow in obedience to the wishes of the armed workers.)

Accounting and control — that is *mainly* what is needed for the 'smooth working', for the proper functioning, of the *first phase* of communist society. *All* citizens are tranformed into hired employees of the state, which consists of the armed workers. *All* citizens become employees and workers of a *single* country-wide state 'syndicate'. All that is required is that they should work equally, do their proper share of work, and get equal pay. The accounting and control necessary for this have been *simplified* by capitalism to the utmost and reduced to the extraordinarily simple operations — which any literate person can perform — of supervising and recording, knowledge of the four rules of arithmetic, and issuing appropriate receipts.

When the *majority* of the people begin independently and everywhere to keep such accounts and exercise such control over the capitalists (now converted into employees) and over the intellectual gentry who preserve their capitalist habits, this control will really become universal, general and popular; and there will be no getting away from it, there will be 'nowhere to go'.

The whole of society will have become a single office and a single factory, with equality of labour and pay.

But this 'factory' discipline, which the proletariat, after defeating the capitalists, after overthrowing the exploiters, will extend to the whole of society, is by no means our ideal, or our ultimate goal. It is only a necessary *step* for thoroughly cleaning society of all the infamies and abominations of capitalist exploitation, *and for further* progress.

From the moment all members of society, or at least the vast majority, have learned to administer the state *themselves*, have taken this work into their own hands have organised control over the insignificant capitalist minority, over the gentry who wish to preserve their capitalist habits and over the workers who have been thoroughly corrupted by capitalism — from this moment the need for government of any kind begins to disappear altogether. The more complete the democracy, the nearer the moment when it becomes unnecessary. The more democratic the 'state' which consists of the armed workers, and which is 'no longer a state in the proper sense of the word', the more rapidly *every form* of state begins to wither away.

For when *all* have learned to administer and actually do independently administer social production, independently keep accounts and exercise control over the parasites, the sons of the wealthy, the swindlers and other 'guardians of capitalist traditions', the escape from this popular accounting and control will inevitably become so incredibly difficult, such a rare exception, and will probably be accompanied by such swift and severe punishment (for the armed workers are practical men and not sentimental intellectuals, and they will scarcely allow anyone to trifle with them), that the *necessity* of observing the simple, fundamental rules of the community will very soon become a *habit*.

Then the door will be thrown wide open for the transition from the first phase of communist society to its higher phase, and with it to the complete withering away of the state.

8

The Growing Anarchy

VOLIA NARODA

(Volia Naroda was the daily paper of the Right Socialist-Revolutionaries.)

**Editorial in *Volia Naroda* on the Growing Anarchy
(No. 123, 20 September 1917, p.1.)**
Against the background of merciless foreign war and defeats of the armies of the Republic, internally the country has entered upon a period of anarchy and, virtually, a period of civil war.

- National class animosity has flared up everywhere — in the north and in the south, in the west and in the east, in Turkestan, near Moscow, in Finland, in the Urals, in Siberia, and in the Caucasus. From words people passed to action, and the singular devastation of Russian life is further complicated by strikes, revolts, upheavals and outright robberies.

In a few more weeks, perhaps a few days, all of Russia will be swept by the fire of dissension, mutual discord and the complete paralysis of all life.

An open revolt flares up in Tashkent, and the government sends armies and bullets to suppress it.

A mutiny in Orel. Armies are sent there.

In Rostov the town hall is dynamited.

In Tambovsk gubernia there are agrarian pogroms; experimental fields are destroyed, also pedigree cattle, etc.

In Novgorod-Voynsk uezd zemstvo storehouses are looted.

Grain reserve stores in Perm guberniya are looted.

Gangs of robbers appear on the roads in Pskov gubernia.

In the Caucasus there is slaughter in a number of places.

Along the Volga, near Kamyshin, soldiers loot trains.

In Finland the army and the fleet disassociated themselves completely from the Provisional Government.

Russia is threatened by a railway employees' strike ...

Unbridled, merciless anarchy is growing. Any cause is used.

Events of colossal importance take place throughout the country. The Russian state collapses. Whole regions secede ...

How much further can one go ...

Don't the leaders of democracy really understand, or are they unwilling to understand that further tolerance is impossible; that the policy of compromises and agreements with bolshevism has already disintegrated Russia and will eventually ruin the revolution, the country, and democracy itself?

In Tashkent the soldiers, egged on by bolshevism, stage a revolt which the Provisional Government is putting down with machine guns. Through its outrages bolshevism not only caused a revolt in Tashkent, but is encouraging the seceding of the entire oblast, because the local population in its turn takes up arms.

Here too the central organ of the Russian Social Democratic Workers' Party hails in its editorial the action of the Tashkent inhabitants, approves of them and promises them support:

'We are ready to support the Tashkent Soviet,' write the Bolsheviks in *Rabochii Put'* — we shall fight in the same ranks with the revolutionary SRs. We shall form a united front with them.'

The Bolsheviks, Social Democrats and Socialist Revolutionaries are with the Tashkents, and with the Finns, and with the Baltic, and with the Orlovsty. They are for everything that causes anarchy, refuses to defend the country, or is against unity.

Their front is one, and the devastation of Russia moves at a gigantic rate.

And the other part of the democracy, the one that sits in session at the Aleksandrinsky Theatre — is its front united, and what does it intend to do?

Does it seriously imagine that it is impossible to support the Provisional Government, to protest against the machine guns and troops sent into Turkestan, and to continue to seek compromises with the instigators of the Tashkent revolt?

That it is possible to argue until exhaustion about the preparliament with those who sow discord and hostility throughout the Republic, who repudiate at bottom what it asserts, who will fashion a toy of the garrison from the preparliament as well as from the future government?...

9

The Minutes of the Bolshevik Central Committee, 16 October 1917

Resolved ...Intensive preparations for an armed insurrection...

(The meeting of the Central Committee held on 16 October was decisive. The committee had agreed six days earlier to stage an insurrection, after much acrimonious wrangling. But only now were the wheels of revolt set in motion. Krylenko's argument that the second revolution had in effect begun seems to have stiffened resolve.

According to Krylenko, what had catalysed the situation was the government's planned evacuation of the garrison, citing the threat of a German advance on the capital. This, Krylenko thought, had suddenly resolved the question which had hung over the revolution since February — how to end the war. Lenin's 'defeatism' was based on the reality that Russia was already defeated. But there was still no guarantee that the Bolsheviks would be able to achieve peace. The question remained of the German attitude to a Bolshevik government.

Without an armistice, either the Germans would march unopposed into Russia, or the new government would have to fight, in which case its position might seem scarcely different to the Provisional Government it had overthrown.This argument had been a major drawback for Bolshevik 'defeatism'. Lenin had hoped for war exhaustion to stifle Germany. 'The chances are a hundred to one that the Germans will at least give us an armistice. And to get an armistice would in itself mean to win the *whole world.*' He also thought that a government which gave land to the tiller and the factories to the workers, might be worth fighting for. If Germany refused an armistice the Bolsheviks themselves could become defencists and would wage 'a truly revolutionary war'.

But now the issue had moved from speculation to practicality. General Cheremisov (Commander-in-Chief of the Northern Front) had called a conference of soldiers' committees to persuade them to withdraw from Petrograd, claiming this was needed to forestall a German advance. The decision was referred to the Petrosoviet, which decided against transfers. In the CC debate, Krylenko anticipated this outcome, and pointed to its significance:

'It will be argued at the Cheremisov conference that it is necessary for the troops to retreat; we will not be able to make an answer to this but must reply that even if it is necessary, it will not be done because there is no faith in the generals: thus the (German) offensive against us is already a fact and it can be used.'

In other words: for the first time, continued hostilities with Germany had become a reason for the Bolsheviks to take power rather than an argument for postponement. For the garrison would no longer defend Petrograd under the command of the Provisional Government, which in any case was more concerned to smash the revolution than the Germans, and which would use the German advance as a cover to ship rebellious troops out of the capital (the army command and the government justified this seeming dereliction on the grounds that the collapse of transport and supply systems was such as to make even an orderly demobilisation a virtual impossibility, let alone continuing the war). By an irony of history, it was now left to the Bolsheviks, those legendary 'defeatists', to save the nation, because the troops would no longer fight for anyone else.

Once the crucial decision had been taken, another obstacle appeared, this time a psychological one, as the members of the Central Committee (whose lives for the most part had been a wasteland of police wanted lists) for the first time faced the enormity of what they were about to do: arrest the government. These minutes make poignant reading, and it is easy enough to identify with the anguished members of the Central Committee, at a moment when Russia seemed poised on a cusp of fate.)

16 October 1917

Present :
Members of the CC, the Executive Commission of the Petrograd Committee, the Military Organisation, the Petrograd Soviet, trade unions, factory committees, the Petrograd Area Committee and the railwaymen.

Comrade Sv(erdlov) in the chair.
Comrade S(verdlov) proposes an agenda:

1. Report on the last CC meeting.
2. Short reports from representatives.
3. The current situation.

1. Report on the Last CC Meeting.
Comrade Lenin reads out the resolution the CC adopted at its last session. He announces that the resolution was passed with two votes against. If the dissenting comrades want to say something, a debate can be held but in the meantime he gives the reasons for this resolution.

If the Menshevik and SR Parties had broken with conciliation, it might have been possible to offer them a compromise. The proposal had been made but it was clear that the Parties in question rejected this compromise. By that time, on the other hand, it had already become clear that the masses were supporting us. That was before the Kornilov revolt. He cites the election figures in Peter and in Moscow as evidence. The Kornilov revolt itself pushed the masses even more decisively towards us. The balance of forces at the Democratic Conference. The position is clear: either a Kornilov dictatorship or a dictatorship of the proletariat and the poorest strata of the peasants. One cannot be guided by the mood of the masses for it is changeable and not to be calculated; we must go by an objective analysis and assessment of the revolution. The masses have put their faith in the Bolsheviks and demand deeds not words from them, a determined policy in both the struggle against the war and the struggle with disruption. On the basis of a political analysis of the revolution, it becomes quite clear that even anarchic outbursts confirm this now.

He goes on to analyse the situation in Europe and shows that revolution is even more difficult there than here; if things have gone as far as a revolt in the navy in a country like Germany, then this shows that things have already gone a long way there, too. Certain objective facts about the international situation indicate that in acting now we will have the whole European proletariat on our side; he shows that the bourgeoisie wants to surrender Peter. We can only escape that when we have taken control of Petrograd. From all this, the conclusion is clear, the armed insurrection talked of in the CC resolution is on the agenda.

As far as practical conclusions to be drawn from the resolution are concerned, it would be better to deal with them after hearing the reports from representatives from the centres.

A political analysis of the class struggle both in Russia and in Europe points to the need for a very determined and active policy, which can only be an armed insurrection.

2. Reports from Representatives.
Comrade Sverdlov of the CC reports on behalf of the CC secretariat on the state of affairs in the localities.

The Party has grown on a gigantic scale; it can be estimated that it now encompasses no fewer than 400,000 (he furnishes evidence).

Our influence has grown in the same way, especially in the Soviets (evidence) and similarly in the army and navy. He goes on to give the facts about the mobilisation of counter-revolutionary forces (Donetsk district, Minsk, Northern front).

Comrade Boky of the Petrograd Committee. He gives information district by district:

Vasil'evskii Island — mood not militant, military preparations being made.

Clockwise from top: the class enemy –
Tsar Nicholas II and his retinue (among
them the assassins of Rasputin) at
General Headquarters, Mogilev, 1916;
the billiard room in the officers'
assembly of the Horse Artillery Guards
Brigade, St Petersburg, 1913; queuing
for bread, February 1917; digging for
victory: the Russian Army in the First
World War.

Clockwise from top: soldatki – soldiers' wives – demonstrate for an increase in food rations; Russian and Austrian troops fraternising in 1917; the women's 'Death Battalion', taking an oath of allegiance before leaving for the front, June 1917. Kerensky hoped that they would shame the soldiers at the front into a more martial spirit; Petrograd, 1917. Tearing down the tsarist emblem.

The revolutionary Red Guard, Petrograd, 1917

Bolsheviks scattering proclamations in the streets of Moscow, 1917

Kerensky tries to encourage his troops

The Vulkan Factory – a Petrograd foundry – Red Guard, 2nd Group

Clockwise from top: Putilov workers on guard at the Smolny, October 1917; Podvoisky, chairman of the Military-Revolutionary committee, and a former publisher, inspects his troops; the Soviet meets at the Uritsky Palace

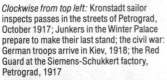

Clockwise from top left: Kronstadt sailor
inspects passes in the streets of Petrograd,
October 1917; Junkers in the Winter Palace
prepare to make their last stand; the civil war:
German troops arrive in Kiev, 1918; the Red
Guard at the Siemens-Schukkert factory,
Petrograd, 1917

American troops arrive in Arkhangelsk, 1919

The Red Army recruits the first volunteers, 1918

The Red Army attacks, 1919

Clockwise from top:
Lenin with his followers
in Kashiro, 1920;
Nadezhda Krupskaya,
Lenin's wife; Lusik
Lisiniova, with the
teddy bear, and friends,
1917; Alexandra
Kollontai

Top: literacy campaigns among Turkmen women; right: feeding starving children in the Volga, 1921 – victims of war, blockade and drought; below: Lenin in Moscow, October 1918

Vyborg District the same but they are preparing for an insurrection; a Military Council has been formed; if there were action, the masses would be in support. They consider that the initiative ought to come from above.

1st City District   The mood is difficult to assess. There is a Red Guard.
2nd (City District)   A better mood.
Moscow District   A reckless mood, will come out if the Soviet calls but not the Party.
Narva District   Not eager for action but no falling off in the Party's authority. The anarchists are getting stronger at the Putilov (factory).
Neva District   The mood has swung sharply in our favour. Everyone will follow the Soviet.
Okhten District   Things are bad.
Petersburg District   An expectant mood.
Rozhdestvensk District   Doubt here, too, on whether they will rise, anarchists have strengthened their influence.
Porokhov District   The mood have improved in our favour.
Schluesselburg   Mood in our favour.

Comrade Krylenko of the Military Bureau announces that they differ sharply in their assessment of the mood.

Personal observations of the mood in the regiments indicate that they are ours to a man, but information from comrades working in the district differs; they say that they would have to be positively stung by something for a rising, that is: the withdrawal of troops. The Bureau believes that morale is falling. Most of the Bureau thinks there is no need to do anything in practice to intensify things, but the minority thinks that it is possible to take the initiative oneself.

Comrade Step(anov) of the Area Organisation. In Sestroretsk, Kolpino, the workers are arming, the mood is militant and they are preparing for a rising. In Kolpino, an anarchist mood is developing.

The atmosphere in Narva is grave because of the dismissals. 3,000 have already been dismissed.

Where the garrisons are concerned, the mood is depressed but Bolshevik influence is very strong (2 machine-gun regiments). Work in the regiment in N(ovyi) Peterhof has fallen off a lot and the regiment is disorganised. Krasnoe Selo — 176th (regiment) is completely Bolshevik, the 172nd (regiment) nearly, but apart from that the cavalry is there. Luga — a garrison of 30,000; the Soviet is defencist. A Bolshevik mood and there are elections ahead.

In Gdov — the regiment is Bolshevik.

Comrade Boky adds that according to the information he has, matters are not so good in Krasnoe Selo.

In Kronstadt, morale has fallen and the local garrison there is no use for anything in a militant sense.

Comrade Volodarsky from the Petrograd Soviet. The general impression is that no one is ready to rush out on the streets but everyone will come if the Soviet calls.

Comrade Ravich confirms this and adds that some have indicated that also at the Party's call.

Comrade Shmidt of the trade unions. The total number organised is more than 500,000. Our Party's influence predominates but it is weak in unions more of the handicraft type (especially among the office workers and the printers) but even there it is beginning to grow, particularly since there is dissatisfaction with pay regulations. The mood is one where active demonstrations cannot be expected, especially because of the fear of dismissals. To a certain extent, this is a restraining factor. Because of certain economic conditions, colossal unemployment can be anticipated in the near future; this, too, makes the mood expectant. Everyone recognises that there is no way out of the situation apart from a struggle for power. They demand all power to the Soviets.

Comrade Shlyapnikov adds that Bolshevik influence predominates in the metalworkers' union but a Bolshevik rising is not popular; rumours of this even produce panic. The mood among metalworkers in Russia as a whole is also predominantly Bolshevik; they pass Bolshevik resolutions but they are not conscious that they are capable of organising production for themselves. The union faces the struggle to raise wages. The issue of control will be linked with this fight.

Comrade Skrypnik from the factory committees. He states that a craving for practical results has been noted everywhere; resolutions are no longer enough. It is felt that the leaders do not fully reflect the mood of the masses; the former are more conservative; a growth of anarcho-syndicalist influence is noted, particularly in the Narva and Moscow Districts.

Comrade Sverdlov gives additional information that as a result of the CC resolution, steps have been taken in Moscow to clarify the position about a possible insurrection.

Comrade Moskvin — *from the railwaymen*. The railwaymen are starving and embittered, organisation is weak, especially among the telegraph employees.

Comrade Shmidt adds that the strike has led to a crisis among the railwaymen. Dissatisfaction with the committee is especially marked at the Moscow junction. In general, the Peter and Moscow junctions are closer to the Bolsheviks.

Comrade Boky. *The post and telegraph employees*. There is no separate organisation. The telegraph apparatus is mostly under the control of the Cadets. The postmen report that they will be able to take control of the post offices at the decisive moment.

Comrade Shmidt. The postal workers' union is more radical than the railwaymen. The lower employees are essentially Bolshevik but not the higher ones: while they keep control of the union, there has to be a struggle with them.

3. The Current Situation

Comrade Miliutin considers that the resolution should be made more concrete on the basis of all the reports. He believes that the slogan 'All power to the Soviets' has come to fruition, particularly in the provinces, where the Soviets are effectively in power in places. Agitation is not really the issue — actions not words are needed now. The matter is not resolved by moods and bulletins but by organised forces. Either we take the first step or it will be taken by our enemies. The resolution does not take enough account of the possibility of this second prospect, i.e. the possibility not of an insurrection, which presupposes our initiative, but of a conflict resulting from objective conditions. Personally, he believes that we are not ready to strike the first blow. We are unable to depose and arrest the authorities in the immediate future.

Another prospect arises: an armed conflict; he shows that this is developing and the possibility approaching. And we must be ready for this conflict. But this is a different prospect from an insurrection. He thinks the resolution should be developed in this direction.

Comrade Shotman says the mood was far more pessimistic at the City Conference and in the Petrograd Committee and the *Voenka*. He shows that we are unable to take action but must prepare ourselves.

Comrade Lenin argues against Miliutin and Shotman and demonstrates that it is not a matter of armed forces, not a matter of fighting against the troops but of a struggle between one part of the army and another. He sees no pessimism in what has been said here. He shows that the bourgeoisie do not have large forces on their side. The facts show that we have the edge over the enemy. Why is it not possible for the CC to begin? No reason emerges from all the facts. To throw out the CC resolution, it must be shown that there is no economic disruption and that the international position is not leading to complications. If the trade union leaders are demanding full power, they know very well what they want. Objective conditions show that the peasants have to be led; they will follow the proletariat.

There is a fear that we will not hold on to power, but just now our chances of retaining power are particularly good.

He expresses the wish that the debate be confined to a discussion of the substance of the resolution.

Comrade Krylenko declares that the whole Bureau is unanimous on one point, that things are near enough to the boil; it would be the greatest mistake to pass a resolution rescinding this resolution. Our task is to bring armed force to the support of an insurrection if one flares up anywhere. But the mood described here is the result of our mistakes.

He differs from V.I. (Lenin) on the subject of who will start it and how. He considers it unnecessary to enter into the technical details of the insurrection too much and, on the other hand, also regards it as inadvisable to make a definite date for it. But the issue of withdrawing the troops is crucial, the very moment to give rise to a fight. It will be argued at the Cherem(isov) conference that it is necessary for the troops to retreat; we will not be able to make an answer to this but must reply that even if it is necessary, it will not be done because there is no faith in the generals: thus, the offensive against us is already a fact and it can be used. Agitation cannot be diminished and there is no point in worrying about who is to begin since a beginning already exists.

Comrade Rakh'ia shows that the masses are consciously preparing for an uprising. If the Petersburg proletariat had been armed, it would have been on the streets already regardless of any CC resolutions. There is no sign of pessimism. There is no need to wait for a counter-revolutionary attack for it already exists. The masses are waiting for slogans and weapons. They will erupt into the streets because famine awaits them. Apparently, our rallying cry is already overdue, for there is doubt whether we are going to live up to our exhortations. It is not our task to reconsider but, on the contrary, to reinforce.

Comrade Grigory (Zinoviev). Evidently the resolution is not being interpreted as an order otherwise it would not be possible to discuss it.

On its substance, he expresses doubt about whether a rising would be successful. First of all, we do not control the railway and post and telegraph. The influence of the *TsIK* is still quite strong.

The issue has to be decided on the very first day, and in Peter, for otherwise demoralisation will set in. One cannot count on reinforcements from Finland and Kronstadt. And we do not have the strength in Peter yet. In addition, our enemies have a huge organised headquarters staff. The noise we have made in recent times is wrong, even from the point of view of the CC resolution. For why do we have to give them a chance to prepare? The mood in the factories is no longer what it was in June. It is clear that there is not the mood now there was in June.

It is said there is no way out of the position in which we find ourselves; I do not think the position is like that yet. I think our attitude to the Constituent Assembly is wrong. Of course, it cannot be regarded as a panacea but the Constituent Assembly will take place in a highly revolutionary atmosphere. Until then, we will be gaining strength. It is not out of the question that with the Left SRs we will be in a majority there. It cannot be that the peasants will hesitate on the land question. I stood for withdrawal from the preparliament but I do not think that this mass is lost to us forever. He talks of international relations and shows that it is our duty to the international proletariat, too, to exercise the greatest caution:

our influence is still growing. The surrender of Peter is not to be expected before the Constituent Assembly. We have no right to take risks, to stake everything on one card.

I propose: that if the Congress meets on the 20th, we should suggest that it does not disperse until the moment the Constituent Assembly meets. In the context of the Provisional Government's complete inertia, our tactics must be defensive, biding our time. One must not totally isolate oneself. The Constituent Assembly does not mean freedom from civil war either but it is a very important stage. The CC resolution must be reconsidered, if possible. We must tell ourselves squarely that we are not going to organise an insurrection in the next five days.

Comrade Kamenev. A week has passed since the resolution was adopted and this is also the reason this resolution shows how not to organise an insurrection: during that week, nothing was done; it only spoiled what should have been done. The week's results demonstrate that there are no factors to favour a rising now. It cannot be said that the resolution was only to inspire the idea, it called for a move from words to action. But nothing was done. We have no apparatus for an insurrection; our enemies' apparatus is far stronger and has probably grown even more in this week. He shows that we did nothing in the past week, either in a military and technical sense or in provisioning. This resolution only gave the government the opportunity to get itself organised. All the masses who do not support us are now on their side. We strengthened them at our own expense. The matter is more serious than in the July days. Socially, the crisis is ripe but there is no evidence of any kind that we must begin the fight before the 20th. It is not a question of now or never. I have more faith in the Russian Revolution. Social battles lie before us and in preparing for the Constituent Assembly, we will certainly not be taking the path of parliamentarianism. We are not strong enough to go into an insurrection with the certainty of victory but we are strong enough to prevent any extremism by the reaction. Two tactics are in conflict here: conspiracy and faith in the motive forces of the Russian Revolution.

Comrade Fenigstein considers that the armed rising is not a question of weeks but of days. That is a political position, and he agrees with it, but he is not in favour of immediately going over to bayonets.

He goes on to show that we have not made technical preparations for an armed insurrection. We do not even have a centre yet. We are going half-consciously to defeat. There are moments when one has to go on all the same. But if this is not one of them, it is necessary to look at things from the practical side.

Comrade Stalin. The right day must be chosen for the rising. This is the only way to understand the resolution.

It may be said that we have to wait to be attacked but it must be understood what such an attack is; the rise in bread prices, cossacks sent to the Donetsk district, etc. — all this already constitutes an attack. How long is one to wait if there is no military attack? The objective result of what Kamenev and Zinoviev propose is that the counter-revolution will be given the opportunity to organise itself; we will retreat endlessly and lose the whole revolution. Why not give ourselves the chance to choose the day and the conditions so the counter-revolution has no opportunity to organise itself. He moves on to an analysis of international relations and he shows that now there ought to be more faith. There are two lines here: one steers for the victory of the revolution and relies on Europe, the second has no faith in the revolution and reckons on being only an opposition. The Petrograd Soviet has already taken its stand on the road to insurrection by refusing to sanction the withdrawal of troops. The navy has already rebelled since it has gone against Kerensky.

Comrade Kalinin does not interpret the resolution as meaning a rising tomorrow but as taking the matter out of the realm of policy into that of strategy and appealing for specific action. Conspiracy is not to be feared, it must always be in view; there is no need to slip on to the path of the parliamentary struggle, that would be wrong. Neither should we wait till they attack, because the very fact of attack improves the chance of victory.

Comrade Sverdlov analyses the resolution. From one point of view, it was an order but it is true that the matter has moved out of the political sphere into the technical sphere. He speaks about the preparations made by the counter-revolution. He takes issue with Kamenev's assertion that the weakness of the resolution is that so far nothing has been done in practice to implement it. The conclusion to be drawn from that is that it is necessary to work more energetically. One does not have to conclude that the majority is against us, it is only not yet for us. In Peter itself, we have the strength; the junkers are not so terrible, especially if we act first. He does not share the pessimistic feelings about the garrison which have been expressed here. The balance of forces is in our favour. The resolution should not be rescinded but amended to make the technical preparations more energetic.

Comrade Skrypnik. If we do not have the strength now, we are not going to have any more later; if we will not retain power now, it will be even worse then. It is said that it is an advantage to be in a defensive position — perhaps! But later we will not even have the strength for defence.

All the arguments used here are only postponements. There is no guarantee of victory. They are repeating here what the Mensheviks and SRs said when the proposal was made to them to take power. Now we are talking too much when we should act. The masses are appealing to us and if we do not give them anything, they will regard it as a crime. What is needed is preparation for insurrection and an appeal to the masses.

Comrade Volodarsky. If the resolution is an order then it has already been disobeyed. If the question of an insurrection is put in terms of tomorrow, we must say straight out that we have nothing to do it with. I made speeches daily but I must say that the masses met our appeal with bewilderment; this week, a change has occurred.

If there had not been a current of thought in the CC wanting to reduce the class struggle to a parliamentary one, we would have been ready for a rising now, but not as it is. The positive side of the resolution is that it forces us to go to the masses with a new slogan. The resolution must be understood as putting us on a course for insurrection and we must not stop our technical preparations.

A concrete motion: to continue to make technical preparations and to bring the question before the Congress, but not to regard the moment as having arrived already.

Comrade Dzerzhinsky thinks that Volod(arsky) is wrong to think that our Party made a mistake when it pursued, as he puts it, parliamentary tactics. On the contrary, it was the change in the situation which led to the change in our decision. Two months ago, illusions still existed and had not been overcome and that was why it was impossible to present the idea of an insurrection then. Conspiracy is just the demand that everything should be technically prepared for a rising. When the rising comes, the technical resources will be there, too. The sames goes for food.

Comrade Ravich. To rescind the resolution would be to rescind all our slogans and our whole policy. The masses have already taken the view for themselves that an insurrection is inevitable. If the masses are too revolutionary, it will start from below, but if there is also a call from above, no one can doubt that the masses will support it. There is no going back.

Comrade Sokolnikov. Kamenev's objections carry no conviction. He blames us for broadcasting our insurrection, i.e. a conspiracy is what is needed. Our most unusual feature, and our strength, lies precisely in the openness of our preparations for a rising. He recalls the events of February, when nothing was prepared either, yet the revolution succeeded. No better balance of forces can be expected.

On the subject of the resolution, there is absolutely no point in interpreting it as an order to act.

If it turns out that events give us a respite then we will, of course, make use of it. It is possible that the Congress will be earlier. If the Congress adopts all power to the Soviets, it will be necessary then to deal with the question of what to do, appeal to the masses or not.

Comrade Skalov argues that the right relationship of forces is needed for power to pass to the Soviets. Once the Soviets are in power, the food problem will be solved. Now we are turning into defencists; if we do not take power, maybe the navy will abandon its position and the army, too. He talks of breaking treaties, etc. He thinks an insurrection cannot be organised before the meeting (of the Congress) of Soviets but it is necessary to take power at the Congress.

Comrade Miliutin. The resolution was not written in the sense it has been given here; it is being interpreted to mean that we should orient ourselves towards an insurrection. That was already planned in September. The discussion is still about the political and not about the technical side of the problem. No one is arguing about our general direction. Those who talk about an insurrection picture it in a very primitive way. The first need is to take power and to replace the old regime, but to act like a stereotype — that is absurd. We gained from the fact that there was no insurrection on (July) 3-5 and if there is not one now, it will not be the end of us. This resolution must be for internal consumption.

Comrade Ioffe argues that the resolution cannot be understood as an order to rise; it is a rejection of the tactics of refraining from action and a recognition that insurrection is a possibility and a duty on the first suitable occasion. In this sense, it is to be welcomed. But it is not true, on the other hand, that it is now a purely technical matter; even now, the moment for insurrection must be considered from a political point of view. The spirit of the resolution is the need to use the first suitable occasion to seize power and that is why it should be welcomed.

Comrade Shmidt. The matter is becoming clearer now, and there is no reason to object to preparations for a revolution.

Comrade Diadia (Latsis). It is grievous that the resolution has not gone into action so far. I am convinced the resolution will be approved. I took the floor to amend the assessment given of the mood of the masses. The eagerness with which the masses seize on arms is an indication of how they feel. Our strategy is also strange. When they talk of junkers, I have already said they can be crossed off.

Comrade Le(nin). If all resolutions were defeated in this manner, one could not wish for anything better. Now Zinoviev is saying down with the 'power to the Soviets' slogan and bring pressure on the government. To say that an insurrection is ripe means there is no need to talk of conspiracy. If an insurrection is inevitable politically, it must be treated as an art. And politically, its time has come.

There is only bread for one day, and that is why we cannot wait for the Constituent Assembly. He moves that the resolution be confirmed, that preparations get positively under way and that it should be for the CC and the Soviet to decide when.

Comrade Zinoviev. This revolution has been compared with the February revolution. There is no comparison because the old regime had nothing on its side and now it is a war against the whole bourgeois world. We did not launch the slogan 'power to the Soviets' in the abstract. If the Congress puts pressure on the Constituent Assembly, this cannot be compared with Menshevik policy. If the insurrection is tabled as a long-term prospect, there can be no objection, but if it is an order for tomorrow or the day after, then this is adventurism. We must not start an insurrection before our comrades have held the Congress and there has been consultation.

Comrade Stepanov. The resolution has historic significance; I saw it as a barometer pointing to a storm. He goes on to object to Kamenev about his arguments about the lack of food.

The Cheremisov conference apart, the reduction in the soldiers' rations could be the moment for an insurrection.

The objective situation is growing from minute to minute and this resolution has played an important role. It has clarified a lot of things for us. He contends that the masses make a distinction between the *TsIK* and the Peter Soviet; he suggests that this resolution be kept intact as a barometer.

Comrade Kamenev shows that the present interpretation of the resolution is a retreat because earlier it was said that the rising must be before the 20th and now it is a question of steering towards a revolution. The question is posed politically. To fix a date for the rising is adventurism. We ought to explain to the masses that we will not summon them to a rising in the next three days but that we consider an insurrction inevitable.

He moves a vote on the resolution, and makes a proposal that the central organ should publish a statement that there will be no appeal for a rising before the congresses.

Comrade Skrypnik proposes an appeal to the masses to get ready for an insurrection.

Comrade Lenin objects to Zinoviev that this revolution should not be seen in contrast to the February revolution.

On the substance, he proposed the resolution:

'The meeting unreservedly welcomes and entirely supports the CC resolution, calls on all organisations and all workers and soldiers to make comprehensive and intensive preparations for an armed insurrection and to support the Centre created for this by the Central Committee and expresses its full confidence that the CC and the Soviet will be timely in indicating the favourable moment and the appropriate methods of attack.'

Zinoviev. He replies to Lenin on the subject of the February revolution. These two months will be the worst in the pages of our Party's history. On the substance, he moves his own resolution:

While going ahead with the work of reconnaissance and preparation, to consider that any demonstrations in advance of a conference with the Bolshevik section of the Congress of Soviets are inadmissible.

Comrade Lenin's resolution voted on in principle. In favour 20, against 2, abstained 3.

An amendment by comrade Miliutin to substitute the words 'armed conflict' is rejected.

An amendment by comrade Skrypnik to take out the words 'expressing confidence' etc. is rejected.

An amendment by comrade Fenigstein: to replace the word 'attack' with the word 'action'. Rejected.

An amendment (introduced by) comrade Volodarsky:

To move comrade Zinoviev's resolution in the form of an amendment to the approved resolution.

Rejected.

An amendment by comrade Fenigstein:

'The centre consisting of the Executive Commission and the *Voenka*'. Withdrawn.

The resolution as a whole:

In favour — 19; 2 — against; abstained — 4.

Comrade Zinoviev's resolution: in favour — 6; against — 15; abstained — 3.

The CC sits alone and adopts the following decision:

The CC organises a Military Revolutionary Centre consisting of the following: Sverdlov, Stalin, Bubnov, Uritsky and Dzerzhinsky. This Centre is included in the Soviet Revolutionary Committee.

10

The Debate in the Council of the Republic, 24 October 1917

(Kerensky's last public speech on Russian soil, made the day before the October rising, is notable for his determination to begin 'judicial investigations' into the 'obvious' fact that 'a certain part of the population' was in a state of insurrection. After the debate, a resolution deeply critical of Kerensky's government was passed: an effective vote of no-confidence made by Kerensky's own principal supporters, this destroyed the residual legitimacy of the Provisional Government.)

Kerensky's Speech before the Council of the Republic, 24 October 1917

Attempts to Thwart the Constituent Assembly
The Provisional Government has authorised me to make the following statement. Of late, the nearer we come to the day of the convocation of the Constituent Assembly — which will establish forever a free, democratic system of government in Russia, an achievement of the great Russian revolution — the more persistent, arrogant and insolent become the attempts of the two wings of Russian public opinion to block and eliminate the possibility of convoking the Constituent Assembly. At the same time, attempts to disorganise the defences of the Russian State and to betray the liberty and independence of Russia (into the hands of) a ruthless and relentless foe who is advancing on our capital are becoming increasingly persistent. The Provisional Government, as I have repeatedly stated, considers it its duty to safeguard the freedom of every citizen ... in the exercise of his political and civil rights, and has therefore remained apparently indifferent to the violent attacks to which it has been subjected in the press, at meetings and at public gatherings. Lately, all of Russia, and the ... capital in particular, has become alarmed ... by those open appeals for insurrection which come from an irresponsible — I would not say extremist, in the sense of (political) trends, but extremist in the sense of absence of reason — section of the democracy which has split off from the revolutionary democracy. At the same time another section of the press was

also agitating and conducting propaganda for supplanting the Provisional Government ... immediately by a dictatorship. (*Voices from the right:* 'By a strong government!') This has been published recently in the newspapers *Novaya Rus, Zhivoe Slovo, Obshchee Delo*. On the other hand, appeals for insurrection have appeared daily in the newspapers *Rabochi Put* and *Soldat*. At the same time, preparations have been started recently for actually overthrowing the present state system by means of an armed uprising.

The Proclamation of Ulyanov-Lenin

In order to substantiate my statements and in order to prevent anyone from reproaching the Provisional Government with making false accusations or malicious fabrications about any party, I consider it my duty to cite here a few of the more explicit passages from a number of proclamations published in the newspaper *Rabochi Put* by a wanted offender against the state, Ulyanov-Lenin, who is now in hiding. Thus, in one of the issues containing a number of these proclamations, Ulyanov-Lenin wrote: 'On the morning of October 16, I learned that ... the idea of an uprising was discussed in detail at a very important Bolshevik meeting in Petrograd. All the most influential individuals from every branch of Bolshevik work in the capital were represented at the meeting, and only the most insignificant minority — two comrades — took a negative stand on this question. Their arguments must be analysed and their hesitation revealed in order to say how disgraceful they are.' The proclamation ends with the words: 'What are you waiting for? Are you waiting for a miracle? Are you waiting for the Constituent Assembly? Wait, you starvelings! Kerensky promised to convoke the Constituent Assembly.' In the next appeal, the same Ulyanov speaks explicitly about the necessity for an immediate uprising, and says: 'Any delay of the uprising is tantamount to death.'

Destructive Movement

At the same time as these appeals were being made, other leaders of the Bolshevik Party were appealing at various meetings and public gatherings for an immediate, open, armed uprising. Especially noteworthy in this respect was the speech of the present President of the Soviet of Workers' and Soldiers' Deputies in Petersburg, Bronstein-Trotsky, as well as the speeches of several other key organisers of the uprising. Proclamations and appeals of a similar type, weighted down, in addition, with an appeal for disobeying combat orders and insubordination to military authorities, were published in yet another organ of this party — the newspaper *Soldat* — which was aimed especially at soldiers and which was supposed to destroy the noxious influence of the publication *Golos Soldat*, an organ of the Central Committee of the Soviet of Workers' and Soldiers' Deputies. I am not going to cite here from newspapers of the opposite trend, which were also closed last night by my order. I merely want to point out — and this is extremely important — the completely clear, definite and indissoluble connection between the actions and statements of the two (extreme) wings. I must also point out that a whole series of articles in *Rabochi Put* and *Soldat* coincide with articles in *Novaya Rus*, even with respect to style and the words used. I want to emphasise this in order to make it absolutely clear to the Council of the Republic that we are now dealing not only with the actions of this or that political party, but with an organised attempt to exploit foolish oversights or offences of individual political parties in the interest of an organisation that is striving at all costs to provoke an enormous, spontaneous, destructive movement in Russia (*Voice from the right:* 'This has already been done!') ... Considering the present mood of the masses and the events that have already taken place in the provinces, an open movement in Petersburg inevitably would be accompanied by the heaviest incidence of pogroms, disgracing forever the name of free Russia. Simultaneously with all the phenomena which I have pointed out and which the Provisional Government and the military authorities, in particular, have been watching closely, a number of preparations have been started for active demonstrations.

Betrayal and Treason
Very characteristic and very important is the admission by Ulyanov-Lenin, himself the organiser of the uprising, that 'the position of the extreme left Russian social democratic wing is particularly favourable'. 'Just think', Lenin writes; 'the Germans only have Liebknecht, without newspapers, without freedom of assembly, without soviets; with the incredible hostility of all classes of the population, down to the last well-to-do peasant; with the excellent organisation of the imperialist bourgeoisie. And yet the Germans are making some attempts to agitate, while we, having dozens of newspapers, freedom of assembly, with a majority in the Soviets, we who are the best organised proletarian Internationalists in the whole world — can we refuse to support the German revolutionaries and the revolutionary organisations?' Thus, the organisers themselves are admitting (this is extremely important for me to note) that the political conditions for the free activity of all political parties are perfect at the present time under the present Provisional Government, which is headed, in the opinion of the Bolshevik Party, 'by a usurper, a man who has sold himself out to the bourgeoisie — Minister-President Kerensky'. I find it necessary to point this out so that everyone will clearly understand that by organising an uprising ... by disorganising the defensive capacity and the vital capacity of the country — intentionally or unintentionally — (*voices from the right:* 'Intentionally') the organisers of the uprising are assisting not the proletariat of Germany, but ... the ruling classes of Germany; they are opening Russia's front to the armoured fist of Wilhelm and his friends.

(*Prolonged applause from the right and the centre. Cries from the right:* 'True!')

The motives are quite immaterial to the Provisional Government; it is immaterial whether this is being done intentionally or unintentionally. But in full awareness of my responsibility, I proclaim from this platform that such actions by a Russian political party constitute treason and betrayal of the Russian state. (*Cries from the right:* 'Name the accomplices!' *Noise from the left, and cries:* 'They are in your midst!') In addition, I must point out that the attempt to thwart the organised movement of the free Russian people towards the Constituent Assembly is occurring just at a time when the Provisional Government, after a series of preparatory measures, is discussing the final aspects of the procedure by which land shall be transferred temporarily, pending the Constituent Assembly, to the disposal and management of land committees. (*Loud applause in the centre and from the left.*) This is occurring just when the Provisional Government – in accordance with the obligations it has assumed and its own convictions, and in spite of all the difficulties that confront it in foreign policy due to the disorganisation and corruption of the army, which have come about not without the participation of supporters of immediate peace — when the Provisional Government was planning to send its delegation to the Paris Conference in the next few days in order to direct the attention of the Allies — among other matters relating to its convictions and its programme — to the necessity of defining explicitly the tasks and aims of war and to measures for hastening the conclusion of the war, i.e. peace. (*Loud applause from the left and the centre.*) If you take into account that all this is occurring less than three weeks before the elections of members of the Constituent Assembly, i.e. three weeks before elections to the Constituent Assembly, ... then you will understand the actual aims of the real enemies of the people and of Russian freedom. (*Loud applause from the right and the centre.*)

The Beginning of the Uprising

Thus, after open preparations of this kind and propaganda for an uprising, the group that calls itself Bolshevik has come to the point of carrying this (uprising) out. For instance, in the afternoon of the day before yesterday the troops of the Petersburg (Military) District received an order not to obey (their) commanders or (any) military authorities unless the orders were countersigned by the commissars of the Petersburg Revolutionary Staff (sic) who were arbitrarily sent to the regiments. This was done at a time when, according to general regulations, commissars of the Provisional Government, appointed in agreement with the Central Committee, existed in both the army and the Petersburg Garrison. The military authorities viewed this action of the Revolutionary Staff (sic) to be not only unlawful but patently criminal. (*Cries from the right:* 'Right!') And it therefore demanded an immediate rescindment of this order, a recognition that no one but the lawful authorities has the right to command the troops, and a notification of commissars of the Provisional Government who were assigned to the troops for the purpose of seeing to it that the actions of individual military commanders were proper in the political sense. I must note that the Central Committee adopted the same point of view in considering the action of the Revolutionary Staff (sic) as being completely inadmissible. But although there was every reason for adopting immediate, decisive and vigorous measures, the military authorities, following my instructions, believed it necessary first to give the people the opportunity to realise their own intentional or unintentional mistake. (*Cries from the right:* 'That is what's bad !') And they granted them time to retract (their stand) upon seeing their mistake. We had to do this also because no tangible results of this order were evident during the first few days after the announcement was made among the troops. I would prefer, in general, that authorities act more slowly, but more surely and, when the time calls for it, more resolutely. (*Applause from the left, cries:* 'Right!') In spite of numerous attempts to ward off the obvious uprising, with all its consequences threatening to bring even greater difficulties to the people and the country, difficulties that are heavy to bear not for the leaders who have the custom and an extraordinary talent for going into hiding (*loud applause from the right*) but for the masses whom they are leading at ... their own responsibility; in spite of the numerous measures adopted, the speeches, persuasions and proposals which have come from various public organisations; in spite of the very impressive statement that was made yesterday by the delegates who arrived here from the front — the Government did not receive any statements retracting the orders that were issued. Not until 3:00 a.m. were we informed that all the points presented in the form of an ultimatum by the military authorities were acceptable in principle. Thus, at 3:00 a.m. the organisers of the uprising were compelled to announce officially that they had committed an unlawful act which they now wished to retract. (*Miliukov from his seat:* 'How original!') But, just as I expected — and, in fact, as I was sure from all the preceding tactics of these people — this was but another case of the usual delaying (tactics) and a deliberate deception. (*Cries from the right:* 'So you have finally learned this!') At this moment the period of grace has expired, and we do not as yet have the declaration that was supposed to have been issued (by the Military Revolutionary Committee) to the regiments. What we have is just the contrary, namely, an unauthorised distribution of arms and ammunition; and, in addition, two companies have been summoned to the aid of this Revolutionary Staff (sic). Thus, it is my duty to establish before the Provisional Council that the obvious, definite, over-all condition of a certain part of the population of Petersburg (must be termed) a state of insurrection. (*Voice from the right:* 'That's what it has come to!') This is the situation from the legal standpoint, and I have proposed that judicial investigations be started immediately. (*Noise from the left.*) Arrests have also been ordered. (*Protests from the left.*) Yes, yes, listen, because at the present time, when the State is imperilled by deliberate or unwitting betrayal and is at the brink of ruin, the Provisional Government, myself included, prefers to be killed and destroyed (rather than to betray) the life, the honour and the independence of the State. (*Loud, prolonged applause. All the members of the Council, with the exception of the Internationalists, and the audience, which includes many military men, rise from their seats and accord the Minister-President a stormy ovation.*)

ADZHEMOV (*from his seat*): Take a photograph of these people (to show that they remained) seated. (*Loud cries from the left.*)

CHAIRMAN: I call the meeting to order.

LAPINSKY *and* MARTOV *are shouting something from their seats, but their words cannot be heard on account of the noise.*

CHAIRMAN: Member of the Council Martov, I call you to order.

MINISTER-PRESIDENT: The Provisional Government might be reproached –

MARTOV (*from his seat*): With confusion.

CHAIRMAN: Member of the Council Martov, I again call you to order.

The Attitude of the Front

MINISTER-PRESIDENT: The Provisional Government can be reproached with weakness and extraordinary tolerance, but, at any rate, no one has the right to say that the Provisional Government, in all the time that I have stood at the head of it, and even before that, has ever resorted to any kind of repressive measures until there was a threat of immediate danger and peril to the State. (*Loud applause from the centre and the right.*) … And I believe that our task of strengthening freedom and our tactics give us the right and the grounds to demand that the country support our decisive measures in a time of need, since no one can suspect us of undertaking these measures for any purposes other than the necessity of saving the State. (*Loud applause from the centre.*) I have to say that the attitude of the front towards the events … in the rear, and especially in Petersburg, is completely clear … I consider it my duty to read only the resolution of the Joint Army Committees located at Stavka: 'The Army', it is stated in this resolution, 'urges all citizens of the Republic to make the utmost sacrifices in the name of the earliest peace which will bring justice to all the toilers of the world and well-being to all the nations. (The Army) therefore insists upon the strictest adherence to the will of the organised majority of the people. It urges the Provisional Government, in agreement with the Provisional Council of the Republic and the All-Russian Central (Executive) Committee, to put a stop at once to the savage military pogroms in towns and villages, and to suppress as resolutely and energetically as possible every form of excess and license. In exercising restraint against all accomplices of the destruction of national integrity, the

Government will be supported by the Army, (which will fight) with all its strength as though it were fighting against the enemies of the people.' (*Loud applause from the the benches, with the exception of the Internationalists.*)

In a State of Insurrection
(*At this point*) A.I. Konovalov, *Deputy-Minister-President, approached A.F. Kerensky and handed him a note. There was a long pause. Having read the note, A.F. Kerensky continued.*)
I have been given a copy of the document that is now being sent to the regiments: 'The Petrograd Soviet is in danger. I hereby order the regiments to be in complete readiness for action and to await further instructions. Any delay or failure to execute the order will be considered a betrayal of the revolution. Signed for the President, Podvoiski. Secretary, Antonov.' (*Cries from the right:* 'Traitors!') Thus, the present situation in the capital is one that in the language of law ... is called a state of insurrection. (*Voices from the right:* 'Traitors!') This is an attempt to incite the rabble against the existing order; it is an attempt to block the Constituent Assembly (*cries from the centre and the right:* 'Right!'), and to expose the front to the serried ranks of Wilhelm's concentrated forces. (*Cries from the centre and the right:* 'Right!' *Noise from the left, and cries:* 'Enough!'*) I use the word 'rabble' deliberately, because all the responsible elements of the democracy and its Central Executive Committee, all the army organisations, and all that free Russia can and must be proud of — the reason, the conscience and the honour of the great Russian democracy — all protest against this ... (*stormy applause on all the benches, with the exception of the Internationalists*) ... They understand perfectly well that the objective danger of this demonstration does not lie in the fact that a part of the local garrison might seize power, but in the fact that this movement, just as in the month of July, could serve as a signal for the Germans at the front to deliver a new blow on our borders, and it could provoke a new (counter-revolutionary) attempt, even more serious, perhaps, than that of General Kornilov. Let everyone recall that Kalushch and Ternopol' coincided with the July uprising. Let everyone remember that only recently I said from this rostrum that the danger which we consider to be serious today could flare up tomorrow if the political situation gives the enemy forces an opportunity to attempt a new adventure. And I ... assert that if a new military catastrophe occurs we will not need to look for the culprits — they are present. (*Cries from the right:* 'Right!' *Cries from the benches of the Internationalists:* 'The guilty ones are they who are prolonging the war behind the backs of the democracy!'*)

Address to the 'Internationalists'
I believe (A.F. Kerensky addressed the Internationalists) that everyone at

the present time must decide whether he is on the side of the Republic, freedom and the democracy, or against these. (*Prolonged applause on all the benches, with the exception of the Internationalists.*) And if there are people who believe that the truth is on the other side, then they must manfully take their place in those ranks, and not behave themselves as they do now. (*Storm of applause from the right and the centre; noise from the left.*)

Appeal for Support

...I have come to call upon you for vigilance, for the defence of all the gains of freedom won by the many sacrifices, by the blood and the lives of many generations of free Russian people. I have come here not with a request, but with the conviction that the Provisional Government, which is now defending this new freedom, and the new Russian State, born to a great future, will receive the unanimous support of everyone, with the exception of those people who can never bring themselves to speak the truth openly and courageously; (that it will receive) the support not only of the Provisional Council but of the whole Russian State. (*Storm of applause on all the benches, with the exception of the Internationalists.*)

...And I was authorised to declare on behalf of the Provisional Government that the Provisional Government has never infringed on the rights of the citizens of ... Russia to enjoy complete political freedom. Proceeding from a definite point of view on the current situation, the Provisional Government believes that one of its most important duties is to avoid provoking any sharp critical disturbances before the convocation of the Constituent Assembly. Now, however, in full awareness of its responsibility to the state and to the future of the country, the Provisional Government makes (the following) declaration: All elements of Russian society, those groups and those parties which have dared to raise a hand against the free will of the Russian people, threatening at the same time to expose the front to Germany, are subject to immediate, final and definite liquidation. (*Storm of applause from the centre and from part of the left. Laughter on the benches of the Internationalists.*) Let the people of Petrograd know that they will meet with a power that is resolute; and perhaps, in the last hour or in the last minute, reason, conscience and honour will prevail in the hearts of those who have still preserved some of these values. (*Applause from the right and the centre.*) I ask for the sake of the country — and let the Provisional Council of the Republic forgive me — *I demand* that this very day, at this afternoon's session, the Provisional Government receive your answer as to whether or not it can fulfil its duty with the assurance of support from this exalted gathering.

(*A.F. Kerensky's speech was drowned in loud, prolonged applause on all the benches with the exception of the Internationalists. All the members of the Council, with the exception of the Internationalists, and the audience rose from*

their seats and once again accorded a stormy ovation to the Minister-President.
General commotion.)

Dan's Speech before the Council
(*Rech'*, No. 251, 25 October 1917, p.2)
The floor was given to Gurvich-Dan, who spoke on behalf of the
Mensheviks.

I agree with the Minister of Labour, Gvozdev, (Dan said) that what we
observe in Petrograd is not a demonstration of the revolutionary proletariat
and the revolutionary army in defence of freedom. The working class, as
a whole, will not go for this criminal venture into which the Bolsheviks are
pushing it. (*Applause from the left.*) There is no doubt in my mind that the
demagogic agitation and the incredible actions which the Bolsheviks permit
themselves are truly criminal in nature and are aimed against the
revolution. (*Applause on all the benches.*) But, while I have wanted to fight
against bolshevism as vigorously as possible, I do not want, nor have I ever
wanted, to become an instrument in the hands of counter-revolutionaries.
(*Applause from the left.*) There is no doubt in my mind that the Bolsheviks
have taken advantage of all the misfortunes that have befallen our native
land. If we want to avert the catastrophe that threatens our country, then
we must adopt the necessary measures, but not look for the solution in a
resort to arms. (*Storms of applause from the left.*) For if the Bolshevik
uprising is drowned in blood, then whoever wins — be it the Provisional
Government or the Bolsheviks — it would mean a triumph for a third force,
which would sweep away both the Bolsheviks and the Provisional
Government, and the whole democracy. (*Applause from the left; cries from
the right:* 'Tell this to the Bolsheviks and not to us!') The Bolsheviks have
openly taken advantage of the real dissatisfaction among the broad masses,
whose needs have not been met. The satisfaction of these needs is
obstructed by classes whose representatives are sitting on the right side.
(*Applause from the left.*) First of all, one must satisfy the people's cry for
peace. (*Applause from the left.*) Not out of weakness, but out of
revolutionary strength, pride and the desire to preserve the revolution, we
must say that we demand immediate negotiations for peace. (*Applause from
the left.*) Yesterday's speech of the Minister of Foreign Affairs played a fatal
role in all the events of the past day. He did not say a single word about
raising the question of peace negotiations at the Allied Conference.
Furthermore, apart from the question of peace, it is necessary to formulate
the land question in such a way that no one would have any doubts that
the Government is taking firm steps in the direction of satisfying the needs
of the people. We, Mensheviks, do not want a government crisis, we want
to defend this Provisional Government. But let us make it possible for the
whole democracy to rally around it.

Martov's Speech and the Resolutions Offered to the Council
(*Rech'*, No. 251, 25 October 1917, p.2)

Following Dan, L. Martov spoke on behalf of the Internationalists. He declared that the Internationalists will not stand in the same ranks with the Kornilovites, and that if a conflict becomes unavoidable as a result of the policy which had been pursued to date, they will not be able to suppress the uprising. (*Applause from the left.*) 'The language of Kerensky, who spoke about the movement of the rabble when the question concerned the movement of a significant part of the proletariat and the army, cannot be called anything else but a language of challenge to civil war. Only a government that is guided by the interests of the democracy can deliver the country from the horrors of a civil war.' (*Applause from the left.*)

... After the recess, A.V. Peshokhonov, presiding, stated that two (resolutions) ... had been submitted. The first formula, submitted by the Mensheviks, the Internationalists, the left Socialist Revolutionaries and the Socialist Revolutionaries, read (as follows): 'The recently developing revolutionary movement with the aim of seizing power threatens to provoke a civil war and create favourable conditions for pogroms and for the mobilisation of Black Hundred counter-revolutionary forces. It will have the inevitable result of frustrating the Constituent Assembly and of bringing about a new military catastrophe and the collapse of the revolution under conditions of economic paralysis and the complete disintegration of the country. The success of the aforesaid agitation is due not only to the objective conditions of war and disorder, but also to the delay in carrying out urgent measures, and therefore it is, above all, necesssary to issue a decree on the transfer of land to the jurisdiction of land committees, and to take a vigorous stand in foreign policy, proposing that the Allies proclaim the conditions of peace and enter into peace negotiations. In order to combat manifestations of anarchy and (to prevent) an outbreak of pogroms, it is necesssary to adopt immediate measures for their liquidation and to create for this purpose, in Petrograd, a Committee of Public Safety consisting of representatives of municipal governments and of organs of the revolutionary democracy, acting in contact with the Provisional Government.'

The second formula was submitted by the cooperative organisations and the Party of the People's Freedom. This formula read: 'Having heard the report of the Minister-President, the Provisional Council of the Russian Republic declared that, in the struggle against traitors to the native land and to the cause of the revolution who have resorted to the organisation of an open revolt in the capital, in the face of the enemy and on the eve of the Constituent Assembly, the Provisional Council will give its full support to the Government and urges that the most decisive measures be adopted for suppressing the revolt...'

The first resolution received 123 votes for and 102 against, with 26 abstentions ... The session closed at 8:30 p.m.

11

In the Winter Palace on 25-26 October 1917

P. MALYANTOVICH

(Malyantovich was the Minister of Justice in the last Provisional Government.)

... Everything was creaking and disintegrating ... Cars were sent late, different ones every time, and they were often out of order. The car assigned to the Ministry of Justice for my personal use was being repaired suspiciously long. The ministry's official complained he could do nothing about it ... A car came at a quarter to ten.

I walked into my study to take my diary, with which I did not part from morning till night, making brief notes of all meetings and conversations.

I took it out from a drawer of my desk and a thought, sudden and persistent, flashed in my mind: 'Is this not your last day?'

The thought at once shaped into a decision. I took out from the same drawer another, completed, diary, a stack of letters, private and official but addressed to me personally, my notes, and folded them into one packet, then looked around the study and shoved the parcel into a big heap of old newspapers, lying on a ledge of the book-case behind the desk ...

After our arrest my secretary and good friend D.D. Danchich, at my request, removed that parcel and took it to a friend of mine ...

Although I was certain Tyurin had made a mistake and I had been summoned not to the General Headquarters but to the Army Headquarters, I went first to the General Headquarters since the two were next to each other. There was no one there.

I went to the Army Headquarters. It was situated to the right of the Winter Palace.

The car drove up, I alighted, walked to the entrance and...understood everything.

There were no sentries at the entrance. Every minute military men of all ranks and arms of the service walked in and out of the building singly or in groups. The door was wide open, or so it seemed, because there were so many people passing in and out that it was never shut.

I walked in; no one knew me, but no one stopped me at the entrance.

Two steady streams of soldiers, officers of all ranks and a fewer number of cadets were flowing up and down the stairs. All looked busy, concentrated and worried.

'Are all these "our men"?' I asked myself. 'How many of them are Bolsheviks? There could be any number of them. Just walk in ... and take the place.'

This is exactly what they did later on: they walked in and sat down and those who had sat there got up and walked out; that is how the Army Headquarters was taken.

I walked up the stairs to the first floor. On the landing near the door in the centre stood a cadet with a rifle. His right hand held the bayonet and he leaned on the rifle like on a cane ... He might as well have been without a rifle and a good cane would have been much more convenient. I asked him:

'Do you know where the Prime Minister is?'

He replied courteously:

'Beg your pardon, I do not know. See the officer on duty, to the left, he will tell you.'

I walked into a large poorly lit room. Directly opposite the entrance door was a window and there were two more doors in the side walls. In the middle of the room was a big table with papers piled on it in disorder. There was no one at the table. Military men in coats or without them, in hats and without them, walked in and out of the entrance and side doors all the time, carrying papers or without them.

No one knew me. I was a total stranger. But no one paid the least attention to me. Some would look up, cast a scrutinising glance and hurry on their way...

I could have taken any papers from the table, folded them unhurriedly and carried them off; I could have planted a bomb, pasted a leaflet on the wall calling for the overthrow of the government ...

A general passed, reading a paper as he walked along. I stopped him and asked whether he knew where the Prime Minister was. He stopped, raised his head, cast a glance over his spectacles like a man just roused from sleep but still not fully awake, and quickly mumbled:

'No idea, my dear sir, ask the officer on duty' — and walked on.

He continued on his way, then stopped suddenly, turned around, again looked over his spectacles but with the glance of a man struck by a sudden idea, and said in an irritated voice:

'The hat, you know, should be taken off!'

That sounded reasonable. I took off my hat and walked again out on the landing, deciding to go straight into the office of the chief of staff. I asked the cadet where it was and he told me.

I came up to the door. Of course, there was no one who could report my coming.

People were passing along the corridor all the time, but at the chief of staff's door there was no sentry, not even a secretary who could announce me ...

A group of men could get into the office unhindered and say calmly: 'Are you the chief of the staff? You're arrested...'

I turned the knob and walked in, without being announced.

Directly opposite the door, facing it, with their backs to the window stood Kerensky, Konovalov, Kishkin, General Bagratuni and some other people I did not know.

A tall man, clean-shaven, foreign-looking, was talking to Kerensky.

Kerensky was in a wide grey coat of English cut and in the grey cap he always wore, something of a cross between a cap and a sportsman's hat.

His face was that of a man who had gone without sleep for many nights, pale, terribly worn and aged.

He stared in front of him, not seeing anyone, with screwed-up lids, darkened eyes full of hidden suffering and restrained alarm.

He extended his hand to me and gave me a vacant and casual look.

I shook hands with Konovalov and Kishkin.

It was clear that I had come at the end of some conversation, although it was only ten in the morning, and that Kerensky was getting ready to go somewhere alone: both Kishkin and Konovalov had no overcoats on.

'What's happening?' I asked Konovalov in a low voice.

'Trouble!' he said looking at me over his pince-nez.

'Where is he going?'

'He is going to Luga by car to meet the troops coming to Petrograd to the aid of the Provisional Government. He wants to see them and find out how they stand before they get to Petrograd.'

'To meet the troops coming to help the Provisional Government? Does it mean that in Petrograd there are no troops ready to defend the Provisional Government?'

'I know nothing', Konovalov waved his arms helplessly. 'It is bad', he added.

'What troops are coming?'

'I think a battalion of cyclists.'

Things, indeed, were in a bad way if to defend the Provisional Government and the state system from the definite danger of an armed uprising in Petrograd it was necessary to go to Luga to meet ... a battalion of cyclists.

Someone announced that the cars were ready. It turned out that one of the two cars was provided at Kerensky's request by an allied embassy. Evidently our garage no longer took orders from the government.

Kerensky hastily shook hands with everyone present.

'And so you, Alexander Ivanovich, remain Deputy Prime Minster', he said, turning to Konovalov, and swiftly strode out of the room.

From that moment we never saw Kerensky again ...

'What about us?' I asked, turning to Kishkin and Konovalov.

We at once agreed that all members of the Provisional Government must be summoned instantly to discuss the situation.

We went down to my car which proved very useful to us because it was the only one we had. We drove to the Winter Palace, stopping at the Saltykov Entrance in the garden.

We walked across the huge vestibule into the adjacent room and then turned left to a staircase, all the walls of which were hung with tapestries. On the first floor the staircase led into a very wide interior hall, dimly lit overhead and with galleries upstairs.

To the right of the entrance to this hall was a temporary tall partition, separating a makeshift hospital for wounded soldiers from the left part of the hall.

To get to the Malachite Hall, where the Provisional Government held their meetings, we had to walk to the left through this hall and three more halls.

All the huge windows of the Malachite Hall faced the Neva. The other premises on that side, i.e. the chancellery of the Provisional Government and the offices of the prime minister and his deputy, reached up to the corner of the palace, pointing to Nikolaevsky Bridge, and occupied part of the wall along the garden opposite the Admiralty.

We began to call all members of the Provisional Government by phone...

The Provisional Government were well aware of the degree of disintegration of the Petrograd garrison and the fleet, although the leading body of the fleet, Tsentroflot, was apparently in favour of supporting the Provisional Government and the same position was held by Cossack units, the officers' training-schools and also, as was said not very definitely, by some units of the garrison.

The situation was very alarming but did not seem to have taken final shape. It seemed that a swing in any direction might occur at any moment, depending on the course of events.

Energetic and successful actions against the Bolshevik insurrection, it seemed, might put an end to the indecision and vacillation of the Cossacks, some units of the garrison and also the Tsentroflot, but then the actions must be successful. It was clear that these units would not take any action of their own accord.

At best the mass of soldiers was everywhere unreliable.

As for the officers, they felt offended by the entire course of events since the Kornilov affair and even more isolated from the soldiers than before and they had no faith in the Provisional Government (or in its determination)...

Up to four in the afternoon access to the Winter Palace was still possible. A.G. Khrushchev, Deputy Finance Minister, came twice, and so did someone else, V.D. Nabokov I think.

An hour and a half or two hours after he had left for the Army Headquarters N.M. Kishkin returned from there to the Winter Palace. His report described the situation as indefinite.

Palchinsky's report was more optimistic. He considered it possible that the Bolsheviks would not make an open attack, that they might limit themselves to a threat in order to terrorise us, that so far only Red Guards were being moved up and, in case of necessity, it would not be difficult to disperse them. The Army Headquarters was ready and the Winter Palace was being guarded.

What units did the Provisional Government have to defend themselves and Petrograd?

There was no definite information on this score. This may seem strange, but it is true. We did not know who was defending the new Russian state order.

I have retained in my memory the following information: two companies, from each of two officers' training-schools, Pavlovsky and Vladimirsky I think, two companies from the Oranienbaum Ensigns' School; two companies from the Mikhailovsky Artillery School with six guns; a part of the Women's Battalion and 200 Cossacks.

Who supplied this information? I do not remember, but I do recall that no exact and reliable report by the military command had been submitted to the Provisional Government.

No one knew the temper and attitude of the other troops — the infantry, cavalry, artillery and special machine-gun and armoured-car units.

'The mood is indefinite, but there is sympathy for the government', some said. Who? I do not know. It was not reported by a person with verified data who was in a position to give information which could serve as a guide for action.

At that time, on the very same day, I would have been unable to tell who said this. Perhaps someone who came to us, when that was still possible, stayed for a while and then left. Perhaps the report was given over the telephone. The telephone worked for a long time. Verderevsky, Kishkin, Nikitin and many others spoke over the phone with different people in the city.

'They are unsympathetic to the Bolsheviks, rather than sympathetic to the government. A neutral position. They will side with the victor.'

And who said that? I cannot remember. Perhaps some definite person or perhaps many at once. In any case that was not definite information, but rather an opinion, a surmise...

It was reported from the city that the population was agitated, very much set against the Bolsheviks. Party meetings were under way: all parties were expressing themselves against the Bolsheviks and their insurrection. In a word, the Bolsheviks were gradually ... 'being isolated'.

Parties were expressing their opinion!

What unusually comforting news!

There will be a public meeting of the Duma. All parties and all organisations will voice their opinion and a common resolution will be drawn up.

'A common resolution!' What an outburst of energy!

All talking machines were set into motion!

Later on, but, bear in mind, on the same day, two new committees were set up: the Committee for the Salvation of the Fatherland and the Revolution, and the Security Committee ... They will also be...'isolating...' But we shall see whom!

The Congress of Soviets opened ...

What courage, what fervour, what determination will be displayed there by the defenders of democracy and the revolution! How solemnly, after having spouted an ocean of words, they will leave the session of the congress to consummate the process of 'isolating' the Bolsheviks ... at the very same moment when, on orders of the Military Revolutionary Committee, all members of the Provisional Government will be taken to the Peter and Paul Fortress by the Bolsheviks under the guidance of 'Comrade' Antonov.

'The population' of Petrograd and its revolutionary leaders were 'isolating' the Bolsheviks with unconsciously panicky alarm and words, while the Bolsheviks, without any words, but with rifles, hand-grenades, machine guns, armoured cars, guns, were gripping in a solid ring the isolated organ of the people's power.

The guns from the turret of the *Aurora* beyond Nikolaevsky Bridge and the guns of the Peter and Paul Fortress stared grimly at the Winter Palace. The cold light of a grey sunless day poured in through the huge palace windows.

A panorama of the city could be clearly seen through the crisp air. From the corner window we could view the crowded expanses of the mighty river. Indifferent, cold waters ... Hidden alarm seemed to hang in the air.

Doomed people, lonely, abandoned by all, walked around in the huge mousetrap, occasionally getting all together or in little groups for brief conversations ...

Around us was a void, inside of us a void and in it we felt the growing reckless determination of total indifference ...

'What will happen to the palace if *Aurora* opens fire?'

'It will be turned into a heap of ruins', replied Admiral Verderevsky calmly, as always. Only his cheek at the corner of the right eye twitched nervously. He shrugged his shoulders, fixed his collar with the right hand and, again tucking his hands into his trouser pockets, turned and resumed his walk. He stopped for a moment.

'Her turrets are higher than the bridges. She can demolish the place without damaging any other building. The Winter Palace is very conveniently located, a good target ...'

And he walked on.

Telephone conversations were carried on continuously with various organisations and persons. It seemed Nikitin was called most of all. They did not clarify our position in the least.

One thing was becoming increasingly clear: we could not count on any real military support other than the forces we actually had. Could we rely on them? How much time had we to spend in the palace? How were we to behave? How would it all end? What orders were to be issued to the troops defending us?

The moment when we should issue a brief and decisive order would come inevitably. What order?

To hold out to the last man, to the last drop of blood? What for?

When a power was not defended by those who organised it – was it needed? If it was not needed, if it had outlived itself, to whom should it be turned over, how, and on whose orders?

Those who organised it and were not defending it, however, were 'isolating' those who wanted to take it and they did not issue an order to hand it over.

We could not cast power out on to the square into the hands of the mob. Neither reason nor a sense of duty allowed us to do that ... This was not a craving for power but only a sense of duty. If this was no longer power, it nevertheless was the prerogative of supreme power given by the people and it could be given back to the people only.

Those who had abandoned us will become our prosecutors and say: 'How dared you renounce what was not your right but your duty!' which meant ... It meant that some political game was being played.

We could yield only to coercion, but the correlation of military forces was such and, what is most important, all the revolutionary organisations which in their totality could (as they had done throughout the revolution) decide the problem of supreme power authoritatively, and in a way obligatory for us, acted in such a manner, both socially and politically, that we were left to our own devices. Completely isolated, in fact, but at the same time having been legally vested with supreme authority, we ourselves had to choose the moment when it was clear beyond all shadow of doubt that we had yielded only to irresistible force. We had to show that we had not overstepped the line beyond which resistance would seem only a craving for power, senseless bloodshed, supported neither by the authority of the people's will nor by an evident preponderance of armed force. In the last case the risk of cruel and bloody action would be justified by victory, because neither in war nor in politics are victors ever judged; the victor himself is both law-maker and judge.

There was no preponderance in armed force. One part of our alternative was lacking.

We did not have behind us the authority of an order issued in the name of people; we enjoyed verbal sympathy but actually we were being abandoned. The other part of our alternative was also lacking.

We were abandoned to our own fate. We ourselves had to find the demarcation line, up to which we had to move and beyond which we dared not step — if we were to preserve the dignity of the bearers of the people's powers and were not to turn into gamblers, indifferent to the senseless shedding of the people's blood ...

What were we to say to the men who came to ask us what to do?

We would issue a brief order.

It is a simple question to answer when there is a real struggle and not the staging of a political game. It is simple, regardless of how many armed forces you have or how weak they are. It is simple because there is only one order to be issued: to fight to the last man, to the last drop of blood. And this meant that we had to emerge at once from the state of waiting, because defence is possible only through attack.

If we had known that the factories had risen, that the population of the capital had come out on the streets to defend the revolutionary gains, its government, that the revolutionary organisations had sounded the call and had gone over from speech-making to the defence of the state, even if all this were doomed to failure — never mind! — the order would have been simple, clear-cut and brief, inspired as it was by one idea, one resolve: to fight to the last man, to the last drop of blood!

When the men came to ask us what to do, what could we tell them?

On the other side there was no hesitation, everything was so simple. There the whole political wisdom, all the 'revolutionary spirit' had long since taken the shape of destructive military orders, brief and imperative.

At that moment we had to have our own soldiers who would obey these brief and imperative orders to pit against these attacking soldiers. The struggle would be waged in the name of different ideologies and practical aims, but all this had to be outside the military struggle of the given moment and by no means be introduced into this struggle. An order that has to be explained is not an order, and if it has to be preceded by a meeting and voting it always spells defeat ...

When the men came to ask us what to do what could we tell them?

And they did come to ask ...

Again, without losing any time for discussions, we all unanimously came to the conclusion each one of us had arrived at individually. It was obvious, on the basis of what I said earlier, that we were not in a position to issue a brief order.

We were not able to issue an order to fight to the last man, to the last drop of blood, if only because we were defending merely ourselves. In that case the bloodshed would not only be fruitless as regards direct results, i.e. would inevitably end in the defeat and ruthless annihilation of our defenders, but would also be aimless politically.

But neither could we issue the other order — to surrender — because we did not know whether the moment had arrived when surrender was inevitable and when it would make the indisputable impression that the government had yielded to irresistible coercion in order to stop needless bloodshed and not to save their own skins, that they had not deserted their posts, throwing their powers overboard with an easy heart, had not renounced the duties entrusted to them by the people.

What military order could we have issued? None.

In war a soldier can be given only two orders: to fight or to surrender...

We learned that several sailors had made their way into the palace and from the upper galleries in the hall dropped two hand-grenades. They were rather poor affairs. The sailors had been arrested. They had two more grenades which they had no time to drop. Palchinsky and Rutenberg brought them into the room.

Manikovsky and Verkerevsky examined them.

'These are not bad and both are charged', Manikovsky said.

The grenades were put in the next room.

Again silence. We again scattered over the room resuming the places we had chosen ...

Firing outside. It did not count, it was merely an accompaniment to the silence ...

Someone came in and said that the Women's Battalion had left, stating: 'Our place is in the front lines, we have not volunteered for this sort of fighting.'

That was the first cheerful news for the entire day — indeed ...

Again noise in the palace, in the distance. It died down ...

Palchinsky reported that the guard had taken a mob of Bolsheviks to be the deputation from the Duma and admitted them into the palace. When the mistake was discovered, the Bolsheviks were disarmed at once. They submitted without any resistance. Some of the disarmed men had, besides a rifle, two and even three pistols.

'How many of them were there?'

'About a hundred.'

The Winter Palace was getting filled, but not with our defenders ...

What a guard: they mistook armed men for members of the Duma! ... Strange! ...

'Unusual cowards', Palchinsky ended his story, 'they will not dare to attack. We will hold out until morning.'

Of course, they were cowards, but what about the clever, brave and staunch people who should have been protecting their government? They...they...were 'isolating' the Bolsheviks ...This thought dissolved into drowsiness. I fell asleep ...

Someone came in, it seemed to be the chief of our guards. He reported that the cadets, from the Pavlovsky or Vladimirsky school, had left.

We listened to the news with indifference. The number of our defenders was dwindling ...

Over the phone different people from various organisations expressed their sympathy and 'advised' us to hold out until morning ...

I shall omit details, the time has not come yet for publishing reminiscences fully ...

The hand of the clock drew near to twelve.

We were told that some of the cadets of the Oranienbaum School had left ...

Well, how much of a military force remained with us, the Provisional Government of the Russian Republic? What difference did it make? The less, perhaps, the better if there was no hope of victory. It would then be possible to avoid useless bloodshed and more easily determine the moment when we could yield to the obvious preponderance of force, and surrender without suffering losses.

Around 1 o'clock at night, or perhaps it was later, we learned that the procession from the Duma had set out. We let the guard know ...

Again noise ...by this time we were accustomed to it. Most probably the Bolsheviks had broken into the palace once more, and, of course, had again been disarmed.

Palchinsky walked in. Of course that was the case. Again they had let themselves be disarmed without resistance. Again there were many of them ...

How many of them are in the palace? Who is actually holding the palace now: we or the Bolsheviks?

About 2 o'clock I was called to the phone. A personal friend was on the wire.

'How are you there?' he asked at the end of the brief conversation.

'Not bad, in cheerful spirits.'

I returned to my place and lay down on the divan ... silence again, not even the sound of firing ...

Suddenly a noise flared up and began to rise, spread and draw nearer. Its varying sounds merged into one wave and at once something unusual, unlike the previous noises, resounded, something final. It was clear instantly that this was the end ...

Those sitting or lying down jumped up and grabbed their overcoats.

The tumult swiftly mounted and its wave rolled up to us. Together with it, painful alarm, like a wave of poisoned air, swept the room and engulfed us ...

All this happened within a few minutes.

From the entrance to the room of our guard came the shrill, excited shouts of a mass of voices, some single shots, the trampling of feet, thuds, shuffling, merging into one chaos of sounds and ever-mounting alarm ...

It was clear that this was the storm, we were being taken by storm ... Defence was useless, sacrifices were aimless ...

The door was flung open, a cadet rushed in. He drew up at attention and saluted. He was excited but determined.

'What are the orders of the Provisional Government?' To fight to the last man? We're ready, if the government issues the order.'

'It's not needed! It's useless! Everything is clear! No bloodshed! We must surrender!' all of us shouted, without having agreed in advance, only looking at each other and reading the same mood and decision in the eyes of all.

Kishkin came forward.

'If they are here, it means that the palace has already been captured ...'

'Yes, all entrances are captured. All have surrendered, only this place is guarded. What are the orders of the Provisional Government?'

'Tell them we want no bloodshed, we yield to force, we surrender', Kishkin said.

At the door the tumult was growing and we were afraid that blood would be shed and that we might not be able to prevent it ... all of us shouted anxiously:

'Go quickly! Go tell them. We want no bloodshed! We surrender!'

The cadet walked out of the room. The whole scene, I think, lasted no more than a minute.

We heard the wave of sounds subsiding.

There was more noise but it sounded different this time.

Evidently the cadet had communicated our statement.

We felt relieved...

'Leave your overcoats. Let us sit down at the table', someone, Kishkin it seems, said. We sat down, I found myself next to Konovalov.

I looked round. I remember all the faces. They were tired but strangely calm...

A noise at our door. It was flung open and a little man flew into the room, like a chip tossed up by a wave, under the pressure of the mob which poured in and spread at once, like water, filling all corners of the room.

The little man was in an open overcoat and a wide-brimmed felt hat pushed back on reddish long hair. He wore glasses and had a short-trimmed reddish moustache and a little beard. His short upper lip tilted towards his nose when he spoke. Colourless eyes and a tired face...

For some reason his shirt front and collar drew my attention and impressed themselves on my memory. A starched high collar propped up his chin. A soft shirt front together with a long tie stuck out from his vest and had rolled up toward his collar. His collar, shirt, cuffs and hands were all very dirty.

The little fellow flew into the room and shouted in a shrill, jarring voice.

We sat around the table and were at once surrounded by a tight ring.

'The Provisional Government is here', Konovalov said. 'What do you want?'

'I inform you, all of you, members of the Provisional Government, that you are arrested. I am Antonov, a representative of the Military Revolutionary Committee.'

12

Mercy or Death to the Whites?

ALBERT RHYS WILLIAMS

(Rhys Williams (like John Reed, an American journalist who was sympathetic to the Bolsheviks), later helped organise — at Lenin's suggestion — an International Brigade to defend the revolution against the forces of the Allied interventionists.)

It was a black outlook for the White Guards hemmed inside the telephone station. But now comes this jubilant news that an armoured car is hurrying to their rescue. They gaze intently down the street for the first glimpse of it.

As it comes swinging in from the Nevsky, they hail it with cheers. Like a great iron steed it lumbers along and stops before the barricades. Cheers again from the Whites. Ill-starred cheers! They do not know that they are cheering their end. They do not know that this is not their car; it has passed into the hands of the Reds. It is a Trojan horse, within whose armoured belly are concealed the soldiers of the Revolution. It slews about until its muzzle is pointed through the archway. Then suddenly it spouts a stream of lead as a garden hose spouts water. Screams now instead of cheers! Tumbling over boxes and one another, the officers, in one shrieking, tangled mass, go crashing through the hallway and up the stairs.

Poetic justice! Here where a few hours earlier these Counter-revolutionists pressed their revolvers against the temples of the Revolution, the Revolution presses its machine guns against their temples.

The White Guards in a Funk
At the top of the stairway the Whites disentangle themselves, not to make a stand, but to run better. Ten resolute men could have held this stairway against a thousand. But there are not ten men to do it. There is not one. There is only a panic-stricken pack, in the clutch of a fear that drains the blood from their faces, the reason from their brains. All courage gone. All prudence gone. Gone even the herd-instinct of unity in the face of common peril.

100

'*Sauve qui peut*' (let him save himself who can) becomes the cry of the older officers.

They fling away caps, belts and swords; insignia of honour now become badges of shame and death. They rip off shoulder straps, gold-braid and buttons. They plead for a workman's costume, a cloak, an overcoat — anything to disguise their rank. An officer coming upon a greasy blouse hanging on a peg becomes a maniac with joy. A captain finding the apron of a cook puts it on, plunges his arms in flour and already white from terror becomes the whitest White Guard in all Russia.

But for most of them there is no cover save the darkness of closets, booths and attic corners. Into these they crawl like hunted animals in collapse. To treachery against their enemies these officers now add treason to their allies. They had led the Junkers into this trap. Now the trap is closing, and the officers abandon them.

First to rally their wits, the Junkers begin to cry out, 'Our officers! Where are our officers?' No answer to their cries. 'Damn the cowards!' they shout. 'They have deserted us.'

Rage at this betrayal fuses the Junkers together. Their best tactics would be to hold the stairway, but they shrink away from it. Red vengeance crouching at the foot fills them with dread. It will not let them move forward. They fall back into a thick walled room with a narrow entrance. There, like rats clustering in a hole, they wait the onrush of the Red tide that may come rising up the stairway, flooding the corridors, drowning them out.

To some of these young fellows, sprung from the middle class, this is a doubly tragic ending. Death at the hands of peasants and workers with whom they have no quarrel! But, caught in this camp of the Counter-revolution, they must share its doom. They know how richly they deserve it. This sense of guilt unnerves them. Their guns fall from their hands. They slink down on chairs and tables, moaning, their eyes fixed on the entrance through which the Red tide is to come crashing in. They listen for the swirl of the first wave flinging itself on the stairway; hammering on the door. Save their own hammering pulses there is not a sound.

Reds, Whites and Girls Petrified by Fear

There is another chamber of torture in this building. It holds Antonov, the Red sentries, and all captives bagged by the Whites during the day. They sit helpless, locked in their prison, while outside rages the battle sealing the fate of their Revolution, and their own fate. No one comes to tell them how the battle goes. Only through the thick walls comes the muffled crackle of rifles, the crash of falling glass.

Now all these noises abruptly cease. What does it mean? The triumph of the Counter-revolution? The Whites victorious? What next? The opening of the door? The firing-squad lining them up before a wall?

Bandages tied round their eyes? The report of rifles? Their own death? The death of the Revolution? So many muse, heads sunk in hands, while the clock above the door pitilessly tells off the seconds. Each stroke may be the last. Awaiting that last, they sit straining to hear the tread of the firing-squad coming down the corridor. But save for the ticking clock, not a sound.

Still another torture chamber, this one filled with women. It is the top floor, with hundreds of telephone girls huddled around the switch-boards. The eight-hour bombardment, the stampede of the officers, their frenzied cries for help, have shattered the nerves of these girls and their minds run wild. They run to wild stories of Bolshevik atrocities, the rape of the Women's Battalion, crimes imputed to these Red hordes swarming into the court-yard below.

In their fevered imagination they are already victims of a like brutality, writhing in the arms of these monsters. They break into tears. They write frantic little last farewells. They cling together in white-faced groups, listening for the first yells of the ruffians, the thumping of their boots along the hall. But there are no thumping boots — only their own thumping hearts.

The building becomes quiet as a tomb. It is not the quiet of the dead, but tense and vibrant, the silence of hundreds of living beings paralysed with terror. The silence is contagious. It passes through the walls and lays hold of the Red throngs outside. They in turn become still, stricken by the same paralysis of fear. They shrink away from the stairway lest it belch out clouds of gas, a fusillade of bombs. Hundreds outside in terror of the Whites within! Hundreds inside in terror of the Reds without! Thousands of human beings torturing each other.

Inside the building this ordeal by silence becomes unendurable. I, at least, can endure it no longer. For relief I run forward, not knowing where; anywhere to get away from the silence. Opening a sidedoor by accident I catapult into the chamber filled with Junkers. They jump as though it is the crack of doom.

'American correspondent', they gasp. 'O! Help us! Help us!'

'How can I?' I falter. 'What shall I do?'

'Something — anything!' they implore. 'Only save us.'

Some one says, 'Antonov.' The others catch up the name, repeating it like an incantation. 'Antonov. Yes, Antonov. Go to Antonov. Downstairs — Antonov. Quick, before it is too late — Antonov!' They point the way.

In a minute I make another headlong entrance before another astounded audience — the captive Reds and Antonov.

'You are all free. The officers have fled. The Junkers surrender. They beg you to save them. Any terms. All they ask is their lives. Only hurry, hurry.'

In a moment this prisoner Antonov awaiting death becomes the arbiter of death. The condemned is asked to be the judge. A startling change! But the face of this little, tired overworked Revolutionist did not change. If the thought of revenge flashed into his mind, it as quickly flashed out again. 'So I am not to be a corpse but a commander', he said wanly. 'Next thing is to see the Junkers is it? Very well.' He put on his hat and walked upstairs to the Junkers.

'Antonov! *Gospadeen* Antonov! Commander Antonov!' they wailed. 'Spare our lives. We know we are guilty. But we throw ourselves on the mercy of the Revolution.'

Sorry ending to a gay adventure! In the morning sallying out to kill Bolsheviks and in the evening begging Bolsheviks for their own lives. Saying '*Tovarish*' as one might say 'swine', then breathing it reverently as a term of honour.

'*Tovarish* Antonov', they implored, 'give us your word as a Bolshevik, a true Bolshevik. Give us your word for our safety.'

'My word', said Antonov. 'I give it.'

'They may not take your word, *Tovarish* Antonov', muttered one poor wretch. 'They may kill us anyhow.'

'If they kill you', assured Antonov, 'they must first kill me.'

'But we don't want to be killed', whimpered the poor fellow.

The Mob Decrees Death to the White Guards
Antonov could not conceal his contempt. Turning into the hall, he started down the stairs. To the taut nerves every step sounded like the detonation of a gun.

The Red throng outside heard the steps and raised their rifles expecting a fusillade. And then this surprise! Antonov, their own leader!

'*Nash! Nash!*' (Ours! Ours!) acclaimed a hundred voices. 'Antonov! Long live Antonov!' rose from another hundred throats. The shout raised in the courtyard was caught up in the street and the crowd surged forward crying, 'The officers, Antonov? Where are the officers and the *Junkers*?'

'Done for', announced Antonov. 'Their arms are down.'

Like the bursting of a dam came the roar from a thousand throats. Yells of triumph and howls of rage proclaiming 'Death to the officers! Death to the Junkers!'

Good reason for the Whites to tremble! At the mercy of those to whom they had forfeited all claims for mercy. Not by fighting, but by fighting foully they had roused this volcano of wrath. In the eyes of these soldiers and workmen the Whites were murderers of the Red comrades, assassinators of the Revolution, miscreants to be exterminated like vermin. Fear only had kept the Reds from plunging up the stairway. Now all cause for caution was gone. The infuriated men stormed forward filling the night with their cries, 'Wipe out the butchers! Kill the White Devils! Kill every one of them!'

A torch here and there in the blackness lit up the bearded faces of peasants, soldier-faces, the faces of city artisans grimed and thin, and in the front rank the open, alert countenances of the big sailors from the Baltic fleet. On all of them, in flashing eyes, and clenched jaws vengeance was written, the terrible vengeance of the long-suffering. Pressed from the rear, the mass lunged forward against the stairway where Antonov stood, calm and impassive, but looking so frail and helpless before this avalanche of men.

Raising his hand and voice, Antonov cried out, '*Tovarishi*, you cannot kill them. The Junkers have surrendered. They are our prisoners.'

The throng was stunned. Then in a hoarse cry of resentment it found its voice. 'No! No! They are not our prisoners', it protested. 'They are dead men.'

'They have given up their arms', continued Antonov. 'I have given them their lives.'

'You may give them their lives. We don't. We give them the bayonet!' bawled a big peasant turning to the crowd for approval.

'The bayonet! Yes, we give them the bayonet!' they howled in a blast of approbation.

Antonov faced the tornado. Drawing a big revolver, he waved it aloft, crying out, 'I have given the Junkers my word for their safety. You understand! I will back my word with this.'

The crowd gasped. This was incredible.

'What's this? What do you mean?' they demanded.

Clutching his revolver, finger on the trigger, Antonov repeated his warning: 'I promised them their lives. I will back that promise with this.'

'Traitor! Renegade!' a hundred voices thundered at him. 'Defender of the White Guards!' a big sailor flung in his face. 'You want to save the rascals. But you can't. We'll kill them.'

'The first man who lays his hands on a prisoner — *I will kill him on the spot!*' Antonov spoke slowly, with emphasis on each word. '*You understand! I will shoot him dead!*'

'Shoot us?' queried the affronted sailors.

'Shoot us! Shoot us!' bellowed the whole indignant mob.

For it was just that — a mob, with all the vehement passions of the mob. A mob with every primitive instinct inflamed and ascendant: cruel, brutal, lusting for blood. In it flamed the savagery of the wolf, the ferocity of the tiger. A huge beast drawn out of the jungles of the city, stirred up by these White hunters, wounded, and bleeding from its wounds, all day exasperated and tormented, at last, in a paroxysm of joy and rage it was about to pounce upon its tormentors and tear them to pieces. At this moment this little man stepped between it and its prey! To me the most emotional thing in the whole revolution is this little man standing in that stairway, so unemotionally looking that mob in the eye; rather, in its thousand glaring eyes. There was pallor in his face, but no tremor in his limbs. And no quaver in his voice, as he said again slowly and solemnly, 'The first man who tries to kill a Junker, I will kill him.'

The sheer audacity, the impudence of it took their breath away.

'What do you mean?' they yelled. 'To save these officers, Counter-revolutionists, you kill us workmen — Revolutionists?'

'Revolutionists!' retorted Antonov, derisively. 'Revolutionists! Where do I see Revolutionists here? You dare call yourselves Revolutionists? *You*, who think of killing helpless men and prisoners!' His taunt went home. The crowd winced as though struck by a whip.

'Listen!' he went on. 'Do you know what you are doing? Do you realise where this madness leads? When you kill a captive White Guard you are not killing the Counter-revolution, you are killing the Revolution. For this Revolution I gave twenty years of my life in exile and in prison. Do you think that I, a Revolutionist, will stand by and watch Revolutionists crucify the Revolution?'

'But if they had *us* there would be no quarter', bellowed a peasant, 'they would kill us.'

'True, they would kill us', answered Antonov. 'What of that? They are not Revolutionists. They belong to the old order, to the Tsar and the knout, to murder and death. But *we* belong to the Revolution. And the Revolution means something better. It means liberty and life for all. That's why you give it your life and blood. But you must give it more. You must give it your reason. Above the satisfaction of your passions you must put service to the Revolution. For the triumph of the Revolution you have been brave. Now, for the honour of the Revolution be merciful. You love the Revolution. I only ask you not to kill the thing you love.'

He was aflame, his face incandescent, his arms and voice imploring. His whole being, focusing itself in that last appeal, left him exhausted.

'Speak to them, comrade!' he entreated.

Four weeks earlier I had spoken to these sailors from the turret of their battleship *The Republic*. As I stepped to the front they recognised me.

'The American *tovarish*', they shouted.

Loudly and fervently I spoke about the Revolution, about the battle waged throughout Russia for land and freedom, about their own betrayal by the White Guards and the justice in their wrath. But the eyes of the world turned to them as the fighting vanguard of the Social Revolution. Would they take the old bloody path of retaliation or blaze the way to a nobler code? They had shown themselves daring for the preservation of the Revolution. Would they show themselves magnanimous for its glory?

It was an effective speech at the outset. But not because of its content. The recitation of the Lord's Prayer or Webster's Oration would have been almost as effective. Not one in a hundred understood what I was saying. For I spoke in English.

But these words — strange and foreign — crackling out in the dark held them and made them pause — precisely what Antonov was working for — that this hurricane of passion might subside a little, to gain time for another impulse to get the upper hand.

The Mob Disciplined by the Revolution

For while this was a mob, it was a revolutionary mob. Deep-rooted in the hearts of at least half this workman-soldier crowd was one powerful abiding loyalty — the Revolution. The word was a fetish. Their dreams and hopes and longings were all woven around 'The Revolution'. They were its servants. It was their master.

True, at this moment another master held them, displacing every idea of the Revolution. Revenge was in the saddle, recklessly lashing the mob along. But this was temporary. The permanent allegiance of their lives was to the Revolution. Given the chance it would rise up, expel the usurper, assert its authority and again control its followers. Antonov did not stand alone against a multitude. In that mob, there were a thousand Antonovs, sharing with him the same high zeal for the Revolution. Antonov was just one unit of that mob, flesh of its flesh, spirit of its spirit, sharing its antagonism to the Junkers and officers, aflame with its same hot passions.

Antonov happened to be first of this mob to rein in his passions, the first in whose consciousness the Revolution replaced revenge. The change made in his heart by the concept of the Revolution would likewise be wrought in the hearts of the soldiers and workers. This Antonov knew. By repeating the magic word 'Revolution' he sought to bring them to their revolutionary selves; he sought to evoke revolutionary order out of chaos. And he did.

Before our eyes we saw again the ancient miracle of the Word — the stilling of the tempest. The howling and the raging died away, save for here and there an angry voice still persisting. But as Woskov interpreted my words, and Antonov spoke again, these centres of dissent subsided. Chastened and in a receptive mood, these soldiers and sailors were substituting for their own will to revenge the will of the Revolution. Only let them understand that will.

'What is it, Antonov?' they cried. 'What do you want us to do?'

'To treat the Junkers as prisoners of war', said Antonov. 'To carry out the terms of surrender. I have pledged these Junkers their lives. I ask you to back my pledge with yours.'

The mob became a Soviet. A sailor spoke; then two soldiers and a workingman. The vote was taken by show of hands. A hundred battle-stained hands went up, and another hundred until nearly a thousand hands were lifted. A thousand clenched fists threatening death to the officers now raised in an open-handed promise of life.

At this juncture arrived a delegation from the Petrograd Duma commissioned 'to liquidate the civil strife with the shedding of as little blood as possible'. But the Revolution was liquidating its own affairs without the shedding of any blood at all. It ignored these gentlemen, and detailed a squad to enter the building and bring the White Guards down. First came the Junkers, and then the officers, ferreted out of their hiding places, one of them dragged out by his heels. Hustled out upon the elevated stone steps, they stood blinking in the torch-light, facing the muzzles of a thousand guns, the scorn of a thousand hearts, the grilling of a thousand pairs of eyes.

There were a few jeers, cries of *'Assassins of the Revolution!'* and then silence — the solemn silence of a court. For this was a court — the tribunal of the disinherited. The oppressed sitting in judgement on their oppressors. The new order passing sentence upon the old. The grand assizes of the Revolution.

'Guilty! All guilty!' was the verdict. Guilty as enemies of the Revolution. Guilty as retainers of the Tsar and the exploiting classes. Guilty as violators of the Red Cross and the laws of war. Guilty on all counts as traitors to the workers of Russia, and to the workers of the world.

The wretched prisoners in the dock shrank before the blast and bowed their heads. Some of them would have found it easier to stand up to a volley from the guns. But the guns were there to guard them.

Five sailors shouldering rifles took their stand at the foot of the steps. Antonov seized the hand of an officer and placed it in the hand of a sailor.

'Number one', he said. 'A helpless, disarmed prisoner. His life is in your hands. Guard it for the honour of the Revolution.' The squad encircled the prisoner and marched through the archway.

With a like formula the next prisoner was handed over, and the next, and the next; each one entrusted to a detachment of four or five. 'The end of the rubbish', muttered an old peasant as the last officer was delivered to his escort, and the procession filed out into the Morskaya.

Near the Winter Palace infuriated mobs fell upon the Junkers and tore them from the hands of their convoys. But the revolutionary sailors, charging the mobs, rescued the prisoners and brought them safely to the prison Fortress of Peter and Paul.

The Revolution was not everywhere powerful enough to check the savage passions of the mobs. Not always was it on time to allay the primitive blood-lusts. Unoffending citizens were assaulted by hooligans. In out-of-the-way places half-savages, calling themselves Red Guards, committed heinous crimes. At the front General Dukhonin was dragged from his carriage and torn to pieces despite the protesting commissars. Even in Petrograd some Junkers were clubbed to death by the storming crowds; others were pitched headlong into the Neva.

13

Lenin – Organiser of the Victorious October Uprising

NIKOLAI PODVOISKY

(Podvoisky was President of the Military Revolutionary Committee of the Petrograd Soviet, the headquarters staff of the revolution. He later played a key role in organising the Red Army, but before the revolution had worked as a socialist publisher.)

The evening of October 17 has remained firmly fixed in my memory.

After a meeting in one of the regiments I hurried to the Smolny Institute. The long corridors of the gigantic vaulted building resounded to the trample of many feet. Soldiers' grey greatcoats, the black jackets and smocks of the Red Guards, the dark pea-jackets of sailors with machine-gun belts strapped round them and bristling with hand-grenades, armed men everywhere — such was the picture presented by the Smolny.

At the entrance were two quick-firing guns, between them and on the flanks stood machine-guns.

A big former class-room of the institute, on the ground floor, was the headquarters of the Bolshevik group; the only furniture in the room was the desks moved up against the walls.

The room was full of people. An important conference of representatives of all districts of the Petrograd Bolshevik organisation and the Military Organisation of the Central Committee was under way. The question of the armed insurrection was being discussed. The chairman was Comrade Sverdlov. In the middle of the room stood a simple little table without a cover.

One report after another told that the workers and soldiers of Petrograd were prepared for the insurrection. Party workers from the districts produced facts and figures showing that the time was ripe...

As chairman of the Military Organisation of the Bolshevik Party I reported to the conference on the Red Guards, the army units and the fleet.

I began with the Red Guards in Vyborg District. They were in close contact with the factory and district Bolshevik organisations and with the factory committees. I mentioned the names of the organisers of the Red Guards. I made special mention of those secretaries of Party groups and chairmen of factory committees who had shown ability in drawing the workers into the Red Guard. These organisers of the Red Guards had worked well to put into force the battle slogans of the Bolshevik Party.

The former Moscow Regiment of Life Guards had given great assistance to the Red Guards of Vyborg District, where it was quartered.

I spoke about the Red Guard of Petrograd District which was developing into an important force. It had had its baptism of fire during the April demonstration when a group of Tsarist officers had attacked the Red Guards in an attempt to take away and tear up their red flag.They were repulsed by armed force.

I spoke of Moscow-Narva District and the giant Putilov Works with its forty-thousand strong army of workers. The February Revolution began with the demonstration and strike of the Putilov workers. As early as 5 March 1917, the Putilov workers adopted a resolution not to lay down their arms until the final victory of the proletarian revolution. The Putilov workers were a well-disciplined Red Guard.

I reported on the soldiers of the Petrograd garrison, on the famous Armoured-Car Detachment amongst whom were many former Petrograd, Moscow and Kolomna workers. The older soldiers amongst them remembered the battles with the Tsarist government in 1905. They had shown no fear of court-martial when, in April, they took two armoured cars to the Finland Railway Station on the memorable day of Lenin's arrival. The 17 armoured cars in possession of the detachment were an important force. The officers of the Provisional Government had got control of this force and with its aid were guarding the railway stations, telephone exchange, telegraph office, post office, the Winter and Marian palaces and the Army Headquarters.

Then I spoke about other units. The Bolsheviks of the Motor Transport Company had all the lorries and army cars in their hands. The Bolsheviks of the Armoured-Car Repair Shops had six cars ready — at a moment's notice they were prepared to place the cars and themselves at the disposal of the staff of the armed insurrection.

The Flame-Thrower and Chemical Battalion and the Engineer Battalion, the 1st Machine-Gun Regiment and others had been disarmed. The soldiers of these units, however, were eager to wash away in blood the insult of the disarmament that had followed their demand during the July demonstrations that all power be invested in the Soviets.

I reported in brief on the ten Guards' regiments. In advance of the others were the Pavlovsky and Grenadier Jaeger regiments and the Petrograd, Lithuanian, Volhynian, Finland and Izmailovsky regiments, where our propaganda had taken root. The Bolsheviks had conducted very extensive propaganda in these regiments even before the July events. K.Y.

Voroshilov was with the Izmailovsky Regiment and had aroused them to revolt in February.

The 180th Regiment and the Siege Artillery of the Peter and Paul Fortress would follow the Bolsheviks. The artillerymen considered it a matter of honour for the fortress garrison that the Colt Machine-Gun Battalion and the Cyclist Battalion, on whose loyalty the Provisional Government had counted, were no longer amongst the defenders of the bourgeoisie.

I listed the troops that would bar the roads to Petrograd from Pskov, Minsk and Mogilev in the event of the General Headquarters making an attempt to come to the aid of the Provisional Government. The garrisons quartered along the Warsaw, Baltic and Vitebsk railways, in Tsarskoye Selo, Gatchina, Luga and other places were all re-electing their company and battalion committees and placing Bolsheviks at the head of them. Groups of the Bolshevik Military Organisation were the only guiding force in these units. All these units would follow the Bolsheviks only in order to overthrow the power of the bourgeoisie and establish the power of the workers and peasants.

The sailors of Kronstadt and Helsingfors, the artillery and infantry at Vyborg, the Lettish Rifles, the soldiers from the armies on the Northern Front, steeled in the battles against the bourgeoisie in the July, August and September days, informed the country of their loyalty to the banner of Lenin in their newspapers *Soldat* (The Soldier), *Volna* (The Wave) and *Okopnaya Pravda* (The Trench Truth). The sailors and the soldiers of Vyborg had shown where they stood as early as March when they threw generals and officers into the sea and drowned them. They were confident of the success of the insurrection, confident that theirs was the force that would crush the bourgeoisie.

Those present listened in rapt attention, trying to catch every word.

I finished my report and went aside. At that moment Yakov Mikhailovich Sverdlov came up to me and whispered:

'Now you can go to Ilyich. He sent for you to report on the preparations.'

Sverdlov took me to Antonov-Ovseenko and Nevsky who were also to go to see Lenin. We were to give him an account of the way in which the Party's Military Organisation was preparing the masses for insurrection. As a precaution we decided to go separately, each of us with a guide.

Night. I was accompanied by Comrade Pavlov, a Petrograd worker born and bred. We went a roundabout way to avoid being followed — it was a lot farther but more dependable. There had been a noticeably keener hunt for Ilyich, dozens of plain-clothes men were roaming the city and camouflaged pickets were to be seen everywhere. The Provisional Government felt their rule coming to an end; they realised how much Lenin was responsible for the masses having become more and more persistent in demanding the overthrow of the bourgeoisie. The plain-clothes men were beside themselves in their efforts to find Lenin.

Avoiding the cadet patrols we continued our way along little used back streets.

We crossed Troitsky Bridge, making for Petrograd District, pretending to be going away from Vyborg District.

When we were quite sure that we were not being followed we went over to Vyborg District. At last we came to the street where Lenin was living. We went round the house carefully to make sure there were no suspicious characters about. The street was deserted. We entered the yard and I was naturally very excited.

We went upstairs to the first floor and looked round. Then we knocked, giving the prescribed signal. The door opened and an unknown man stood before us. Vladimir Ilyich was so well disguised that I only recognised him by his voice when I heard the words, 'Good-evening, Comrade Podvoisky.'

While we were on the way I had given considerable thought to the sequence in which I would make my 'report'.

In actual fact there was no report — just a simple, heart-to-heart talk. When Vladimir Ilyich had seated us he began with Antonov-Ovseenko, asking him to give his views concerning the insurrection. Antonov-Ovseenko said he was not in a position to judge the situation in the Petrograd garrison but he was well acquainted with the Helsingfors Fleet and, to some extent, with the Kronstadt Fleet. The sailors were ready for action. They could come to Petrograd by railway or, in case of necessity, could approach the city from the sea. Good propaganda work had been done amongst the troops quartered in Finland and they supported the uprising in every way. As far as the Petrograd garrison was concerned he believed that after the work done by the Military Organisation the success of the insurrection was assured. He was convinced of this by the numerous meetings held by the Party during September and October and the resolutions passed at them.

Nevsky, whom the Military Organisation had sent specially to Helsingfors to find out whether it would be possible for the fleet to participate in the insurrection directly in Petrograd waters, said that the fleet would certainly take part — Antonov-Ovseenko was right — but the movement of the fleet to Petrograd would be a matter of the greatest difficulty. After the arrest of the officers, which would be necessary in the first hour of the uprising, their places would be taken by men with little experience, and who were not well acquainted with the charts of the mine fields, so that it was doubtful whether they would be able to steer the vessels through them. Deployment of the ships, should it become necessary to fight at Petrograd, would also give trouble since the sailors in command were unable to direct a battle. Nevsky was in favour of leaving the ships in Helsingfors and bringing the sailors to Petrograd by rail.

Then came my turn. I said that the Military Organisation was making the most intensive preparations for the uprising, that at one of the recent meetings of the bureau of military organisations it had been decided to send authoritative comrades to the front — to the 12th, 5th and 2nd armies, to the South-Western Front, and to Minsk, Bryansk, and other places to prepare our organisations at the front and in the provincial garrisons for the insurrection and to find out what degree of support would be given to Petrograd by troops in other places. It was very important for us to show the comrades, especially those on the Northern Front, the significance which the 12th and 5th armies would have in preventing the approach towards Pskov of the Cossack units and Mountain Division that had been brought up and concentrated on the approaches to that city (near Marienburg).

I said that the Military Organisation attached great importance to the contacts with the army at the front that had been decided upon, but the fulfilment of the plan required some time. It would therefore be expedient to postpone the insurrection for ten days or so. The more so since time was obviously working in our favour: every day brought new forces to our side, while the ground was slipping more and more from under the feet of the Provisional Government. We would also be able to use those days to complete preparations in the Petrograd garrison. The regiments that had taken part in the July demonstrations (the Pavlovsky, the Grenadier, Moscow, 1st Reserve and others) had been partially disbanded and were partially demoralised and would only take part when they were sure that the other units were participating; we still had to check whether those units that had formerly been reactionary (the Preobrazhensky and Semyonovsky regiments) were now ready to take part in the insurrection. I called the attention of Vladimir Ilyich to the fact that Kerensky could rely on special composite detachments and other reactionary units from the front that might hinder the success of the insurrection.

The attention with which Vladimir Ilyich listened to my account of the preparations changed to extreme impatience when I spoke about postponement.

'That's just it!' he said, interrupting me, 'that's just why it must not be postponed! Every delay on our part will make it possible for the government parties, who are in possession of the powerful state apparatus, to make more resolute preparations to crush us with the aid of reliable troops recalled from the front. They, of course, are most certainly informed of the impending insurrection ... they are preparing for it. During the period of delay they will make still greater preparations. That's how matters stand! The insurrection must take place before the Congress of Soviets — it is especially important that the congress, confronted with the accomplished fact of the working class having taken power, should immediately give legal strength to the new regime by decrees and the setting up of government machinery...

Lenin asked me to continue and prepared to listen.

I continued by outlining the situation in the Petrograd garrison and the Red Guard. I gave the details of what I had reported that day to the conference of Petrograd Party organisations and the Military Organisation. After telling of the situation in the army units I went on to speak about the Red Guards. I pointed out that the workers were becoming more insistent every day in their demands for arms. The number of young workers joining the Red Guards was increasing. Ilyich was particularly pleased that military training, formerly carried out in secret, in places far from the factories and working-class districts, had now been transferred to the factory yards and to the riding-schools of the army units in the neighbourhood. But then his face showed that he was worried about something. Vladimir Ilyich got up from his seat, came over to me, took me by the hand, led me to a sofa standing in the corner of the room, sat me down beside him and asked:

'Are you quite sure the information you have given me is correct? Have you checked up on it?'

I told him that leading members of the Military Organisation, including myself, were visiting the Red Guard detachment and military units every day. Soldier and officer members of the Military Organisation supervising the instruction of the Red Guard, and the leaders of the Bolshevik groups in the army, reported each day to the Bureau of Military Organisations at the Central Committee on the progress of military instruction and on the growth of Bolshevik influence amongst the soldiers.

It seemed to me that Vladimir Ilyich was satisfied with my report. I was pleased myself; it had turned out all right, the picture was complete, exhaustive information had been provided on all points — the 'rehearsal' I had had obviously helped me. And then Ilyich began asking me for fuller details. Who reported it? When was it reported? Under what circumstances? How did I know that we could rely competely on that factory? Who was the secretary of the Party organisation there? What people were there on the factory committee? When was the last election of a company or battalion committee? Who had been sent from the factory or regiment to the Petrograd Soviet after the elections?

I knew that all these questions were 'legitimate' but they were so unexpected that I kept going hot and cold. And still Ilyich continued 'checking up details'. What people were there in the district Duma? In the district Soviet? What connections had such and such a factory with the staff of the Red Guard? How were the factories and the army units linked up? And the district Party committee? How was it linked up with the army units of the district? Where did the Military Organisation expect to get arms from? Who was teaching the workers to shoot and how? Lenin then asked questions about the leadership of the Red Guard detachments and battalions, but even here I was no better off and felt as uneasy as an inexperienced boxer in the ring...

'You said that at such and such a factory there is a good military organisation, there are 300 men in the Red Guard, there are rifles and cartridges, and, you said, there are even machine-guns. Who is the commander there, do you know him?'

'Yes. I know him.' And I told Ilyich all I knew about him.

'You say he is an excellent man? Would give his head for the revolution? And what are his military qualifications? Can he shoot, from a revolver, say? And could he handle a cannon if it were necessary? Could he bring up something essential in a car, in case of need? Can he drive a car? And then, do your Red Guard commanders know anything about the tactics of street fighting?'

It appeared that I knew nothing about any one of the commanders from that point of view. Vladimir Ilyich stood up, placed his fingers in his waistcoat pockets and shook his head reproachfully.

'Ai-ai-ai, and that's the chairman of the Military Organisation! How are you going to lead the insurrection if you do not know what your commanders are like? It is not enough for them to be good agitators, good propagandists, that they make good reports and are excellent organisers of the masses. Insurrection is not a meeting to hear reports, insurrection is action with arms in hand. There you not only have to act with self-sacrifice but also with skill, otherwise the slightest mistake may cost the lives of Red Guards, revolutionary sailors and soldiers ... A mistake may lead to the defeat of the insurrection.'

I saw what a tremendous mistake we had been making. I then realised that the Petrograd Organisation of the Bolshevik Party had mustered huge masses of workers and soldiers for the insurrection, but had been paying little attention to purely military matters although that was the primary duty of the Military Organisation. There was only one thing I wanted at that moment — to go straight back, roll up my sleeves and try to make up for lost time...

Noting my confusion, Vladimir Ilyich tried to help me out of the awkward position in which I found myself.

'My dear fellow', he said, 'insurrection is the most crucial form of warfare. It is a great art. Of course, bold commanders can do wonders by their own example, audacity and courage. But what sort of commander for an armed uprising is a man who cannot shoot? Such commanders must be immediately replaced by others. Leaders who do not understand the tactics of street fighting will ruin the insurrection. And remember, please, that soldiers are all right in their way, but in our struggle we must depend mostly on the workers.'

From that moment on I began to look at insurrection through the eyes of Vladimir Ilyich. It was now quite clear to me what had to be done in the few days that were left before the uprising. We had to make sure that the Red Guard would not only be the leading political force, but also the leading military force that would determine the success of the insurrection.

'And are you sure', continued Vladimir Ilyich, 'that the commanders of the army units will not let you down? Are they not Tsarist officers?'

I informed Comrade Lenin that during the four months of enforced underground existence the influence of the Bolsheviks in the army units had increased very greatly. Only those commanders had remained at their posts in the units who recognised the control of the soldiers' committees. The soldiers' committees, as I had already reported, were in the majority of cases under the influence of the Bolsheviks.

Even in a regiment like the Semyonovsky, we were able to get our resolutions passed without any special difficulty. It was true that the Preobrazhensky Regiment was still not ours, but we were confident that we would win it over. I then named all those commanders – mostly of machine-gun companies and some of the Guards' regiments – who during the past few days had unconditionally come over to our side.

'What tremendous power is wielded by the revolution!' said Vladimir Ilyich with great satisfaction. 'The main thing now is to direct it so as to win and without the application of military science we cannot win.'

'The most important thing now', continued Lenin, 'is to select a core of selfless workers, especially the youth, who are ready to die rather than retreat or give up a position. They must be formed into special detachments beforehand to occupy the telephone exchange, the telegraph office and, most important of all, the bridges.'

The bridges... The working-class districts of Petrograd were interconnected and were linked to the centre by eight bridges — Liteiny, Troitsky, Palace, Nikolayevsky, Okhta, Great and Little Sampson and Tuchkov. It was absolutely essential that we keep these bridges in our hands.

After that Lenin touched on the question of arms.

'You said that the workers were more and more persistently demanding arms. Where do you propose to get them?'

It was our pride, the pride of the Military Organisation, that in most regiments we could take almost all the arms from the storehouses because the Bolshevik military groups in every regiment, on the ships and in the artillery were a force to be reckoned with. The Cossacks were the only units we had not yet succeeded in influencing with our propaganda. In all other units in the region and in the nearest front-line areas we were in a position to obtain arms in almost any quantity.

When I told Vladimir Ilyich this his face did not express pleasure or satisfaction but some sort of perplexity: what is the man talking about, he seemed to say.

'Just a minute... The more arms we take away from the soldiers the less will remain for them. Is that not so?' said Vladimir Ilyich.

Hm...That was something that I had not thought about.

'That won't do! You must get into closer contact with the arsenals and the munition stores', continued Comrade Lenin. 'There are workers and soldiers there, too. Work out a plan and ensure its fulfilment so that we can take arms straight from the stores at the very moment they are needed. It is good that we have the Sestroretsk Arsenal, but that is not enough. I'm sure that if you help the Bolsheviks of the Peter and Paul Arsenal, of the New Arsenal on Liteiny and the Old Arsenal in Vyborg District to develop their work in the proper way they will open the storehouses for the distribution of arms to the workers the moment they are needed. Is that not so?'

Never before, despite the experience of 1905, had I realised how much an armed insurrection is organically connected with the arming of the widest sections of the working class. Nor did I realise that the greatest revolutionary enthusiasm amongst the masses was far from enough to ensure victory. Victory could only be achieved by skilled leadership. It was only Lenin's masterly analysis of the problems of the armed uprising and the part to be played by the masses, the leaders and the weapons, that ensured the general participation of workers and soldiers in the insurrection and guaranteed success.

We began to talk of the Military Revolutionary Committee as the body that must lead the insurrection. The Military Organisation of the Central Committee of the Bolshevik Party, owing to its great influence amongst the masses, had already begun to play an exceptional role in the Military Revolutionary Committee, set up by the Petrograd Soviet. It took little heed of the representatives of other organisations in the committee, and there were many of them. It seemed to us that it was too unwieldy to be an operative leadership.

Comrade Lenin asked me what I thought of the work of the Military Revolutionary Committee.

'The Military Revolutionary Committee', I answered, 'is actually an extended bureau of the Military Organisations of the Central Committee of our Party.'

'And that is wrong!' said Vladimir Ilyich. 'It should not be a bureau, but a non-party insurrectionary body which has full power and is connected with all sections of the workers and soldiers. The committee must ensure that an unlimited number of workers and soldiers are armed and participate in the insurrection. The greater the initiative and activity of each member of the Military Revolutionary Committee, the stronger and more effective will be the influence of the entire committee on the masses. There must not be the slightest hint of dictatorship by the Military Organisation over the Military Revolutionary Committee. The main task of the Military Organisation is to see that the committee follows the correct

Bolshevik line. The main thing is the victory of the insurrection. The Military Revolutionary Committee must serve that purpose and that alone.'

At the same time Lenin pointed out the way in which the work of the Military Revolutionary Committee would take on a mass character.

'Call daily conferences of representatives of all army units in Petrograd and act through them.'

Towards the end of our talk I asked Vladimir Ilyich a question:

'Would it not be expedient to print beforehand millions of copies of the decrees on land, peace, workers' control of production and the organisation of a Soviet Republic?'

Vladimir Ilyich looked up at me and burst out laughing.

'You're getting a long way ahead of yourself! First we have to win and then print decrees.'

We parted with great warmth. It was long past midnight. I flew back as though on wings. Lenin's words kept hammering at my head: 'The masses are there. Organise their military leadership. Put as many weapons as possible into their hands. That is what must be done.'

That same night every single member of the Military Organisation immediately got down to the job of putting Lenin's instructions into effect.

★ ★ ★

The Smolny was as crowded with people as it had been five days before. The workers had been armed and were setting out to defend Petrograd against the attacking troops of General Krasnov's army corps. On this occasion they again displayed their extraordinary might and the strength of their organisation. The Smolny had practically been turned into an armed camp; units were being hurriedly formed from workers sent by the districts; they were equipped somehow by the Red Guard Headquarters — or rather they were given greatcoats, cartridge pouches, haversacks, rifles and cartridges. Many of the workers had taken up rifles and formed ranks for the first time in their lives. The Republic, however, was in danger, a blow was being struck at socialist power and the volunteers, sent by the factory committees, had only one thing on their minds: to fight for Petrograd and to prevent the counter-revolution capturing the city and crushing Soviet power. The workers elected their own commanders. On the spot each unit set up a minimum staff — officers in charge of supplies, munitions, communications and a commandant.

The marching feet of the Red Guards resounded through the streets; behind them followed a motor lorry with stores, equipment and munitions. This was but one of the Red Guard battalions and it was followed by a second and a third. The fourth was awaiting its turn, the men excited and with their nerves on edge.

News from the front was scanty. We knew that Comrade Chudnovsky's advanced troops had been unable to stem the attack and were in a difficult position. Chudnovsky was wounded and his detachment had lost contact with other units at the front and was threatened with annihilation. There was no commander-in-chief; the Krasnoye Selo and Tsarskoye Selo garrisons and the Red Guard units were all operating on their own... Comrade Antonov-Ovseenko went to the front himself but returned dismayed at the lack of order and the confusion there. Tired out and depressed, he had scarcely realised what was going on and had reacted weakly to an extremely critical situation. Weeks of sleepless nights had sapped his energy and will-power. We settled down to a discussion of the situation. With the command disunited and improperly organised, it seemed that the enemy could defeat us easily with very small forces, and during the ensuing panic and the retreat of our troops to Petrograd, could effect the counter-revolution.

The situation was extremely serious.

Despite the revolutionary enthusiasm of the masses and their readiness to sacrifice themselves, there was little organised resistance to Kerensky's advance owing to our poor leadership. The tone of his proclamations and 'orders' became more and more confident.

The chief difficulty arose from the fact that the soldiers were flushed with recent victory and did not appreciate the approaching danger. The regiments that had accomplished the socialist revolution in cooperation with and under the leadership of the Petrograd workers, considered that their work was done and that they were heroes. They were ready to admit that the defence of Petrograd from enemies within the city was their affair, but as far as Kerensky's troops were concerned — well, they were still somewhere near Gatchina, let the local garrisons fight them, they were nearer ...

Orders, in the soldiers' sense of the word, had long since ceased to be effective. This had been a positive factor when it had helped us get the regiments out of the hands of the counter-revolutionary officers. Now, however, it had become the opposite — the soldiers had got into the habit of deciding for themselves what they should and should not do.

My order to the troops of the Petrograd garrison to move against Kerensky was obeyed by only a few of the regiments, the majority refused to go to the front on the excuse that it was essential to defend Petrograd.

Krylenko went round the barracks. When he returned he told us that his persuasions and exhortations had met everywhere with rebuff.

In order to put an end to that mood I went to the regiment that had been the first to rise against Tsarism, the Volhynian. I mustered the soldiers and demanded action. The regiment, through its committee, informed me unceremoniously that it would not fulfil the order. The same thing happened in a number of other regiments.

I felt that the whole of our front line of defence was beginning to collapse as a result of this refusal.

I got into my car and rushed off to the Smolny to ask Vladimir Ilyich for his advice.

Hurriedly I told him of the failure to get the soldiers to act. I said that as the Volhynian and other tried and trusted regiments refused absolutely to leave we would not be able to get a single army unit out of the city.

Lenin answered calmly:

'You must get them out. This very moment. At no matter what cost.'

'Krylenko tried and failed', I answered, 'nor did they listen to me.' Then I added, 'We can't do anything with the regiments.'

Lenin went into a terrible rage, his face became unrecognisable, he fixed his sharp eyes on me and, without raising his voice, although it seemed to me that he was shouting, said:

'You will answer to the Central Committee if the regiments do not leave the city instantly. Do you hear me, at this very moment!'

I shot out of the room like a bullet and in a few minutes was again at the barracks of the Volhynian Regiment. I mustered the soldiers and said very few words to them...

The soldiers must have seen something extraordinary in my face. Silently, they rose to their feet and began to get ready for the campaign.

Other regiments followed them...

That evening, rain set in. It poured all night long. At 2 o'clock in the morning Vladimir Ilyich unexpectedly arrived at the regional headquarters where a conference of Military Organisation workers was in progress... Lenin's overcoat was soaked through and the water ran off his cap in streams.

His very first questions showed that he was closely following Kerensky's offensive and had a very real appreciation of the critical situation at the front. He turned to Antonov-Ovseenko, Mekhonoshin and me and demanded that we give him a detailed report on the situation at the front.

In answer to my question as to the meaning of this sudden arrival — did the Council of People's Commissars not trust the military leadership that had only just been elected at the congress? — Lenin answered simply but firmly:

'It is not a question of mistrust but simply that the workers' and peasants' government wants to know how its military authorities are functioning, how they are organising the defence of Petrograd.'

In Vladimir Ilyich's tone, now and a few hours before when the question of the regiments leaving for the front had been discussed, I felt the full power of the dictatorship of the proletariat.

Until then my relations with Vladimir Ilyich had been most cordial. But at that moment, from the way he spoke I saw the full extent of the responsibility for the fate of the country and the revolution which the people had laid on the shoulders of Vladimir Ilyich as the leader of the workers' and peasants' state, the full extent of the responsibility which lay on each of us as members of the Party.

Lenin sat down at the map of operations spread out on a table. Antonov-Ovseenko began outlining the general plan of operations, pointing to positions held by our forces and the positions and strength of enemy forces that he knew hardly anything about.

His lack of information and the condition of Antonov-Ovseenko himself were all too obvious, although Lenin pretended not to notice anything and fixed his eyes on the map. After the report, to which he listened with great attention and without once interrupting the speaker, Lenin began to ask questions with the keenness of a profound strategist and military leader: Why was this point not guarded, had the strategic importance of this station been taken into consideration, why had this step been taken and not another, why had the support of Kronstadt, Viborg and Helsingfors not been assured, why had that point not been worked out in detail or this opening blocked. Owing to his weariness Antonov-Ovseenko's answers to Lenin's poignant questions were far from satisfactory. The impression created was that we were not fully aware of the seriousness of our position at the front, that we were not capable of weighing up the situation fully, in short, that we were not to be trusted to conduct operations against Kerensky.

Lenin continued asking questions and each of them, in reality, contained the answer of a masterly strategist — he was telling us what we had to do.

'How is the railway line Gatchina-Lissino-Tosno defended? What forces are there on that line, are they reliable?' he asked. Not only the question itself but the tone in which it was asked told us of a tremendous anxiety to strengthen that line and in that way make it impossible for the enemy to seize the Petrograd-Moscow Railway which would mean that Moscow would be deprived of Petrograd's help.

His question about where the Red Guards from the Lessner, Putilov, Baltic, Tube works and other big factories were operating showed that Lenin regarded it as very important that the armed forces of the workers should be on the decisive sectors.

'Why has the cavalry not been brought from Novgorod and sent into Chudovo and Volkhov district to defend that highly-important railway?

'Are the soldiers and the Red Guards ensured all the necessary supplies? How do you propose to arrange this?

'What task has been allotted the garrison of Luga?

'Have you thought of demolishing the railway bridges and lines, and has provision been made for it so that the enemy will be prevented from advancing?

'What about the artillery?'

Lenin's questions so clearly showed the essence of his strategic and tactical plan, which was so obviously calculated to rout the Krasnov-

Kerensky gang rapidly and effectively, that we were anxious to do only one thing: to end that conference and immediately set about putting Lenin's ideas into effect. The trouble was, however, that the front had no commander-in-chief. It was no use depending on Antonov-Ovseenko – he simply had to be put to bed.

I did not feel it convenient to place the question of the command before Lenin in such a sharp form: it would have looked as if we regarded Antonov-Ovseenko as responsible for our failures whereas it was perfectly clear that all of us, workers of the Military Organisation, including myself, were responsible for the failures.

We had made a large number of mistakes, we had not been as active as the situation demanded and had not made use of all forces and means at our disposal for the defence of Petrograd. We had been following the masses but had done nothing to make ourselves the military leaders, the strategists of the masses.

There were only two ways out of the situation: either tell Comrade Lenin that we were unsuitable, that we could not take responsibility for operations, or somebody else must undertake the command.

I asked for an interval of a few minutes and called into another room those members of the Military Organisation who were present at the staff conference which Comrade Lenin had interrupted. I told the comrades that we had made a great mistake in nominating Comrade Antonov-Ovseenko Commander-in-Chief of the Petrograd Military District, that he had been several weeks without sleep and was so worn out that he had lost the energy necessary for the task.

I asked which of the comrades thought he could assume command of the front. No one answered.

I thereupon put forward my own candidature and said that in face of the great danger I considered it my duty to the Party to take upon myself this terrific responsibility, ignoring all the conventions and the 'awkwardness' of self-nomination. The Military Organisation of the Party, whose chairman I was, were used to me, we worked well together and I was sure that they would help me much more actively than another whom they did not know. Krylenko, Mekhonoshin, Nevsky and other comrades gave me their hearty support. I asked Antonov-Ovseenko his opinion. He was against my candidature, he said that I could not do any better than he had done. The other comrades, however, did not agree with him.

After that I returned to Lenin and told him that I would undertake the task of clearing up the situation at the front.

Without another word Lenin ordered me, in the name of the government, to take over command of the front as Commander-in-Chief of the Petrograd Military District. I told him that next day I would report on what measures I had adopted during the night and then asked for permission to get down to work.

Lenin went away. No doubt he had had a very clear conception of the confusion prevailing even before he came to us. At a conference of regimental representatives of the Petrograd garrison Vladimir Ilyich spoke very sharply of the faults of our command.

'This cannot be denied. On account of this we have lost some ground. Those faults, however, can be overcome. Without losing a single hour, a single minute, we must organise ourselves, organise a general staff; it is essential that it be done today... The political and military task is: the organisation of the general staff, the concentration of all material forces, the provision of everything needed by the soldiers; that must be done without losing a single hour, a single minute...'

Lenin went away and we settled down to work with renewed energy. In the first place I transferred our headquarters to the Smolny – all the threads led to that place — and set about regrouping our forces according to a plan that had formed in my mind on the basis of the questions and remarks made by Vladimir Ilyich.

I appointed Comrade Yeremeyev as chief of staff. The Military Organisation personnel were ordered to go immediately to army units and arrange for those that still remained to leave for the front next day and to call to arms the workers of all the factories, stopping some of the factories if there was no other way out. They were to make the first call on the Putilov Works and the big factories in Viborg, Vasilevsky Island and Moscow districts.

At that moment I was given a note from Comrade Antonov-Ovseenko in which he said he would do everything to help me. I proposed that he sleep well and then go to the front to set up a central command, organise communications between units and their bases and the centre, and the delivery of supplies and munitions.

Representatives of our district Party organisations, district Soviets and factory committees were called to headquarters and instructions were given to send those workers incapable of bearing arms to dig trenches, and to requisition shovels for this purpose. The line of trenches was mapped out and engineers mobilised from the 6th Reserve Sapper Battalion and from the factories.

We felt desperately in need of a highly-qualified military specialist as a consultant, but could not find one. The most suitable man would have been the commander of the Preobrazhensky Regiment, but he had been wounded and was unable to take part in the work. In drawing up the plan of operations and in carrying it out we had to depend on untried people. We decided to entrust the plan of operations to a battalion commander from the Izmailovsky Regiment. When they had studied the plan the commanders of the regiments and other units immediately began to reform as brigades. Brigade commanders were appointed.

Early in the morning of the 30th Dybenko appeared at the Smolny. He was ordered to occupy a certain sector of the line and take command of the left group. Without losing any time Dybenko set out with a detachment of sailors for the positions.

Very soon the sailors Lenin had sent for arrived from Helsingfors. They occupied the positions allotted them on the coast. The cruiser *Oleg* and the destroyer *Pobeditel* stood by to defend the approaches to the Petrograd-Moscow Railway in fulfilment of Lenin's instructions.

That same day thousands of Petrograd workers went out to dig trenches, and six regiments, made up to strength, left for the front.

The arrival of these regiments at the front, the appearance of the artillery organised by Comrade Sklyansky who had just arrived, the strengthening of the front by the Helsingfors sailors who cemented the units together, the direction of operations directly at the front by Antonov-Ovseenko — all served to bring about a sharp change at the front. The turning-point had come and in this a decisive role was played by the help Vladimir Ilyich gave us.

At 12 o'clock noon Lenin again visited our headquarters — it was now quartered in the Smolny — and insisted on a table being placed in my office for him so that he could be kept up to date on all instructions and reports...

Soon he sent V. Bonch-Bruevich, an executive of the Council of People's Commissars, to help me and he brought with him his secretary and wife V.M. Velichkina. Every five or ten minutes Lenin kept sending somebody to help me — in the matter of supplies, mobilisation of the workers,demolitions. Airmen, agitators, doctors, gunners, all came to me... Vladimir Ilyich was gradually carried away by the work and, without apparently noticing it, whenever he left my room, gave direct instructions to one comrade or another. The work was kept going at top speed, every cog in the Petrograd defences was kept turning, but Lenin was still not satisfied. It seemed to him that things were going too slowly, without sufficient determination, without the necessary energy, and he himself, parallel to me, in his own office, began calling representatives of one organisation or another, or from this or that factory, asking for information on the number of men capable of carrying arms, on technical equipment, on what, in general, they could provide for the front, and in what way this or that factory could be of use for the defence. Then came his order to the Putilov workers to put armour-plating on railway engines and wagons, place guns on them and send them to the front. He proposed to Narva District that they requisition cab-horses and harness to take the forty guns that stood ready at that factory to the front.

Representatives of the Baltic Fleet came on some business or another and Vladimir Ilyich instructed them to check up on the readiness of the crews to put to sea at a moment's notice and to report at such and such a time.

The officers of the Motor Transport Company arrived. Lenin arranged with them for the company to send all its lorries to the front and instructed them to send out soldier-drivers to mobilise in Petrograd a sufficient number of lorries to transport munitions to the front.

'Give them credentials with special authority', he said.

The motor transport people took hurried leave of Lenin to carry out his instructions.

Lenin began sending commissars to different factories and organisations to take everything that was necessary for defence.

Several times in the course of three to five hours I had 'tussles' with Comrade Lenin, protesting against his 'predatory' methods of defence work. He apparently took notice of my protests, but in a few minutes they were forgotten and ignored. In actual fact there were two headquarters: in Lenin's office and in mine. Lenin's office was a sort of mobile staff since he also had a table in my office, but the more often Lenin went to his own office where all kinds of operatives were being constantly sent for on his instructions, the clearer it became that separate, casual instructions were merging into one single chain, into a regular system, welded together by some invisible but clearly felt general plan.

It is true that these instructions did not have anything to do with operations or the army units and were, in essence, merely the mobilisation of everything and everybody for defence. Nevertheless this seeming dualism got on my nerves to such an extent that I demanded very sharply and quite unjustly that he release me from my post of commander-in-chief.

Lenin lost his temper completely as he had never been known to do before.

'I'll hand you over to the the Party court, we'll shoot you! I order you to continue your work and not to interfere with mine!'

I had to submit...

Only next day did I appreciate the significance of the tremendous work Lenin had done, especially after I had analysed the conference he had called of representatives of working-class organisations, district Soviets, factory committees, trade unions and army units. Vladimir Ilyich ordered me to attend that conference.

'The workers of Petrograd', said Lenin at the conference, 'are going as volunteers to the Pulkovo Heights, without commanders, without transport, without food and supplies, often without warm clothing. It is our duty to organise assistance for these heroes.'

And Lenin, addressing himself in turn to the leaders of the Party groups and factory committees of the Putilov Works, the Arsenal, the Obukhov Works, the Tube Works and other factories, appealed to them to make use of all the resources of their factories for the defeat of the counter-revolution that had raised its head. And he there and then gave an example of initiative in dealing with this problem.

'The Putilov workers make cannon but there is no way of getting them to the front — there are no horses. Nevertheless a way out of the situation can be found: a branch railway line passes the Putilov Works where the guns can be loaded on to wagons and sent to the front-line positions.

'We have not got enough artillerymen. Can we not find the necessary gun-layers and gunners at the Arsenal, the Obukhov Works and other factories? Of course we can!

'We should take those cadets who fought against Soviet power by the scruff of the neck and force them to fight against the Cossack officers.

'The Bolsheviks of the Baltic and Neva shipyards and the naval port must ensure that the naval vessels undergoing repairs there be commissioned without loss of time.'

Later when I thought over that conference I realised more and more that Lenin had a special ability to concentrate our forces and resources to the extreme limit in time of need. We had dispersed our forces, mustered and then distributed them again without any plan. As a result our actions were not coordinated and this led to irresolution and lack of initiative among the masses. They did not feel the iron will and the iron plan where, as in a machine, everything fitted perfectly and worked smoothly in its proper place. Lenin hammered one single idea into everybody's head — everything must be concentrated on defence. Out of this basic idea he evolved a plan which could be understood by all, a plan in which there was a place for everyone, for his factory and for his fighting unit.

Everyone at the conference had a clear conception of his own plan of future work and saw what contribution he could make towards the defence of the Republic. Therefore, each one was fully aware of the responsibility placed upon him by the dictatorship of the proletariat.

Lenin strove constantly to get the people to understand that the leaders could not do everything for them, that they themselves, with their own hands, would have to build a new life and defend their own state; in this he proved himself to be a real people's leader, able to show the people the way forward and induce them to take the first step forward fully conscious of their aim, instead of following blindly behind the leaders.

After the conference Lenin spoke separately to those of the workers' representatives who had come late.

That day Lenin's method of selecting an organiser became clear to us; he not only made the comrade personally responsible for the work given to him, but also told him that he really would be held personally responsible; this was a method that Lenin usually adopted with the People's Commissars under him, as well as with all Party and Soviet officials.

With this in mind, Lenin tried to show everyone at the conference with whom he spoke that he had noted his name and would see to it that the job he had given him would be carried out. He wrote down the names of those comrades and exactly what they had to do by a certain day and hour.

Everything that Lenin did in those days was for all of us the first school of state administration, a broad and peerless school of practical education.

Next day, I tried to estimate all that Lenin had said and realised that to make a good practical leader one must not fix all one's attention on one separate question, but be able to see the connection between his work and all the active forces of the revolution.

Immediately after the conference, workers' detachments, lorries, carts, guns, improvised cavalry, the squadrons of the 9th Cavalry Regiment, began pouring day and night through the Moscow Gate and along the Moscow Highway.

Cars with messengers and liaison officers raced to and from the front line. A real workers' and peasants' war, embracing gigantic masses of people, developed to defeat the counter-revolution.

All Petrograd was on its feet. Under such conditions victory was certain. The enthusiasm with which the workers went to the front, their desire to fight, their readiness to give up their lives for the happiness of the Republic made heroes of those who, for the first time in their lives, held a rifle in their hands. This enthusiasm welded the front into a single whole.

That day many of the units, with great fortitude, began flanking movements on the front. The heroic Red battalions had no experienced commanders, they were often cut off from their bases, tormented by hunger and cold, and menaced by the most terrible thing of all — to be encircled by the enemy. Many of the Red Guards wore light, torn boots and their working clothes. They had to carry huge supplies of cartridges on their backs as transport had not yet been properly organised. The scene of the fighting was a swampy plain with a few elevated points. The daily rains made the terrain of each hollow almost impassable. Some of the troops moved up to their knees in water the whole day. A detachment of sailors stood in icy water a whole night waiting to attack Kerensky's armoured train.

The enemy were suffering appreciable losses. We struck blow after blow.

Our troops would have brought matters to a head by 1 November but for the fact that we had an insignificant number of cavalry, scarcely enough for reconnaissance, while the enemy forces consisted mainly of cavalry. This made it possible for them to transfer troops rapidly to any threatened point and, as our reconnaissance was not functioning properly, we got the false impression that the enemy possessed greater forces than they did. Then, as formerly (and also later, during the Civil War), our agitators played an important role in the defeat of Krasnov. They made their way into the enemy's ranks and exposed to the Cossacks the real objects which the opposing sides pursued in the newly begun war. The Cossacks lost all desire to die for a cause alien to their interests. After five days of fighting, exhausted by our constantly increasing attacks, the Cossacks surrendered. Kerensky fled. The Cossacks arrested Krasnov and sent a delegation to the Gatchina Soviet (that had just been arrested by Krasnov) with the offer to surrender on condition that they be allowed to return to the Don.

I proposed to the Gatchina Soviet that they send the delegation to us in the Smolny. In the meantime, however, Dybenko, on his own initiative, sent representatives to Krasnov to demand his surrender. Krasnov got Dybenko to agree to his departure to the Don together with the Cossacks who would retain their arms. An agreement consisting of eight points was drawn up between them.

In this way Dybenko had tied the hands of the government. We were opposed to the Cossacks being allowed to return to the Don with their arms, as we had no reason to believe that they would fulfil their promise not to fight against Soviet power. I insisted on Dybenko's being tried by court-martial and the agreement with Krasnov renounced.

Lenin shared my opinion. Other comrades, however, who considered themselves well informed with regard to the mood of the Cossacks, demanded that the agreement be ratified on the grounds that the Cossacks would under no circumstances permit themselves to be disarmed and would fight to the last man since they would not want to return to the Don 'dishonoured' and that they would not be accepted there without their arms. They argued that it was to the advantage of Soviet power to accept Krasnov's surrender and thus put an end to Kerensky's offensive because every delay in crushing the revolt would strengthen the impression amongst the masses that Kerensky had greater forces and greater possibilities for resistance than was actually the case, while the speedy crushing of the revolt, on the contrary, would raise the prestige of Soviet power. The rout of Kerensky's revolt outside Petrograd would deprive him of the forces necessary to launch revolts against Soviet power in other places. The situation at the front and in the army units would also be determined by the defeat of Kerensky.

The impression created by the statements of the seventeen Cossacks delegated direct from the masses of the Cossack troops participating in the revolt gave these arguments still greater strength. The Cossacks said that they had not been fighting against the working-class government or against the new regime but against the Bolsheviks who, they had been informed, had seized power with the aid of the Germans, German gold and German prisoners of war, for the purpose of betraying Russia and selling her to the Germans. As they learned more about what had been happening in Petrograd they began to understand the real nature of the October Revolution and a conference of Cossacks from the various units demanded that a delegation be sent to the new government. Until then they had considered it their duty to support Kerensky. The delegation defended Krasnov, a slippery demagogue who knew how to play on the feelings of the Cossacks. The delegates insisted that Krasnov, too, had only been doing his duty and could not disobey orders given by Kerensky in Gatchina when the revolution in Petrograd was still unknown to the troops at the front. The Cossacks agreed to arrest and hand over the other officers but insisted that Krasnov go with them.

The question was placed before the Petrograd Soviet which was in session at the time. The Soviet took a decision to allow the Cossacks, headed by Krasnov, to proceed to the Don under arms. The Military Revolutionary Committee issued them a pass to the Don Region and Krasnov and the Cossacks gave their word of honour that they would not fight against Soviet power.

It is an interesting fact that the 1st and 4th Cossack regiments, quartered in Petrograd, at first wavered when Krasnov sent delegates to them asking for their support, and then decided to come over to our side. The presence of the Cossacks in our ranks had a serious moral effect on the insurrectionists and did a great deal towards demoralising them. This greatly influenced the outcome of the struggle.

The Petrograd Cossacks, who had elected their own Cossack Committee, also spoke in favour of allowing Krasnov and his Cossacks to leave for the Don under arms...

After the departure of the Cossacks (some of them who did not wish to return remained in Petrograd), the local Soviets of Gatchina, Peterhof, Krasnoye Selo and Tsarskoye Selo dealt very speedily with the cadet and officer groups that had taken part in the revolt.

After Kerensky's offensive against Petrograd had been defeated we received almost daily reports that Kerensky's supporters were raising revolts first in one place, then in another, and that in some places they even succeeded in restoring the old regime. All this, however, was their death agony. The revolution was celebrating its victory, or as Lenin put it, Soviet power marched in triumph throughout Russia...

14

Letters to Her Family

LUSIK LISINOVA

(Lusik, a young student, was killed by machine-gun fire on 1 November 1917, during the battle for Moscow. Next day, the Whites were routed and Soviet power established. She was buried in Red Square.)

Letter to Anaid

9 May 1917

My dearest Anaid,
I usually write to you in moments of depression, and this is true now, too. However, I have a great source of satisfaction, a remedy which calms me, and that is my work. I am doing a lot of work. I mean in the field of propaganda. When my handiwork helps to turn raw material into a conscious worker, when I awaken his class-consciousness...then I feel satisfied, then my strength is doubled, then I am alive. I do not feel depressed, and set out for work in high spirits. This knowledge helps me to do a lot of studying, to live according to a schedule (otherwise there can be no work), to give up the carefree company of my fellow-students and study, and study. How happy I am that my work was of use when we were still underground, and that now I have a certain amount of experience, and that I can work! There is a fierce struggle on against all who are not with us Bolsheviks... I'm now off to draw up a list and purchase two libraries for two factories; then I'll go home and conduct a class for a group of Social-Democratic women... Anaid, you can't imagine what strength, what talent there is among the workers!... You probably think that like all the other girls who attend the Higher Women's Courses I am sentimentally inclined and speak with tears in my eyes of freedom and the 'poor workers'. No, far from it. I came to know them before through my work, and I know them well now. They (the workers) have the advantage of a class to whom the future belongs, which is just beginning to develop, and whose strength is just awakening.
  ...Don't worry about me. I'm happy and well. I think I have changed quite a bit. No matter, I will have to change quite a bit more. I have to leave the house now, and it's freezing could outside. Hailstones are rattling against the window pane. The sound is a sad, wild, but lively song,

129

and the grey sky is wretched and lonely. But the sun will come out soon, the buds will burst, and the last doubts of winter will be swept away, as with a broom, by life itself.

All my love,
Lusik

Anaid, never forget that I'm living a full life.

Letter to Golya

20 May 1917

Hey, Golya, you've finally responded to me from our dear home. I was getting so worried I wanted to send you a telegram, but I was afraid I'd frighten Mother. I was so glad to receive your letter. It made me feel so good and happy. One of the girls here is singing to a guitar. She has a lovely voice. She's singing 'Those were beautiful days but they're gone...' It brings everything back: Kodjory and Anik and all of you, and the sadness associated with this song. It's a very strange feeling. My life here is full of new impressions. Yesterday two very fine comrades came over at 12 o'clock to see us (Natalka and I had been reading until then). After a short conference we set out for Red Square and then to see the Church of the Saviour. We were the only ones there in the middle of the night. The sombre Kremlin and its towers stood out strangely and sternly against the May night in Moscow, for the nights now are nearly white. There was the quiet Moskva River and our quiet and pleasant conversation, and those fine boys, Ruben and Alyosha, one of our best agitators and a very fine comrade. It was wonderful, even better than in Kodjory in the nights... It's so hard to study now in this awful, stuffy, stupid room when the air is so full of spring, beauty and life. Still, there is a sort of sadness about it all, but it is not unpleasant. And when we walked with Alyosha and Ruben at sunrise we spoke of this sadness, and of our Party work, and of beauty, and of so many things, and we were silent a lot, too...

About 10 people have been sitting here in our room this past hour, debating... Shurka is playing the guitar, Yulka Kirillyants and Katyukha are singing, but Ter is arguing. Ruben has him by the hair, and the place is full of laughter and noise, while I'm sitting on my bed, writing this letter.

The night is so fantastic you could die. The whole gang is going to Tsaritsino tomorrow.

...I can't tell you how I miss my little boy. Just wait, I'll teach him to sing the *Internationale*, that proud and mighty anthem, and I'll turn him into a Bolshevik.

I'll close here, Golya, my sweet and sensitive one, with such rare eyes, whom I love so dearly. And I love my dearest Mamma, and Anaid, and Anik, and Daddy Onik. Kiss Karen for me and give him a hug. Well, that's about all. Love to everyone,
Your
Lusik

Letter to Anaid

Undated

My dearest, sweetest Anaid,
I have such a need to talk to you now, to tell you about myself. It's spring now, a real spring, the kind we never have at home. It's elemental, sweeping up everything as it advances, so full of sunshine, so evident in all ways, so overpowering. I can't tell you what I feel today. You know, I'm overcome by an insinuating, but consuming warmth and the tantalising spring air. You know, Anaid, I have such a need to do something important, something great, something grandiose in order to pull up all that is wavering and doubtful by the roots.

No, Anaid, I am not satisfied by the events. Democracy has as yet too little under its control.

You know, Anaid, I feel so strong. I sense all that lies hidden within me. These forces are not only within me, they are a part of all those who are workers of the new, emerging era, of the class which will make this era a reality.

Anaid, I wish I could embrace this pulsating, vibrant life. Everything breathes, everything wants to be alive. How much strength there is in each movement, in each breath! I have learned to be less impulsive, to watch others and evaluate everything... You should have heard the church bells today! Today's Saturday. We went down to the Moskva River and stood there on the bridge for a long while and it seemed to me that the river wished to tell me something. It's high now, broad and threatening.

Then I went walking by myself for quite a long time along the streets of my dear Zamoskvorechye District. Anaid, why is everything the way it is? Why does so much remain a mystery? Why are so many things alluring? I want so to be alive at moments like this, to blossom outward or to envisage something that is great, and wonderful, and grandiose.

My dearest, will you ever understand my feelings reading this silly letter? These past two days I have been in communion with Nature, and it seems to me that I can enter into the being of every speck of dust, that I understand the life of each blade of grass and know that there is still so much that is mysterious and unknown to me.

...I am often encouraged by the very good attitude the workers have towards us. After long and heated arguments at various meetings with student 'revolutionaries', workers who formerly did not participate in our work realised we were right and our friendship grew; it became possible to establish much closer ties with the older workers. I visited a working woman yesterday and spent the entire evening at her place. We spoke of many things. Such talks are always encouraging...

Letter to Her Family

Undated

The revolutionary forces are now fighting Kornilov's troops near Petrograd. The revolutionary troops of Moscow have been sent to their aid. I am sitting here and thinking, and cannot fall asleep. The workers have all been alerted. They are ready to fight at the barricades in the city and in the field. Arms that had been hidden are now carried openly... One unit after another passes by my window (I live on the outskirts), singing revolutionary songs...

They are now sung with mighty force, as a warning and with true revolutionary spirit.

Tell Mamma not to worry about me. I'll be very careful, honest.
Love, and don't worry,
Lusik

From a Letter to Her Younger Sister Anik

30 August 1917

My own dear Anik,
I'm on my way to the canteen for dinner. I've been reading Lilly Brown's *The Woman Question*; I don't especially like the book, though it's a very impressive one; however, it is very good in spots. If you chance upon Kollontai's *The Social Basis of the Woman Question*, be sure to read it. When I read it it gave me a great feeling of satisfaction... Our spirit is militant. The Red Guard is being formed and part of the training is taking place right here in our canteen...

From a Letter to Her Mother,
Yekaterina Zakharovna

11 September 1917

My dearest Mamma,
If you only knew how often I think of you and how I miss you. I embrace

you. Tell the girls to write and tell me how you are.

I was at the opening of the First Workers' Theatre. It was rather a let-down, but fun, because there was a whole gang of us and because we put on a demonstration: after the orchestra played the *Internationale* we all began to shout, 'Long Live the Third International!', 'Down with the War!' and everyone present felt better. This is all for now.

Love and kisses,
Your
Lusik

From a Letter to Anik

13-24 October 1917

My dearest girl, Anik,
I received your letter and 2 postcards. Today is my second day out of bed for good. I have my nose in the air and keep smiling, for everything in life makes me happy.

I am very grateful to my friends for taking care of me. They are all very busy, but there was hardly a time when I was alone. They brought me food from home, cocoa, buns, coffee, butter, cheese, and my dinners. It even made me feel embarrassed. Two days ago I went to see the doctor.

I was very much afraid it was my lungs and asked him about it with trembling knees; imagine my joy when he said that they are in perfect order and that I had no cause to worry at all. Whew! How happy I was when I left his office. Autumn was shining brightly all about me, with its golden leaves and hoarfrost and the beautiful sun, so gentle and jolly and, at the same time, so sad, as it was taking leave of the earth. I couldn't help feeling that the sun and every person knew that I had got up from my sickbed that day, that I was happy and that my lungs were in perfect order.

Hooray! Perhaps the Soviets will take over power in Petrograd tomorrow... Yes, of course, there will later be, or perhaps even now, a terrible bloodbath... there has never yet been a time when the bourgeoisie surrendered a single position without a fight, to say nothing of surrendering power, so that we must expect this as an inevitable part of all proletarian revolutions, can the triumphant international revolution be kindled... ' Long live the international Soviet of workers' deputies!'

...Oh, Anik! I can't tell you how elated I feel. A great feeling of triumph is like a lump in my throat. You know, there are sad times and hard times, but still, it is wonderful, for that's what we're like. You understand whom I mean, don't you? Our group, a close-knit group of Social-Democrats. That's all for now.
Your
Lusik

Letter to Anik

Undated

My dearest child, my sweetest Anik,
I received your letter. I can't believe that you were ill with typhus. I'm so worried. Ever since I received your letter I keep dreaming of you. Anik, I wrote you a letter for future action which I pondered over quite a bit. My dear, how right I was when I sensed your depression. I can feel how 'depressed about everything' you are. Yes, about everything (oh, how well I understand you!), for everything sends a piercing pain to your heart, it is a throbbing wound, and endless and incurable sadness. I understand you so well that I begin to feel it in my own bones. I think it is because I myself have but recently, perhaps during these past months, thrown off the same sadness, perhaps for ever. Anik, it followed me everywhere and consumed all my energy; if it did not (for instance, when I was working underground or immediately after the Revolution, when there was so much to be done), it was because of the great enthusiasm which prevailed, and, also because I was beginning to acquire a staunch outlook which has become my support. Anik, this sadness is necessary, this 'sadness about everything' is the faithful companion of all the best people, the strong fighters who love the beauty of the future and yearn for it.

Only now, when I see the road of future development, when I can almost clearly visualise what is to be done and, chiefly, when my psychology is changing... only now have I lost this nameless companion, sadness, and I mean a sadness 'about everything'.

My dearest, I was so upset to learn you have been feeling bad, but at the same time (see what a fool I am), I am glad you are the way you are. I've been thinking of how happy you will be when you throw it off completely and so am happy in advance.

My little girl, you are so much deeper than I and so much better. You write that we are not alike, and perhaps you are right. I do not take things to heart as you do, and that is why I find life easier. But you, Anik, are quite different: life will be more difficult for you, but you will make things easier for others. And then, you are better, much better, and your soul is more beautiful and more refined.

Dearest, write and tell me about that 'one fine and beautiful day'. Do write to me about that day, Anik. Please. You are right when you say, 'may there be more days like this, though I cannot study on such days'. More light and joy and then...at times, perhaps, one should just not care.

A few words about myself. After completing my training for the elections I got a regular job, 5 hours a day (10 to 3 p.m.) in the Commissariat (it's office work). The best part of all is that my evenings are free and I'll be able to study and conduct my study groups. I'm feeling fine... I'm going to the theatre the day after tomorrow to see 'Orestea' and to a lecture by the famous Professor Friche tomorrow on 'The Poetry of the *Internationale*'. I think it will be interesting.

By the way, when I gave Alyosha your regards he was pleased and said that he had been wanting to ask me to write something 'nice' to you from him for a long time, but was afraid you 'couldn't care less'. That's just 'by the way'.

Shurka and I were reading the *Deklamator* yesterday and we came upon Turgenev's poem in prose called 'The Sparrow' (do re-read it) and I suddenly felt so refreshed from the fine day and the lively spirit of the poem...' We'll have our say yet', Anik, because there is so much strength and youth in us. Perhaps you don't feel it now, but never fear, your youth and strength will soon make themselves known, they will practically be bursting out of the shell that contains them.

Love,

Lusik

I want your days to be happy. Kiss everyone for me. Write soon.

Letter to her mother

I'm finally home. I've had some tea and I'll soon be going to bed. I was on my feet all day, conducting 3 meetings in the factories, organising the Red Cross and the Youth League, going to the Soviet of Workers' Deputies. It's night now, with cold rain and snow, but I'm feeling fine. The one drawback is that this state of expectation is bad for the nerves.

The officer cadets and our forces are now lined up in the Kremlin. There may be a battle tonight. Which side will be the victor?

Dearest Mamma, don't worry about me. I won't be in any of the dangerous places at all. I'll either be assigned to a hospital or else I'll be in the Soviet; in a word, I'm not going to join any of the combat units. Besides, I don't go out in the streets unnecessarily, and I never go out alone.

Mamma dearest, I won't even be going to any factory meetings, since everyone has already been alerted as to the situation. Well, this is all for now. Love and kisses. My health, far from becoming worse, is improving. I'll look through the papers now and then go to bed.

Your

Lusik

Don't worry about me.

From a letter written by A. Kolpakova,
Member of the Youth League.

Dated 15 November 1917

...We buried Lusik yesterday. Lusik has been buried...on Red Square.
Yesterday was a bright, sunny, frosty day. Heading the procession was a
standard-bearer. The district Party banner waved proudly in the wind, its
silk shining. 'Workers of the World, Unite!' The red cloth beat and
flapped in the wind and, at times it unfurled so triumphantly it sent a
shiver down your back, with the band playing a march behind us... It was
awesome... The Red Guards from the Mikhelson Works, among whom
were some young men from the group Lusik taught (this was her first
study group) asked to assist in the funeral... Lusik was accompanied by a
unit of Red Guards...

15

The Battle for Power
and Peace in Russia

CLARA ZETKIN

(Written within days of the Bolshevik Revolution, this article by the legendary German socialist and fighter for women's rights, Clara Zetkin, was one of the first foreign publications to assess the potential significance of October.)

Once again the eyes of the peace-seeking peoples of Europe are turned towards Russia, and with more passionate longing than ever before. The duration and intensification of this ghastly world war has increased in all countries the desire for peace and the powerful revolutionary event in Russia brings peace within striking distance, provided that the belligerents want peace because they are compelled to desire it.

Just as in March, the Revolution has risen again with all of its terrifying and magnificent strength. Its nature is the same and yet not the same. Once again the upheaval is spearheaded by the Socialist-led proletariat of the great industrial centres and by a considerable part of the peasantry, the petit-bourgeoisie and the army. But as far as its aims are concerned, and the paths it is taking to reach those aims, this Revolution is far more decisive than the February Revolution. The latter forced the Russian bourgeoisie (including the liberalised Zemstvo Aristocracy) to let go of its ideal of a dressed-up bourgeois coup d'etat which merely placed the reins of government into other hands and with a bittersweet mien began to smash Tsardom which had proved to be such an excellent patron of capitalism. It remained, however, a bourgeois-political revolution...

Politically speaking, the February Revolution resulted in constantly changing provisional governments. No matter how the different parties and personalities coalesced, two characteristics remained constant. Its domestic policy was determined by a coalition of revolutionary democracy and the bourgeoisie, and by Socialists of the most diverse factions and the Cadets. The foreign policy was determined by the alliance of Russia with the Western Powers. Thus international imperialism, in revolutionary Russia, too, united nationally what should have been divided by irreconcilable class contradictions and divided internationally what should have been fused by indestructible class solidarity.

Class contradictions, however, are not to be scoffed at. They cannot be argued away by the most refined periwigs nor can they be coaxed away by the most cunning *Realpolitiker*. They cannot be tamed by brutal jailers and hoodlums, nor can they be talked away by democratic eulogies. As long as the means of production are not taken out of private hands, they will make their appearance in history again and again and insist upon their prerogatives. Strikes, hunger riots, Jacqueries, the restriction and abolition of just proclaimed political freedom, abrogation of just promulgated progressive measures: All of this clearly indicates that in spite of all the lip service rendered to revolutionary democracy in Russia, the class contradictions continued to have their effect in the form of class struggle.

The longer the alliance between the revolutionary democracy and the bourgeoisie lasted and the firmer it became, the more it fettered the revolutionary forces of this country. The renewal and the reconstruction of the country on a higher plateau seemed to move further and further into the distance. There were no thorough social reforms in favour of the proletariat, the peasantry and the petit bourgeoisie. Even the safeguarding of the political heritage of the February Revolution by a Constituent Assembly was postponed from month to month. There was no decisive action to realise the demand of revolutionary democracy: A peace without annexations and indemnities with the guaranteed right of the self-determination of nations. To be sure, given the circumstances of the times, it would have been difficult to carry out these redeeming deeds whose effects should not have been to favour one group of belligerent states over the other and to place the beginnings of democratic development under the dragoon boots of the reactionary forces. However, the effect had to be looked upon from the point of view of further political development, and peace seemed to be the only successful means of overcoming the imperialism of all states and the *sine qua non* for Russia's revolution to change the country from the bottom up.

With increasing bitterness and even despair the broad Russian masses witnessed how one provisional government after another continued to waste the blood and the treasure of the people for imperialist desires to obtain world power. The myriad forms of the people's sufferings defy description. A change of mood could be detected among the workers, peasants and soldiers whose organisation, the Workers' and Soldiers' Soviet, constituted the backbone of revolutionary democracy. It seemed detrimental to them to continue to share political power with the bourgeoisie. The need of the moment seemed to be to seize the entire governmental might with one's own hands. It was through this realisation that the slogan triumphed which the left wing of Russian Social Democracy, the Party of the Bolsheviks, had maintained from the very beginning. The leadership of the Soviets changed from the moderate to the radical Socialists whose influence is being strengthened by the similar left wing of the Social Revolutionaries, the Internationalists. Concepts turned into willpower and willpower became action.

The gigantic shadow of the Revolution hovered menacingly over Petrograd when in July the capital's proletariat rose up in order to force the then provisional government to stick to the announced peace formula. Bloodily suppressed in a manner worthy of Tsarism, it nevertheless accomplished the expulsion of leading imperialists from the government as well as a more explicit explanation of the peace formula which was supposed to block the war-prolonging diplomatic game. And now at the beginning of November, the mighty Revolution has returned even more strongly. Inspired and guided by the slogans of the Bolsheviks, the Petrograd Soviet led the working people against the Kerensky Government by raising the flag of rebellion. The All-Russian Congress of Workers' and Soldiers' Soviets received it from its hands and made it its own universal banner. The coalition government of revolutionary democracy and the imperialist bourgeoisie no longer exists.

The Bolsheviks have reached their goal in a bold assault which has no parallel in history. Governmental power is in the hands of the Soviets. What has transpired is the revolutionary dictatorship of the proletariat or more correctly: The dictatorship of the working population because, around the industrial proletariat of the great modern economic centres of Russia (the axis of crystallisation for the revolutionary forces) are grouped the peasants and petit-bourgeois citizens in their work garments and military uniforms. The idyll of revolution as the work of all strata of society is finished. The revolutionary democracy must maintain its power in a difficult civil war.

Do not these facts turn everything upside down that we learned and taught about the developmental maturity of societal phenomena and people as indispensable prerequisites for such an 'upheaval' as is occurring in the East of this world? And must not the 'backwardness' of the economic development of Russia and its masses doom from the beginning the insurrection of the Bolsheviks and thus the revolution itself? This is the opinion not only of the foreign Socialists but also of the moderate Social Democrats and Social Revolutionaries in Russia itself... Three-quarters of Russia consists of agricultural lands. The great centres of capitalist industry that possess a modern proletariat are sparse and separated by long distances. The means of communication are still in their infancy. The proletarians themselves are still caught up in rural sentiments and rural thinking. The broad masses are illiterate. They are without strong organisations with well-filled treasuries and without political training by ballots, electoral campaigns and parliamentary speeches. What a frivolous sacrilege to demand the dictatorship of the proletariat under such circumstances!

As convincing as all of these arguments sound, they are in our opinion not accurate, even though we do not mean to deny the incredible difficulties which the above-mentioned conditions pose. The 'necessary maturity' of phenomena or people for a revolution is a formula which receives content and life by historical reality and this historical reality cannot be pressed into preconceived schemata. Historical materialism is no collection of ready-made prescriptions by society doctors, quacks and druggists. It is the heretofore most perfect tool for the exploration, illumination and comprehension of the historical development of humankind. The development of the economy and the societal phenomena in Russia must be viewed within the context of that country and not compared to the countries of old European culture. Its development includes aspects of Asia, Europe and America. And if the Russian people did not experience the culture which in Central and Western Europe was primarily the achievement of the urban bourgeoisie (fine arts and especially architecture, the most socially oriented of all art forms, make this obvious), it also means that it is not encumbered with all of the bourgeois traditions and ties which, in our country, enervate the decisiveness of the masses. But setting all this aside, what is really important is: Phenomena and people are ready for revolution when the broad strata of the population find certain conditions intolerable and if they no longer believe in the ability and the desire of their superior ruling organs to be able to alleviate the unbearable burden. The revolution occurs when they solely trust in their own strength and are imbued with the feeling that: the old primeval state of nature has returned, in which each human faces other humans.

Among the followers of Cromwell, the number of illiterate singers of psalms was certainly large and very few conquerors of the Bastille were 'literate' enough to even be able to read Père Duchesne. The Russian proletarians and peasants are ripe for revolution and for the seizure of power because they want the revolution and state power and they are not afraid to fight for it.

The conquest of the entire political power in the Empire, the seizure of state power, is one thing. But the revolution cannot be content to bring about political changes in Russia. It must also hammer out a new economic and social philosophy. The social content of this revolution is its life blood. The government of the Soviets wants to give the land to the peasants. It wants to hand over to the working class the control over industrial production. It desires transformations which will encounter mountains of difficulties, but which will lend the greatest historical significance to the Bolsheviks, a significance not only within the framework of Russia but of the world. The most important prerequisite for the realisation of the revolution is peace. The revolutionary government faithfully endeavours this peace, true to the principles which the Bolsheviks proclaimed to the masses ever since the outbreak of the war:

Russia's proletariat stands in irreconcilable opposition not only to the imperialism of the Central Powers but the imperialism of all states including that of Russia. The proletariat of Russia feels the closest solidarity not only with the workers of the Entente Powers, but with the workers of the entire world, including the workers of the Central Powers.

Guided by this concept, the revolutionary government of Russia is determined to make peace. It has taken the initial steps towards an armistice without feeling any obligations towards the secret treaties by which Russian imperialism chained the land and the people to the chariot of war of West European imperialism.

Whatever may be the outcome of the bold struggle of the Russian working class for power and peace: It has not been in vain. This struggle will create deep and ineffaceable marks upon history. Not just from its victory, which the proletarians of all countries passionately desire, but from the mere fact that it occurred, new creative impulses will radiate in all directions.

(Women's Supplement of the *Leipziger Volkszeitung*, 30 November 1917)

16

The Front

LARISA REISNER

(Reisner, born into a middle-class family with socialist leanings, was well-known in pre-revolutionary Petersburg as a writer and art critic. She threw in her lot with the Bolsheviks, becoming a commander of the Volga flotilla, an emissary to the King of Afghanistan and later a Commissar of the Naval Headquarters in Moscow (where she lived with and secretly married Karl Radek).

She wrote voluminously and her other works include *Hamburg Barricades* (on the revolutionary struggles in post-war Germany) and *Coal, Iron and Human Beings*.)

There are large, grimy, gloomy buildings in Moscow in which thousands of workers', peasants' and soldiers' offspring receive their schooling. They lead hard lives in the crowded dormitories, and the air in the lecture halls is foul and damp, not at all like the air which the old-regime students breathed as they walked down the vast, sunny corridors of St Petersburg University. These new people, 'marching Left', must in the space of several fleeting years absorb the old bourgeois culture and not only digest it, but smelt its best qualities and elements into the new ideological forms; these are the new people of the Workers' Faculties, tomorrow's judges, the heirs and successors of this decade.

The revolution takes a great toll of the physical energies of its professional cadres... But a few years from now there will hardly be anyone left from those who stormed the Winter Palace and made up the vanguard that proclaimed the social revolution in October of the great year, who fought at St Petersburg, Kazan, Yaroslavl, Warsaw, the Perekop, in the Caspian sands, in Siberia, the Urals, Archangel and in the Far East... And so the new proletarian culture, our great Renaissance, will not be brought about by the soldiers and commanders of the revolution, nor by its defenders and heroes, but by very new and very young people who are now sitting in those stuffy, dirty lecture halls, digesting science, selling their last shirt in order to eat, and absorbing Marx and Lenin through every pore of their bodies...

These tumultuous, uncompromising young people are materialists. They have calmly and courageously tossed out of their lives and outlook all the laws and platitudes, all the sweet dreams and mystical consolations of bourgeois science, aesthetics, art and mysticism. If you say 'beauty' to them they will boo as if they were insulted. 'Creativity' and 'emotions' cause a stampede. And this is only right.

However, while booing and ridiculing bourgeois sentimentality, you young people, you proletarian children, must not be caught in the old bourgeois trap which has weathered these years so well and which now clicks its old springs again. If you reject the bourgeois-individualist loves, passions and inspirations, you must not ever forget the immortal recent years which have just departed in the delirium of typhoid and starvation.

These aesthetes from the 'Apollo', these refined connoisseurs and lovers of Russian literature winced fastidiously at the sight of the magnificent naked woman, Venus. In a similar way they hold their noses at the revolution. How can one pronounce such primitive and banal words as 'heroism', 'the fraternity of peoples', 'self-sacrifice' and 'killed at his post'! And not only say this, but do all these rough and wonderful things, which make a refined person feel sick! For instance, take a flock of ships, several dozen barges and tugboats encased in iron, and twenty thousand sailors from Kronstadt and the Black Sea Fleet which make up their crews. They fought for three years across thousands of miles from the Baltic Sea to the Persian border, eating bread baked with ground straw, perishing, rotting and shaking with chills on filthy cots in poverty-stricken, lice-infested hospitals; they were victorious, having vanquished a stronger enemy, an enemy three times as strong as they, with the aid of worn guns and airplanes which fell from the sky for lack of quality fuel; moreover, they received letters from home in which they were told that life was bare, hungry and bitter... They most certainly were inspired, were they not? They had to invent words that would overcome the inborn, unavoidable cowardice of the flesh, of the blood, of thin human skin which could be punctured so easily with a rusty nail, did they not?

The red liquid runs out so quickly, and then all is over. One had to see beyond the blood and the dirt, beyond the weary social insurance offices that would not even issue a rubber leg for the one that had been torn off, that would drain the last ounce of strength from the wife standing in the endless waiting lines if he, a sailor of the revolutionary destroyer *Karl Liebknecht*, were mashed to a pulp tomorrow on the shattered deck. And what about dying? Deprived of the clergy's God and Satan, both of whom had evaporated with the revolution, and without the benefit of any consoling lies, he would barely manage to whisper, 'You can have my boots' before he died.

Is it beauty or not when a battery of guns fire point-blank from an ambush upon a ship and the captain shouts to the terrified crew from the bridge words that will make them tear their stomachs from the deck, rise up and run to their battle stations? 'In the name of the Republic, fire the stern gun!' And the stern gun fires.

There is creativity, too. Our own brand, and not the bourgeois kind. Thus: several very formidable ships of the Whiteguard fleet, well-equipped and excellently armed by the British, were to be blown up. And so a hitherto-unknown engineer and Communist named Brzhezinsky invented a superb mechanism. He attached a mine-thrower to the keel of an ordinary sailboat, equipping several sailboats in this manner. There were many men who volunteered for this desperate job. The only reason the plot failed was because it was betrayed by a fisherboy. Comrade Popov, an old Communist, perished. No longer did one see him about in his long coat and light trousers, accompanied by a lively white Spitz which even followed him to the offices of the Fleet HQ. He died gloriously, disclosing nothing to his torturers. Is this revolutionary psychology or not?

I dedicate this book to the students of the Workers' Faculties. They may curse upon reading it, unable to stomach such heretical words as:

'They loved.'

'He died gloriously.'

'Psychology.'

But I want them to read this to the end, this story of how it all happened, from Kazan to Enzeli. How victories were won and how defeats bled us to death. On the Volga, on the Kama and on the Caspian Sea during the Great Russian Revolution. That is all.

Kazan-Sarapul

At night the bells striking on the deck of the destroyer sound surprisingly like the chimes on Peter and Paul Fortress.

However, instead of the Neva River, resplendently serene, instead of the dull granite and golden spires, the clear chiming rings out over the uninhabited banks, the pure capricious waters of the Kama and the remote and scattered villages.

It is dark on the bridge. The moon barely picks out the long, swift, narrow bodies of the ships. Flurries of sparks rise from the stacks, and the milky smoke settles over the water in a white mane. Here amidst the wilds, the ships with their haughty prows seem to be not a modern cultural invention, but warlike and elusive steeds of the sea.

The lighting is unusual: faces can be seen as clearly as in the daytime. The silent figures are etched just as clearly. The gunner's movements, as with a single sweep he removes the heavy canvas from the gun, are epic, perfected by years of repetition and thus as facile as a ballet dancer's.

The hands of the signalman waving the two red flags are both eloquent and laconic, dancing in the night wind. It is the conventional and ceremonial dance of commands and replies.

A green morning star rises above the guarded anxiety of the ships being readied for battle, over the reflections cast by the red-hot furnace which has hidden its smoke and heat in the depths of the hold. The star rises on high, higher than the mast and the bridge.

Somewhere to the right a sly light flashes and is gone. It may be the Whiteguards, or perhaps it is one of Kozhevnikov's units scouting around far in the rear of the Whiteguards to appear unexpectedly from the dense brush that covers the steep bank of the Kama and greet our *Mezhen*.

These banks are unusually beautiful when seen by the first rays of dawn. The Kama near Sarapul is broad and deep, flowing between yellow cliffs of clay, branching between the islands, carrying the reflection of the silver firs on its smooth, oily surface. It is free and calm. The silent destroyers do not break the charmed silence of the river.

In the shallows hundreds of swans spread their wings, dazzling white in the piercing rays of the late October sun. Ducks scoot over the surface in a small tattered cloud, while an eagle soars high above a distant white church. Although the opposite bank is occupied by the enemy, not a single shot is fired from the low bushes. We have obviously not been expected in these parts, and they have had no time to prepare for our coming.

The head and shoulders of the engine-man, so pale and sooty, appear in the engine hatch. He wipes the soot and sweat from his face and deeply breathes in the tangy morning air that has become autumnal and frosty overnight.

The pilot on the bridge, a shaggy-haired, stocky wood-goblin with his grey locks and sheepskin coat, predicts an early frost.

'There's a smell of snow in the air', he says and returns silently to locating the narrow path the ships will follow among the treacherous ripples formed by the shallows, the fog and underwater rocks. Over a hundred miles have been covered during the night.

The tracery of the railway bridge and the white houses of Sarapul appear in the distance. The crew is resting, the men washing at the tap and playing with two black puppies that have been nurtured with such loving care amidst the cannonade and endless raids.

There is a shout from the lookout: 'Men on the left bank!'

Once again there is tension in the air. However, the people on the bank have seen who we are, and red flags wave joyously. Farther on, on the bridge and beyond the sandy embankment, other red flags take wing and flap in the wind. Small figures of infantrymen in grey greatcoats run along the bank waving, shouting and sending joyful greetings to our iron decks.

We pass the bridge and turn left. Intermittent shooting breaks out behind the last ship in our wake. The Whiteguards are shooting at the bridge guard that gathered to watch our flotilla pass.

Through our glasses the embankment of Sarapul is clearly discernible. The town, occupied by Azin's division, is encircled by Whiteguard forces. Now, with the appearance of our flotilla, contact with the armies dislocated farther down will be re-established.

We are getting close. Everywhere, on the roof of a houseboat, on the railings, on the road are Red Army men, blouses, kerchiefs and beards, and all of them excited, proud and so very dear to us. The band on the hill is playing the *Marseillaise*, with the drummer, gazing raptly at the ship, forgetting his cue and the French horn far ahead of the angry conductor, playing for all it was worth, stopping for nothing, like a horse that has thrown its rider. The rope's end has been tossed ashore, the side of the ship gently touches the pier and the crew streams down the gangplank.

A lively exchange follows.

'How did you get through? Did you get their ships?'

'We beat them and chased them up the Belaya River.'

'Go on!'

'It's the truth.'

A young woman makes her way through the crowd. She is weeping. The people pass the word around: 'She's a sailor's wife.' Then lamentation fills the air. The weeping of a wife and mother, the piercing, monotonous wail: 'They took him off on a barge. They dragged him onto the barge. He was a sailor, just like you.' The woman turns this way and that, sobbing inconsolably, stroking the rough sleeves of the sailors' pea jackets, her one last memory. Yes, war is a cruel thing and civil war is monstrous. The retreating enemy has committed so many conscious acts of 'civilised' barbarity.

Chistopol, Yelabuga, Chelny and Sarapul, all these towns have been drenched in blood. These once sleepy towns have been entered in the history of the revolution as burning brands. In one spot the Whiteguards tossed the wives and children of Red Army men into the Kama River, never sparing a single wailing infant. In another there are still caked puddles of blood on the road, with the flaming crimson of the autumn maples an echo of the massacre.

The wives and children of these murdered men do not run off to foreign lands, they do not then sit down to write their memoirs of the way their estate with its Rembrandts and library was put to the torch, or of the cruelties of the Cheka. No one will ever know, no one will ever trumpet over sensitive Europe of the thousands of Red Army soldiers executed on the high bank of the Kama, buried by the current in the slimy shallows, tossed up against the wild bank. Recall, you who were in the crew of the *Prompt*, the *Nimble*, the *Zealous*, the floating battery *Seryozha*, the *Vanya-Communist* and on board of all our iron-clad, clumsy arks, was there a single day on which the silent back of a murdered Red Army man did not float by, the back of the soldier's head covered with thin hair (the result of typhus), with a hand dancing in the water, sometimes surfacing, sometimes trailing deep below? Was there a single place on the Kama where the people did not wail as they told you of their grief and where, among the happy and exuberant who so awkwardly caught your rope ends (for workers are no sailors), there were not a dozen workers' widows and hungry, weak and dirty children? Do you recall the wailing that could not be drowned out even by the clanking of the anchor chain, even by the pounding of your hearts, even by the straining voice of the chairman of the local executive committee who greeted you from half a mile away with the shouted news that Samara had been recaptured by the Red Army...

Meanwhile, another woman has joined the first. She is very small and old. Her face is covered with the same scars of grief. 'Don't cry, dear, tell us what happened.' And the younger one begins to speak, but her words are drowned by her sobs, and it is impossible to understand her.

This is what happened. As the Whiteguards retreated, they herded six hundred Red Army men, sailors and workers onto a barge and sailed off. No one knows where they headed. To Ufa, perhaps, or maybe to the Votkinsk Works.

An hour later the piercing sound of the siren summons the scattered sailors to the pier. The commander issues a new order: the flotilla is setting off up-river to search for the barge with the prisoners. As the commander hurries the crews, he repeats with great emphasis: 'It's six hundred men, comrades.'

They were not expecting us. The approaches to the trenches, barbed wire and pickets are all exposed from the river and are in clear view. The destroyers advance stealthily, looking for a convenient position, while the commanders search out their targets. The hatch in the mess leading to the powder-magazine is ajar. The crew is hurriedly passing up shells. A command follows:

'Fire!'

A fiery bolt emerges from the barrel. The empty case falls with a clang. Ten or fiteen seconds later an ash-white and black fountain of smoke rises amidst the running line of enemy soldiers. The sighting is changed and the gun fires again.

Now the *Prompt* opens fire. The *Durable*'s stern gun hits a building.

By making the best of the general commotion, we should be at Galyany before dark (it is thirty-five miles up-river from Sarapul).

Another ten miles and we reach our goal. The red flags are lowered, for it has been decided to catch the enemy unawares, posing as the Whiteguard force of Admiral Stark which the Izhevsk Whiteguard forces have been awaiting so eagerly. The ships proceed at full steam, coming out from behind an islet and the turn of the river, passing the piers of Galyany, the village on the hill, and turning around farther up the river, a very difficult manoeuvre in such a narrow and shallow spot.

'You are to fire only at my command', the signalmen pass the commander's order from destroyer to destroyer.

The situation is as follows: some fifty or sixty yards away on the bank near the church we can clearly see a heavy 6-inch gun. Farther up on the hill is a crowd of curious peasants and armed soldiers. A second gun is mounted on the bell-tower; perhaps it is only a machine-gun. A barge with a landing force of Whiteguard soldiers is moored by the left bank. We can see the white tents of their camp in the bushes and the smoke from field kitchens. Soldiers are reclining on the bank, watching our manoeuvres with interest. In the middle of the river, under special guard, is a floating grave, silent and motionless.

The *Nimble*'s megaphone, keyed low, passes the order for action to the other ships. The *Zealous* approaches the barge and, still concealing its true identity, makes certain that it contains the precious cargo. The *Nimble* sets its sights on the 6-inch gun which it will hit point-blank at the enemy's first sign of activity. At the same time, it keeps watch over the infantry.

But how can the barge be towed out of the narrow trap formed by the shallows, the islet and the shoal? Luckily, the *Dawn*, an enemy tugboat, is under steam at the pier. Our officer, wearing an impressive naval cap, sends the captain of the tugboat the following command:

'In the name of Admiral Stark, commander of the flotilla, I order you to approach the prison barge, take it in tow and follow us down the Belaya River to Ufa.'

The captain of the *Dawn* has no reason to doubt the authority of the command and hurries to carry it out. The minutes drag on endlessly as the clumsy boat, its water-wheels slapping loudly, approaches the barge, makes fast the cables, chugs and works up steam. Our crew holds its breath. The men are terribly pale. They believe their eyes, yet are afraid to believe this fairy tale coming true, this doomed barge, so close and still so far away. They whisper to each other:

'Is it moving?'

'No, not yet.'

The *Dawn*, thoroughly intimidated by our captain's stern command to hurry up, plays its part well. There is movement on the barge now. The chief warden and his men put down their rifles and help to weigh anchor. Slowly the hulking tub begins to move. First, its prow turns with an effort. For a second the taut cables become slack. Then they begin pulling their resisting quarry again. The order from the *Nimble* reassures the worried jailers:

'The commander orders you to preserve complete calm. We shall take the lead and act as your convoy.'

'We're low on firewood', the *Dawn* protests feebly.

'You'll put in some on the way', the commander replies.

Then the destroyers begin moving slowly away towards Sarapul, not wanting to arouse the suspicion of the Whiteguards who are watching the operation from the bank.

Meanwhile, inside the barge's hold a state of alarm prevails. Where are they being taken? And why? And by whom?

One of the prisoners, a sailor, makes his way over the filthy floor to the stern. A hole has been bored with a penknife in one of the stout planks. It is the only opening through which they can glimpse a bit of the sky and the river. He keeps his eye at the hole, watching the strange ships and their silent crews. The faces of his comrades, merged into a single lifeless, motionless face, watch his expression: now a ray of hope, now apprehension again.

'They're all the same. They're all long and grey. Are they Whiteguard ships or not? Can't you tell?'

'They're not.'

'Not what, damn you?'

The observer topples off the footstool.

'They don't have iron-clad ships like these. These are our ships, from the Baltic fleet. They're manned by regular crews.'

However, the wretched prisoners, who have been sleeping and eating on top of their own excrements in the rotting hold for three long weeks, men who are naked save for the bits of canvas they have wrapped around themselves, do not dare to hope,

When they finally reach Sarapul and the people weep and shout on the piers, when the sailors arrest the Whiteguard jailers and, fearing to descend into the filthy hold, call to the prisoners to come up, they are met by curses and moaning. None of the four hundred and thirty men can believe they have been rescued. Only yesterday the guards traded crusts of bread and a kettle of water for their last shirt.

Yesterday at dawn the torn bodies of the three Krasnoperov brothers and of twenty-seven others were hauled out of the common cells on seven bayonets. For the past twenty-four hours no one has dropped any bread (a quarter of a pound per man) down the hole in the ceiling. And this has been the only food in their daily ration for the past three weeks.

Since they were not fed, it could only mean there was no use wasting even left-over crusts on a doomed herd. It could only mean that during the night or in the sombre hours of dawn they would meet their end. They did not know what this end would be, but theirs would be a terrible death. Then, suddenly, they were taken somewhere. The hatch opening onto the night sky was opened. They were being summoned up now in strange, compassionate voices, calling them by a name that was outlawed and exiled: 'comrades'. Was this new treachery? Another trap?

And yet, weeping, crawling up one after another, they are resurrected from the dead. It is impossible to describe the scene on deck. Several Chinese soldiers who have no family in this cold country embrace a sailor's feet and, speaking in a language we cannot understand, proclaim their dedication to the fraternity of men who would die for each other.

In the morning the town and the army greet the prisoners.

The prison barge is towed to the bank. The gangplank is lowered onto the *Razin*, a huge iron barge armed with long-range guns, and four hundred and thirty-two staggering, bearded, deathly-pale men pass through a corridor of sailors to step onto the bank. The parade of torn canvas, of caps made of twisted straw gives them the fantastic appearance of a procession from hell. Although the crowd is numbed by the sight, the first sparks of humour are kindled.

'Hey, who dressed you up so nice, comrades?'

'Look, it must be the uniform of the Constituent Assembly: a scrap of canvas and a noose for each.'

'Don't step on my boot, can't you see my toes are sticking out.' And the man stuck out a foot wrapped in filthy rags.

As the barge approached the bank they began singing the *Marseillaise* in voices made hoarse by the damp of the hold. The singing continues until they reach the town square. Here a spokesman for the prisoners greets the sailors of the Volga Flotilla, their commander and the Soviets. The faces, the words and the tears are hard to describe, as families are reunited with a father, a brother or a son and sit around the rescued man as he eats and tells them of his imprisonment and then takes leave of them to go over to the comrades, the sailors, to thank them for saving him.

Scattered among the crowd of soldiers and sailors are the gold-braided caps of the few officers who have been on the three-month trip from Kazan to Sarapul with us. I don't know whether they have ever been greeted by such deep respect and affection as they are this day. And if there exists the wonderful unity of spirit, courage and self-sacrifice between the intelligentsia and the masses, it was born when the mothers of workers, their wives and children blessed the sailors and officers for delivering their dear ones from torture and execution.

Markin

Every day the boatswain of the flagship *Mezhen* reports with a broad smile that the temperature of the water in the Kama is dropping.

Today the thermometer stopped at 1°. The temperature of the air is zero. Solitary ice floes float along with the current. The water has become heavy and sluggish with a constant mist curling over it, a sure sign of frost. The crews of the ships which have been all through this difficult campaign from Kazan to Sarapul are getting ready for a winter ashore. The men have perked up in anticipation of their coming leave. In another day or two the flotilla will leave the Kama for the winter.

It is only now, when the hour of our involuntary retreat is near, that everyone has realised how precious and unforgettable these banks, captured from the enemy, have become, as have every turn and bend of the river and every shaggy fir tree along the steep cliffs.

How many difficult hours of waiting there have been, how many hopes and fears, not for one's self, of course, but for the great year of 1918, whose fate has often depended on the accuracy of someone's aim or on the courage of a scout! How many joyous hours of victory will remain here on the Kama! The ice will cover over the harsh waters that have been pummelled by shells and criss-crossed by ships. It will forever conceal from us the deep holes that have become the graves of our best comrades and most bitter enemies.

Who knows against whom and in which waters we shall have to fight next year, and which comrades will man the iron-clad bridges of the ships which have become so familiar and so dear to each of us?

With a heavy beat of water-wheels and a signal lantern swinging from the mast in the darkness, one of the 'transport' ships passes on its way to Nizhny Novgorod.

The remaining vessels see their departing comrade off by sounding their whistles and horns, and the sound lingers in the air. Each whistle and horn is as familiar as the voice of a friend. There is the sharp cry of the *Rochal*; the short, piercing whistle of the *Volodarsky*; and *Comrade Markin* with its low, deafening horn.

This farewell naval salute recalls bitter memories, for the ships use it only when in extreme danger.

Thus did the *Vanya-Communist* appeal for help when it was set afire by enemy shells and became a burning inferno in the icy waters of the river, its rudder broken its telegraph shattered, its siren wailing on and on, and on.

Fountains of water were rising more frequently around it. Then black moving spots appeared on the surface of the river. These were the men of the crew who had struck out for the bank. The current carried off charred timbers, pails and footstools and all the while, enveloped in steam and scorched by flames, the terrible, crazed siren of death wailed on. Misfortune had struck unexpectedly.

The day before the naval flotilla had scored a significant victory over the Whiteguard ships: after a two-day battle at the village of Bitki the enemy was forced to escape upstream, and our ships broke through to its rear, where the Whiteguard forces were entrenched on both banks. The pursuit continued for another twenty-four hours. Not until the morning of the third day did the flotilla drop anchor in a blue, turquoise and amber stretch of the Kama, so beautiful in the clear November sunshine.

We were to stop and wait for the arrival of a landing force, since the scouts had brought back the disquieting news of impressive riverside fortifications in the town of Pyany Bor. An assult launched from the river without the support of a landing force was doomed to failure; besides, our supply of shells was very low. There were only some eighteen to fifty shells per ship or barge. While waiting for the infantry, which was always late in arriving, the cutters set out on reconnaissance. The sailors looked on as the elusive boats darted off, barely visible amidst the clouds of spray. The enemy opened a hurricane of fire, a quite useless barrage.

Fiery arcs played in the high columns of water raised by the exploding shells, and feathery, snow-white and rainbow fountains rose and fell incessantly. A flock of frightened swans took wing from the shallows. A hydroplane zoomed off and up past them, filling the air with the cries of the swans, the flapping of white wings and the buzzing of its propeller.

This was too much for Markin. Markin, commander of the *Vanya-Communist*, our best ship, a man used to danger, enamoured of it like a boy, could not watch the morning's war game from the sidelines. He was tantalised by the high sandy cliff and Pyany Bor, by the silent, mysterious, watchful edge of the woods and by the shore battery, tucked away somewhere and waiting patiently.

No one could later recall when his ship weighed anchor and slipped along the forbidden bank nor how it had managed to move so far away from the other ships. All of a sudden Markin spotted a camouflaged battery. It was practically opposite his ship and very close to it. The barrels of the big guns were trained on the ship.

A single ship cannot take on a shore battery, but this morning of victory was such a heady, reckless one that the *Vanya-Communist* did not retreat, did not slip away, but kept steaming towards the shore arrogantly, chasing the gunners from their posts with the fire of its machine-guns. The ship's doom was preordained.

The destroyer *Nimble* approached the *Vanya-Communist*. One may not believe in premonitions, yet imagine the anxiety of all those who were on the bridge of the *Nimble*. This was not fear, for no one was susceptible to this base disease. It was an unusual, wrenching state of expectancy which I, too, experienced as the *Nimble*, still completely unawares, approached the *Vanya-Communist*.

A short exchange between the two ships was Markin's last. The flotilla commander spoke through a megaphone.

'What are you shooting at, Markin?'

'At the shore battery.'

'Which battery?'

'Over there, behind the stacked firewood. See the shiny barrel?'

'Reverse and retreat immediately!'

But it was too late. No sooner had the engines of the *Nimble* accomplished a great backward leap, no sooner had the *Vanya-Communist* tried to follow, than the Whiteguards on the bank, sensing that their prey was escaping, opened barrage fire. Shells fell like rain, zipping over the bridge with a howling sound, rolling like tenpin balls and rending the air. A few moments later the *Vanya-Communist* was swathed in a cloud of steam, with a yellow tongue of flame dancing inside it as the ship careened with a broken rudder. That was when its siren cried out for help.

Despite the terrible barrage, the *Nimble* returned to the side of the doomed ship, hoping to take it in tow, as we had near Kazan when the *Tashkent* was shelled and then towed out from under direct fire.

However, there are times when even the greatest feats of courage are useless. The very first shell that hit the *Vanya-Communist* smashed its steering line and telegraph. The ship was out of control, spinning around. When the *Nimble* finally managed to approach it, it was unable to take the floundering ship in tow.

The *Nimble* was forced to retreat.

It is a miracle we were able to slip away from the Whiteguards then, for they were firing point-blank. The amazing speed of the destroyer and its heavy guns made it possible for it to escape from the trap. How strange it was to see two large seagulls, undaunted by the shelling, flying before its prow, disappearing now and then beyond the fountains raised by the exploding shells.

Comrade Poplevin, Markin's first mate, was among the survivors. He was a silent, exceptionally modest and courageous man, one of the best in the flotilla. For a long while after his face retained a blue paleness. This stamp of death was especially apparent when the autumn sky was clear and blue and the water peacefully lapped against the golden Kama banks.

Poplevin avenged the death of his comrade and his ship. At night, when even the strongest of the men became exhausted, he would climb to the bridge and stand there alone under the stars, looking and listening, attuned to even the smallest movement of the night. Never did this sacred vengeance ebb.

He waited all night for Markin, but he did not appear. The silent helmsmen at the wheel, the gunners at their posts and the lookouts whose binoculars suddenly clouded over from unspilt tears, all grieved for him.

Markin had perished, a man of blue eyes and a fiery temperament, possessing an animal's keen sense for discovering the enemy, a man of harsh will and great pride, strong words, compassion and heroism.

The *Vanya-Communist* had perished; the burning-hot guns on the destroyers were practically out of ammunition, but still the long-promised landing force had not arrived. At twilight the canvas was removed from four long cigar-shaped objects on the cutter.

The torpedo men, the pilot of the flagship and the commander held a long conference as they pored over a map. They were silent when they came out of the captain's cabin, and shook hands with special emphasis. The commander accompanied four sailors and the officers to the deck. Several minutes later the cutter, carrying the torpedoes, disappeared beyond the island.

It returned towards morning. No longer were the long, black, cigar-shaped torpedoes on the stern. All we could do now was wait. Indeed, the next day the Whiteguards, having celebrated the sinking of the *Vanya-Communist* with a general drinking bout, launched an attack.

They advanced in a column, as solemn as if on parade. This was the very first time that Admiral Stark, commander of the Whiteguard flotilla, was taking part in an operation. The *Oryol* was flying his flag. However, the solemn procession would have to stop when it came abreast of the island. The *Trud*, the first ship in the column, had its prow literally blown off. The torpedoes had accomplished their mission.

Now there are two charred and mangled shells of ships lying practically side by side beneath the icy waters of the Kama. They are the *Vanya-Communist* and the Whiteguard *Trud*. And who knows but that underneath the murky surface of the river, on the dark bottom, the current has not brought the bodies of Markin and of those despicable ones who mowed down the last of his shipwrecked crew with machine-gun fire, to lie side by side.

Upon leaving the Kama now, the sailors were taking long and reluctant leave of each other. Perhaps it would be forever.

Nothing brings people closer together than shared danger, sleepless nights on the bridge and those endless, unnoticeable to an outsider but supreme efforts of will and spirit which make victory possible.

History will neither notice nor be able to estimate at their true value the great and small feats which the sailors of the Volga naval flotilla accomplished each and every day; it is doubtful whether the names of those who by their voluntary discipline, courage and modesty helped to create a new fleet are even known.

Undoubtedly, individuals do not make history, but Russia has known so few outstanding individuals and it was with such great effort on their part that they managed to fight their way through the layers of old and new officialdom; it was so rarely that they were able to express themselves in a real and challenging, not verbal or paper struggle. Now, since the revolution has such personalities, individuals in the highest sense of the word, it means Russia is recovering and gathering strength.

They are many. There were many in our midst. At decisive moments they came forward from the ranks of their own account and their weight was fully felt, for they knew their heroic mission and raised the wavering and pliable masses to their own level.

There was the imperturbable and laconic Yeliseyev, an excellent gunner who could hit a rowboat twelve miles away from a long-range gun. The eyelashes had been singed off his blue eyes when a gun had exploded.

There was Babkin, ever ill and feverish, his eyes seemingly drunken, who had so little time left and who dispensed the treasures of his carefree, compassionate and unbendable will with a royal flourish.

He was the one to set the mine-field on which the Whiteguard *Trud* blew up.

There was Nikolai Nikolayevich Struisky, pilot of the flagship and Chief of Operations of the flotilla during the second half of the Kama campaign. Struisky was one of our best specialists and a highly-educated seaman who served the Soviets faithfully all through the Civil War. He had been one of several former Tsarist junior officers who had been forcefully mobilised and practically brought to the front under convoy. They arrived on board the *Mezhen* hating the revolution, convinced that the Bolsheviks were German agents, implicitly trusting every word printed in the bourgeois *Rech* and *Birzheviye Vedemosti*.

The morning following their arrival they took part in a battle. At first, there was glum distrust, the cold correctness of men forced into an alien, unjust and hateful task.

Everything changed after the first volleys. Half-measures are impossible when the lives of dozens of men who blindly carry out your every order, and the life of the destroyer itself, that magnificent war horse, hinge on a single word of command. A steel bond extended from every man to the bridge, to the voice that commanded the ship, its speed, fire and the helm spinning round in the tense hands of the helmsman.

A true seaman cannot sabotage a battle. Forgetting politics, he responds to fire with fire, forcefully attacking and putting up a stubborn resistance, performing his professional duty brilliantly and coolly. He is not a free man after that. He is bound to the commissar, the crew and the red flag on the mast with a victor's pride, the proud knowledge of their need in him, and the absolute power which he, an officer and intellectual, is given in time of danger.

Ten days aboard filled with events that bring people closer together; the first victory and then the first enthusiastic reception, during which the workers of a town liberated from the Whiteguards gather at the pier with a band playing the *Internationale* and shake the tapered, aristocratic fingers of the 'Red officer' who steps down on 'alien' shore, looking round hesitatingly, not daring as yet to believe that he, too, is a 'comrade', that he, too, is a member of the 'great army of toilers' of which the hoarse trumpet of the provincial band blasts so passionately, awkwardly and joyously.

And suddenly this officer of the former Imperial Navy is horrified to find tears welling up in his eyes as he realises that these are not a 'bunch of German spies', but Russia itself, so terribly in need of his experience, his academic knowledge and his highly-trained brain. Someone is making a speech. Ah, what a saucy, untutored, coarse speech, which but a week before would have brought a scornful smile to his lips. Now the officer listens to it with a pounding heart and trembling hands, fearful of admitting to himself that the Russia of these peasant women, deserters and village boys, of Comrade Abram, the agitator, the muzhiks and the Soviets is his Russia which he had defended and will defend to the end, feeling no shame for its lice, poverty, hunger and errors, not knowing yet, but sensing that it alone is defending justice and looking to the future.

A week later, having put on a clean collar and washed the grime and gunpowder from his head and face, having buttoned every gold, eagle-crested button of his tunic on which the dark areas left by his former epaulets and insignia had not yet faded, Comrade Struisky set out to have a talk with his Bolshevik chiefs. As he spoke he gripped the arms of his chair as tightly as during a storm at sea.

'Firstly, I do not believe that you and Lenin and the others in the sealed train carriage received money from the German.'

He paused, as after firing a volley. Somewhere in the back of his mind there remained the Naval Academy, the dinners aboard the *Standard* and the gold sabre presented to him for valour in the First World War. Explosions and defeat. The October Revolution belatedly understood.

'Secondly, Russia is on your side, and so are we. I shall say the same to all the junior comrades who wish to know my opinion. Thirdly, we took Yelabuga yesterday. As you know, there were nearly a hundred peasant caps found on the bank. The whole ravine was spotted with their brains. You saw the blood and the bast shoes yourselves. We were half an hour late. This must not happen again. We can proceed at night. Naturally, the channel is dangerous and there might be an ambush in the form of a shore battery, but . . .' And here he took from his pocket a dog-eared volume of *Actions of River Flotillas During the American Civil War.*

17

Women and Revolution

ALEXANDRA KOLLONTAI

(Notorious among detractors as a propagator of 'free love', Kollontai's ideas on the subject of communal provision, as a way of releasing women from domestic drudgery in times of absolute material scarcity, became the basis of sensational scaremongering in the West. It was claimed that the 'Bolsheviki' were nationalising everything, even the women. Though her work sometimes reflected the utopian dreams of the period, Kollontai's real achievement in the field of social policy was to help lay the foundations for an array of welfare provision and of social rights which put the Soviet Union far in advance of other countries.

The excerpts included here are from articles written in 1918 and 1919.)

A Commission for Women...
The war and world revolution have brought essential changes in the character and form of all workers' communist movements; 'the ideal type' of German party work, adapted exclusively to the period of peaceful parliamentary activity, has ceased to be a model for us. The revolutionary struggle has generated new problems, new fighting methods of work. The war and the revolution have shaken what seemed to be the most stable foundations of life. And also, the position of woman has changed before our eyes.

Up until the war, the process whereby women were drawn into the national economy was carried out with considerably less speed than it has been for these last four and a half years of feverishly rapid development and the growth of female labour in all fields of industrial life. The old family, too, seemed firm and unshakeable; the Party had to fight against its way of life and traditions every time it wanted to bring the woman worker into the class struggle. The fact that housework was dying out and the transition to the state education of children, were regarded not as mature, living, practical problems of the present day, but as a 'historical tendency', as a lengthy process. The feelings of the women workers were strongest in the economic field — the inequality of men's and women's pay — and in the political field — the absence of voting rights and the inequality in citizenship.

This inequality, on economic and political grounds, together with the enslavement of the woman to her family and the running of the house, created a psychological division between men and women workers, and provided the soil from which grew those independent organisations of women workers which sprang up in all countries alongside the general workers' socialist parties, in the form of societies or unions of women workers, clubs and so on. The more actively the socialist parties became engaged in the business of propaganda amongst women workers, the quicker these specialised organisations for women workers died out.

But only a radical change in the whole existence of the working-class woman, in the conditions of her home and family life, as she acquires equal status with men in civil law, will wipe out once and for all the barrier which to this day prevents the woman worker letting her energy flow freely into the class struggle.

The war provided an impulse towards a radical break in the social position of women. It remains for the revolution to complete this task. The war drove the 'wet-nurse' to the front; ninety women out of a hundred were forced to provide for themselves and their children. The problem was becoming acute: what to do with the children of all those millions of women who had to spend the greater part of their day in preparing military supplies — grenades, shrapnel and bullets? It was in this way that the question had to be posed — not as a theoretical problem and not as something desirable in the remote future, but as a practical measure: state security for maternity and childhood. The capitalist governments were forced to worry about the fate of the 'soldier children' and unwillingly, and half-heartedly, they brought about a situation in which the care of children is the responsibility of the state.

The departure of bridegrooms and fiancés to the war, and the woman's fear for the fate of her loved one, provided a natural reason for the increased number of babies born outside marriage. And once again the bourgeois capitalist state was forced, under the pressure of war, to inflict upon itself a blow, to encroach upon one of its most sacred rights — on the prerogative of legal marriage. It was forced for the sake of the soldiers' well-being to make equal under the law both legal and extra-marital mothers and children. Germany, France and England were eventually forced to this revolutionary act.

The war not only disrupted the sanctity and stability of the indissoluble church marriage, but also encroached on yet another of the foundations of the family — housework. Rising prices, queues which exhausted the housewife, the system of delaying stocktaking until supplies had run out — all this led to a situation in which the women themselves hastened to do away with the domestic hearth, preferring to use communal facilities.

The work of destroying the social slavery of women as it was then, was carried through by the great workers' revolution. Women workers and peasants participated in the great liberating struggle on an equal footing with men. The former specialisations of the female sex collapsed as the social structure rocked on its twin pillars, private property and class government. The great fire of the world uprising of the proletariat called woman from her baking tins into the arena of the barricades, the fight for freedom. Woman ceased to feel secure in her own home, alongside her familiar flagstones, drinking troughs and cradles, when all around bullets were whistling and, amazed, she heard the cry of the worker fighters: 'To arms, comrades! All of you who cherish your freedom, who have grown to hate the chains of slavery and deprivation of civil rights! To arms, workers, to arms, women workers!...'

The revolution accustomed women workers to great mass movements, to the struggle for the realisation of communism. The revolution in Russia won full political equality and equality of citizenship for women. The revolution fulfilled the demands of women workers from all countries: equal pay for equal work. The revolution made it impossible for women ever again to be tied to their families. The revolution also abolished the previous forms of workers' movements, which had been shaped by the age of peaceful parliamentary rule. We are cut off from the period of the Second International only by four years, but by a whole geological shift in the field of social and economic relations...

However profound are the changes which have been accomplished before our eyes in the life and economic struture of our country, brought about by the war and the revolution, however far Soviet Russia has marched forward along the road to communism, the legacy of the capitalist order has still not been eradicated; the conditions of life, the working-class family's way of life, the traditions which hold captive the mind of woman, the servitude of housework — all these have still not died away. And in so far as all the factors which prevented a working-class woman from taking an active part in the liberating movement of the proletariat before the war are still operative, in so far as even now the Party still has to take into account both the political backwardness of women, and the bondage of the woman worker to her family, so the necessity of intensive work among the women proletariat, with the help of a party machine set up specifically for this purpose, remains as pressing as ever.

The setting up of a commission for agitation and propaganda among women workers in the centre and in the provinces will undoubtedly speed up this work. There was a time when the thought of specialised work within the Party, which I had been advocating since 1906, met with opposition even among my own comrades. But now, after the decision carried by the All Russian Congress of Women Workers and approved by the Party, it only remains for us to get down to its practical implementation. Our Party does not allow a separate women's movement or any independent unions or societies of women workers, but it has never denied the efficacy of a division of labour within the Party and the setting up of such special party machines as would promise to increase the number of its members or deepen its influence among the masses.

At the moment Soviet Russia is in need of many new fresh forces both for the struggle with the enemy and for the construction of the communist society. To create, to educate these forces from the many millions of the female working population — such are the tasks of the party commision for agitation and propaganda among women workers.

On the History of the Movement of Women Workers in Russia

What year could be said to mark the beginning of the working women's movement in Russia? In its essential nature, the movement of women workers is inseparably linked with the entire proletarian movement as one indivisible whole. The woman worker, as a member of the proletarian class, as someone selling her labour, also rose in revolt with the workers every time they opposed the violation of their human rights, participated together and on an equal footing with the workers in all worker uprisings, in all the 'factory revolts' so hated by Tsarism.

For this reason, the beginning of the movement of women workers in Russia coincides with the first signs of the awakening of class self-consciousness among the Russian proletariat, and with its first attempts, by means of combined pressure, strikes and walk-outs, to achieve more tolerable, less humiliating and miserly conditions of existence.

Women workers took active part in the worker revolts at the Krenholm factory in 1872 and at the Lazeryev textile factory in Moscow in 1874. They were involved in the strike in 1878 at the New Cotton-Spinning Plant in Petrograd and led the weavers' strike in the famous workers' demonstration in Orekhovo-Zuyevo, during which factory buildings were wrecked. As a result, the Tsarist government was compelled to hurry through its legislation prohibiting night work for women and children, which came into force on 3 June 1885.

It is indicative that the spontaneous wave of strikes that shook proletarian Russia in the 1870s and the early 1880s affected mainly the textile industry, in which the majority of the work force is made up of cheap female labour. The disturbances of the 1870s and early 1880s occurred for purely economic reasons, provoked by unemployment and the continuing crisis in the cotton industry. However, is it not remarkable that this downtrodden 'factory girl', without rights, oppressed by labour beyond her strength and politically ignorant, despised even by the female half of the urban petty bourgeoisie and held at arm's length by peasant women who clung tenaciously to old traditions, should be in the front ranks of those fighting for the rights of the working class, for the emancipation of women? The harsh conditions of life itself compelled the factory girl to oppose openly the power of the bosses and the enslavement of capital. However, in fighting for the rights and interests of her class, the woman workers was unwittingly also preparing the way for the emancipation of women from those chains that still weighed upon them in particular and created inequality of status and conditions among men and women workers, even within the framework of one single working class.

During the new and intensified wave of worker disturbances in the mid- and the late 1890s, working women were once again invariably active participants in worker revolts. The April revolt at the Yaroslavl factory in 1895 received vigorous support from the women weavers. Nor were women workers less active than their male comrades during the economic strikes of 1894-5 in St Petersburg. When, in the summer of 1896, St Petersburg became the scene of the historic strike by textile workers, the women weavers courageously and unanimously walked out of the workshops together with the men weavers. What difference does it make that at home hungry children are waiting for their working mother? What difference does it make that this strike brings with it the threat of dismissal, of exile or prison? The common class cause is more important, more sacred than maternal feelings, concern for the family, for personal and family well-being!

At a time of disturbances and strikes the woman worker, oppressed, timid, without rights, straightens up to her full height and becomes equal as a fighter and comrade. Ths transformation takes place unconsciously, spontaneously, but it is important and significant. It is the path along which the workers' movement is leading the woman worker to liberation, not only as one who sells her labour, but also as a woman, a wife, a mother and a housewife.

At the end of the 1890s and the beginning of the twentieth century there were a number of disturbances and strikes at factories employing mainly women: at tobacco-processing factories (Shanshal), at spinning and weaving mills (Maxwell) in Petrograd, etc. The working-class movement in Russia is gaining strength, organising itself, taking shape. So also is class resistance among the female proletariat.

None the less, until the momentous year of the first Russian revolution, the movement was basically economic in nature. Political slogans had to be concealed or advanced in disguised form. A healthy class instinct prompts the woman worker to support strikes, and not infrequently the women themselves organise and carry through 'factory revolts'. However, no sooner had the workers returned to work, victorious or defeated, than the women were once again isolated from one another, still unconscious of the need for organisation, for constant comradely contact. In those years it was still exceptional to find a woman worker in the illegal party organisations. The broad objectives of the socialist workers' party had still not seized hold of the working woman, and she remained unresponsive to universal political slogans. The life led by six million proletarian women in Russia at the beginning of the twentieth century was still too dark, too unenlightened, and their existence too much in the grip of hunger, deprivation and humiliation. A 12-hour, or at best an 11-hour working day, a starvation wage of 12-15 roubles a month, accommodation in overcrowded barracks, the absence of any form of assistance from the state or society in case of illness, pregnancy or unemployment, the impossibility of organising self-help as the Tsarist government savagely persecuted any attempts at organisation by the workers — these were the conditions surrounding the woman worker. Her back was bent by the intolerable burden of oppression, and her soul, terrified by the spectre of poverty and starvation, refused to believe in a brighter future and the possibility of fighting to cast off the yoke of Tsarism and capital.

At the beginning of the twentieth century, women workers avoided politics and revolutionary struggle. The socialist movement in Russia can, it is true, take pride in an abundance of charming and heroic women who, by their energetic work and selflessness, helped to consolidate the underground movement and prepared the way for the revolutionary explosion that occurred in the years that followed. However none of these women, from the first women socialists such as Sofia Bardina or the Leshern sisters, full of charm and inner beauty, to the iron-willed Sofia Perovskaya, were representatives of the female proletariat. In the majority of cases these were the young girls to whom Turgenev dedicated his prose poem 'The Threshold', girls from a wealthy, aristocratic background who left their parental homes, broke with their prosperous past and 'went to the people' to spread revolutionary propaganda and fight against social injustice, striving to redeem the 'sins of their fathers'. Even much later, in the 1890s and the beginning of the twentieth century, when Marxism had already put down deep roots in the Russian workers' movement, the number of women workers involved in the movement was very small. The active women members of the underground organisations in those years were not women workers but women from the intelligentsia — students, teachers, medical assistants and writers. It was rare to find a 'factory girl' at an illegal meeting. Nor did the women workers attend the Sunday evening classes held just outside the city limits of Petrograd, which were then the only legal method of spreading, under the innocent guise of geography or arithmetic, the ideas of Marxism and scientific socialism among the broad working masses. Working women still fought shy of life, avoided combat...still believed that their lot was the oven, the wash-tub and cradle.

The First Revolution of 1905
The picture changes radically from the moment when the red spectre of revolution first overshadowed Russia with its fiery wings. The revolutionary year of 1905 sent deep shock waves through the working masses. The Russian worker sensed his strength for the first time, for the

first time realised that he was bearing on his shoulders the whole national wealth. The Russian proletarian woman worker, the unfailing collaborator in all the political demonstrations of the proletariat in the revolutionary years of 1905-6, was also awoken from her slumbers. She was to be found everywhere. If we wanted to relate the facts of the mass participation of women in the movement of the time, enumerate all the active manifestations of protest and struggle by women workers, recall all the selfless actions undertaken by proletarian women, their loyalty to the ideals of socialism, then we would have to reconstruct scene by scene the entire history of the Russian revolution of 1905.

Many still remember those years full of romanticism. The image of the woman worker, still 'incomplete', but already stirring into life, with her searching, hope-filled eyes turned on the speaker at crowded meetings charged with infectious enthusiasm, lives once again in the memory. The faces of women, filled with concentrated energy and unshakable resolution, can be seen among the serried ranks of the workers' procession on the memorable 9 January, bloody Sunday. A sun, unusually bright for St Petersburg, illuminates this purposeful, solemn and silent procession, highlighting the women's faces, so numerous among the crowd. The penalty for naive illusions and childish trustfulness strikes the women; the woman worker, young girl, working wife, is a common figure among the mass victims of that January day. The slogan 'General Strike' that flies from workshop to workshop is picked up by these women, yesterday still lacking class consciousness, and compels some of them to be the first to walk out.

The women workers in the provinces did not lag behind their comrades in the capital. In the October days, exhausted by work and their harsh existence on the edge of starvation, women leave the factories and, in the name of the common cause, courageously deprive their children of their last piece of bread... With simple, moving words the woman worker appeals to her male comrades, suggesting that they too leave their work; she keeps up the spirits of those on strike, breathing energy into those who waver... The woman worker struggled tirelessly, protested courageously, sacrificed herself heroically for the common cause, and the more active she became, the more rapidly was the process of her mental awakening achieved. The woman worker began to take note of the world around her, of the injustices stemming from the capitalist system. She became more painfully and acutely aware of the bitterness of all her sufferings and sorrows. Alongside common proletarian demands one can hear ever more distinctly the voices of the women of the working class recalling the needs and requirements of women workers. At the time of the elections to the Shidlovsky commission in March 1905, the refusal to admit women as worker delegates provoked murmurs of discontent among women: the sufferings and sacrifices that they had only recently passed through had brought the men and women of the working class closer together, put them on an equal footing. It appeared particularly unjust at that moment to turn to the woman fighter and citizen and underline her age-old lack of rights. When the Shidlovsky commission refused to recognise the woman chosen as one of the seven delegates from the Sampsionevsky textile works, the indignant women workers representing several textile works decided to present to the commission the following protest declaration: 'Women deputies representing women workers are not allowed onto the commission under your chairmanship. We believe such a decision to be unjust. Women workers predominate in the factories and mills of St Petersburg. The number of women employed in spinning and weaving mills is increasing every year becuase the men are moving to factories that offer better pay. We, the women workers, bear a heavier burden of work. Because of our helplessness and lack of rights, we are kept down more by our comrades, and paid less. When this commission was announced, our hearts filled with hope; at last the time is coming — we thought — when the woman worker in St Petersburg will be able to speak out to the whole of Russia in the name of all her sister workers about the oppression, wrongs and humiliations of which the male worker can know nothing. And then, when we had already chosen our deputies, we were informed that only men can be deputies. However, we hope that this is not your final decision...'

The refusal to allow women workers the right of representation and their expulsion from political life constituted a blatant injustice for all that section of the female population that had carried on its shoulders the burden of the liberation struggle. Women workers repeatedly attended pre-election meetings during the election campaigns for the First and Second Dumas, and noisily protested against a law that deprived them of any voice in a matter so important as the election of a representative to the Russian Parliament. There were instances, for example in Moscow, when women workers came to meetings of electors, broke up the meeting and protested against the way the elections were being conducted.

That women workers were no longer indifferent to their lack of rights is also shown by the fact that, of the 40,000 signatures on petitions addressed to the First and Second State Dumas demanding that electoral rights be extended to women also, a large majority were those of women workers. The collection of signatures was organised by the Alliance for Female Equality and other bourgeois women's organisations, and was conducted at plants and factories. The fact that women workers willingly signed petitions drawn up by bourgeois women also reveals that the political consciousness of women workers was only just awakening, that they were taking their first, hesitant steps, still stopping half-way. The women workers were becoming aware of their deprivation and lack of political rights, but were still unable to link this fact with the common struggle of their own class, were unable to find the correct path that would lead proletarian women to their full and comprehensive emancipation. The woman worker still naively accepted the hand held out to her by bourgeois feminists. The suffragettes turned to the working women, hoping to draw them onto their side, get their support and organise them into purely feminine, supposedly non-class, but essentially bourgeois alliances. However, a healthy class instinct and a deep mistrust of the 'fine ladies' saved women workers from being attracted to feminism and prevented any long or stable fraternisation with bourgeois suffragettes.

The years 1905 and 1906 were marked by a particularly large number of women's meetings eagerly attended by women workers. The women workers listened carefully to the voice of the bourgeois suffragettes, but what was offered to them did not satisfy the urgent needs of those enslaved to capital, and did not evoke any whole-hearted response. The women of the working class were exhausted by the burden of intolerable working conditions, hunger and the material insecurity of their families; their immediate demands were: a shorter working day, higher pay, a more humane attitude on the part of the factory administration, less police surveillance, more freedom of action. All these demands were alien to bourgeois feminism. The suffragettes approached the women workers with narrowly feminine causes and aspirations. They did not and could not understand the class nature of the emerging women workers' movement. They were particularly disappointed by the domestic servants. On the initiative of the bourgeois feminists, the first meetings of domestic servants were held in St Petersburg and Moscow in 1905. The domestic servants eagerly responded to this call to 'organise' and turned up at the early meetings in large numbers. However, when the Alliance for Female Equality tried to organise them to its own taste, i.e. to set up an idyllic, mixed alliance between lady employers and domestic employees, the domestic servants turned away from the suffragettes and, to the disappointment of the bourgeois ladies, 'hastened to join their own class party, organising their own special trade unions'. Such is the state of affairs in Moscow, Vladimir, Penza, Kharkov and a number of other cities. The same fate befell attempts by another political women's organisation even more to the right, the Women's Progressive Party, which attempted to organise domestic employees under the watchful eye of their mistresses. The domestic servants' movement overflowed the boundaries predetermined for it by the feminists. Look at the newspapers from 1905 and you will see that they abound in reports of direct action by domestic servants, even in the most remote regions of Russia. This action took the form either of mass strike action, or of street demonstrations. The strikes involved cooks, laundresses and maids; there were strikes according to profession, and strikes that united all 'domestic servants'. This protest by domestic employees spread like an infection from place to place. The demands made by the domestic servants were usually limited to an 8-hour working day, a minimum wage, more tolerable living conditions (a separate room), polite treatment by the employer, etc.

This political awakening of women was, moreover, not limited to the urban poor. For the first time in Russia, the Russian peasant woman also raised her voice persistently and resolutely. The end of 1904 and the whole of 1905 is a period of continuous 'petticoat rebellions', sparked off by the war against Japan. All the horrors and deprivations, all the social and economic ills that stemmed from this ill-fated war, weighed down on the peasant woman, wife and mother. The conscription of reserves placed a double burden of work and worry on her already overloaded shoulders, and forced her, hitherto dependent and fearful of everything that lay beyond the circle of her domestic interests, to meet face to face previously unsuspected hostile forces, and to become consciously aware of all her humiliation and deprivation, drain to the last drop the whole bitter cup of unmerited wrongs... Illiterate, downtrodden peasant women left their homes and villages for the first time and hurried into town to wear down the steps of government offices in the attempt to obtain some news of their husbands, sons and fathers, to petition for financial assistance and defend their interests... The total lack of rights that was the peasant's lot, the lies and injustice of the existing social order, stood in all their naked ugliness before the bewildered peasant woman... She returned from town sober and hardened, bearing in her heart an inexhaustible supply of bitterness, hatred and anger... In the summer of 1905 a whole series of 'petticoat rebellions' broke out in the south. Filled with anger and with a boldness surprising for women, the peasant women attacked military and police headquarters where the army recruits were stationed, seized their menfolk and took them home. Armed with rakes, pitchforks and brooms, peasant women drove the armed guards from the villages. They are protesting in their own way against the intolerable burden of war. They are, of course, arrested, tried and given severe punishments, but the 'petticoat rebellions' continue. In this protest, defence of peasant interests and of purely 'female' interests are so closely interwoven that there are no grounds for dividing them and classing the 'petticoat rebellions' as part of the 'feminist movement'.

Following the 'political demonstrations' by the peasant women there come a series of 'petticoat rebellions' on economic grounds.

This is the period of universal peasant unrest and agricultural strikes. The 'petticoats' sometimes initiated these disturbances, drawing the men after them. There were cases when, having failed to involve the men, the women marched to the manors by themselves to present their demands and ultimata. Arming themselves with whatever came to hand, they went ahead of the men to meet the punitive detachments. The downtrodden peasant woman, oppressed for centuries, suddenly became one of the central figures in the political drama. During the whole revolutionary period the peasant women, standing always united with their menfolk, guarded and defended peasant interests, and with amazing tact and sensitivity referred to their special, 'women's' needs only when that did not endanger the common peasant cause.

This did not mean that the peasant women were indifferent to their needs as women, that they ignored them. On the contrary, the mass emergence of peasant women onto the political arena, their mask participation in the common struggle, reinforced and developed their feminine self-awareness. By November 1905, the peasant women of the Voronezh province sent two of their own deputies to the peasant congress with instructions from the women's gathering to demand 'political rights' and 'freedom' for women on an equal basis with men.

The female peasant population of the Caucasus defended their rights with particular vigour. The Guria peasant women at village meetings in the Kutaisi province adopted resolutions demanding political equality with men. At rural and urban meetings held to discuss the introduction of Zemstvos in Transcaucasia, the deputies representing the local population included Georgian women who insisted upon their rights as women.

While demanding political equality, the peasant women naturally always raised their voices in defence of their economic interests; the question of 'allotments' of land concerned the peasant woman as much as it did the peasant man. In some regions, peasant women who had enthusiastically supported the idea of expropriating private land, cooled in their support for this measure when the question arose as to whether the women would be included in the count to determine the size of the land allotment. 'If the land is taken from the landowners and given only to the men', the women argued anxiously, 'then we will face real slavery. At present we can at least earn a few kopecks on our own account, whereas if that were to happen, we will simply be working for the men.' However, the fears of the peasant women proved to be completely unfounded; simple economic calculation obliged the peasantry to insist that land also be given to the women. The agrarian interests of the male and female sections of the peasantry were so closely interwoven that the men, in fighting to abolish the existing agricultural bondage for themselves, inevitably defended at the same time the economic interests of their womenfolk.

However, in fighting for the economic and political interests of the peasantry as a whole, the peasant woman also learned how to fight for her own specific needs and requirements as a woman. The same held true for the woman worker; with her unfailing participation in the whole liberation movement she, even more than the peasant woman, prepared public opinion to accept the principle of female equality. The idea of civic equality for women, now implemented in Soviet Russia, was spread through society not by the heroic efforts of individual women with forceful personalities, not by the struggle of the bourgeois feminists, but by the spontaneous pressure of broad masses of working and peasant women, who had been roused into life by the thunder of the first Russian revolution in 1905.

In 1909, in my book *The Social Basis of the Women's Question*, I said, arguing against the bourgeois feminists, against whom the whole of my book is directed: 'If the peasant woman does succeed in achieving in the near future an improvement in her domestic, economic and legal position, this will naturally be thanks only to the combined, united efforts of peasant democracy directed at obtaining the fulfilment of those peasant demands which, in one form or another, continue to be heard in the peasant milieu. Attempts by the feminists to "clear the way for women", are here irrelevant... If the peasant woman does free herself from the present agrarian bondage, she will receive more than all the feminist organisations put together could give her.'

These words, written ten years ago, have now been fully vindicated. The Great October Revolution has not only fulfilled the basic, urgent demand of the peasantry of both sexes that the land be transferred into the hands of those who work it, but has also raised the peasant woman to the honourable position of a free citizen equal in every respect, and now enslaved only by old methods of agricultural work and by still persisting family traditions and mores.

That of which the working and peasant women could only dream in the days of the first Russian revolution in 1905 has been translated into reality by the Great October Revolution of 1917.

Woman in Russia has achieved political equality. However she owes this achievement not to cooperation with bourgeois suffragettes, but to a joint, united struggle with her comrade workers in the ranks of her own working class.

18
Friends and False Friends of the Working Class

BUKHARIN AND PREOBRAZHENSKY

(Written at the height of the Civil War, with White armies at the gates of Moscow and Petrograd, *The ABC of Communism* was a fiery defence of the idea of October and of the heroism of the Russian working class. And it was a terrible damnation of parliamentary socialism, and of the cynical politics of class appeasement which had stood by while the working class of Europe was plunged into the bloodbath of the First World War, and stood by again while the interventionist powers tried to strangle the first socialist revolution.)

Internationalism of the Workers' Movement Essential to the Victory of the Communist Revolution

The communist revolution can be victorious only as a world revolution. If a state of affairs arose in which one country was ruled by the working class, while in other countries the working class, not from fear but from conviction, remained submissive to capital, in the end the great robber states would crush the workers' state of the first country. During the years 1917-18-19 all the Powers were trying to crush Soviet Russia; in 1919 they crushed Soviet Hungary. They were, however, unable to crush Soviet Russia, for the internal conditions in their own countries were critical, and the governments were all afraid of being overthrown by their own workers, who demanded the withdrawal of the invading armies from Russia. The significance of this is, in the first place, that the realisation of proletarian dictatorship in one country is gravely imperilled unless active assistance is given by the workers of other lands. It signifies, in the second place, that, under such conditions, when the workers have gained the victory in only one country, the organisation of economic life in that country is a very difficult matter. Such a country receives little or nothing from abroad; it

169

is blockaded on all sides.

If, however, for the victory of communism, it is essential that there should be a world revolution and that the workers in various lands should render mutual aid one to another, this implies that the international solidarity of the working class is an essential preliminary to victory. The conditions for the general struggle of the workers are like the conditions for the working class struggle in each individual country. In any one country the workers cannot win strikes when these are isolated affairs; they can only win strikes when the workers in separate factories combine for mutual support, when they found a joint organisation, and when they conduct a united campaign against all the factory owners. It is just the same for the workers living in the various bourgeois states. They can only gain the victory when they march shoulder to shoulder, when they do not quarrel among themselves, when the proletarians of all lands unite, feeling themselves to be a single class with interests common to them all. Complete mutual trust, a brotherly alliance, united revolutionary action against world capitalism — these along can bring victory to the working class. THE WORKERS' COMMUNIST MOVEMENT CAN CONQUER ONLY AS AN INTERNATIONAL COMMUNIST MOVEMENT.

The need for an international struggle on the part of the proletariat has long been recognised. In the forties of the last century, on the eve of the revolution of 1848, there already existed an international secret organisation known as the Communist Federation. Marx and Engels were its leaders. At the London conference of the organisation they were instructed to write a manifesto in its name. Such was the origin of the Manifesto of the Communist Party, in which the great champions of the proletariat gave the first exposition of communist teaching.

In 1864 there was constituted under Marx's leadership the International Working Men's Association, now commonly spoken of as the *First International*. In the First International there were associated a number of working-class leaders from various countries, but unity was lacking. Moreover, the organisation was not yet based upon the broad masses of the workers, but rather took the form of an international society of revolutionary propagandists. In 1871 the members of the International took part in the rising of the Parisian workers (the Commune of Paris). There ensued everywhere a persecution of the branches of the International. It collapsed in 1874, having been greatly weakened by internal dissensions, by the struggles between the adherents of Marx and those of the anarchist, Bakunin. After the break-up of the First International, the growth of socialist parties began in various countries. The more rapid the development of industry, the more rapid was the growth of these parties. The need for mutual support was felt so strongly, that in 1889 there was held an international socialist congress attended by delegates of the socialist parties of numerous countries. Thus the *Second*

International came into being. The Second International remained in existence till 1914, when the war gave it its death blow. The causes of its failure will be discussed in the next section.

In the Communist Manifesto, Marx already sounded the war cry: 'Proletarians of all lands, unite!' Here are the concluding lines of the manifesto: 'The communists disdain to conceal their views and aims. They openly declare that their ends can only be attained by the forcible overthrow of the existing social order. Let the ruling classes tremble at a communist revolution. The proletarians have nothing to lose but their chains. They have a world to win. Proletarians of all lands, unite!'

It thus appears that the international solidarity of the proletariat is not a toy or a fine phrase, but a vital necessity, without which the working-class movement would be foredoomed to failure.

The Collapse of the Second International and its Causes

When the great world war began in August, 1914, the socialist and social-democratic parties of the various belligerent lands (with the exception of Russia, Serbia, and at later date Italy), instead of declaring war upon the war and instead of inciting the workers to revolt, rallied to the side of their respective governments, and gave their assistance to the campaign for plunder. On one and the same day, the socialist deputies in France and Germany voted the war credits in parliament, thus solidarising themselves with the robber governments. Instead of joining forces in a rising against the criminal bourgeoisie, the socialist parties took up separate stands, each under the banner of its 'own' bourgeois government. The war began with the direct support of the socialist parties; the leaders of these parties turned their coats and betrayed the cause of socialism. The Second International died an ignominious death,

It is interesting to note that, only a few days before the betrayal, the socialist press and the leaders of the socialist parties were holding forth against the war. Gustave Hervé, for example, the traitor to French socialism, wrote as follows in his newspaper *La Guerre Sociale* (The Class War, subsequently rechristened Victory): 'We are to fight in order to save the Tsar's prestige! . . . How delightful to die in so glorious a cause!' Three days before the outbreak of war, the French Socialist Party issued a manifesto against it, and the French syndicalists wrote in their journal, 'Workers! If you are not cowards, protest!' The German social democrats held numerous great meetings of protest. The memory of the resolution passed at the Basle international congress was still fresh, a resolution to the effect that in case of war all possible means must be employed 'to incite the people to revolt and to hasten the collapse of capitalism'. But within a day or two these same parties and these same leaders were insisting upon the need for 'the defence of the fatherland' (this meaning the defence of the robber state of their 'own' bourgeoisie). In Austria the *Arbeiter Zeitung*

(Worker's Gazette) actually declared that the workers must rally to the defence of 'German humanity'!

In order to understand the inglorious collapse of the Second International, we must study the development of the working-class movement prior to the war. Before this conflict, capitalism in Europe and the USA had largely owed its development to the frantic plunder of the colonies. The loathsome and sanguinary aspects of capitalism were here displayed with exceptional clearness. By brutal exploitation, by robbery, fraud and force, values were extracted from the colonial nations, and were transmuted into profit for the sharks of European and American financial capital. The stronger the position of any state capitalist trust in the world market, the larger were the profits it could derive from the exploitation of the colonies. Out of these surplus profits the trust could afford to pay its wage slaves a trifle more than the ordinary wages of labour. Not of course to all the wage workers, but only to those who are usually spoken of as skilled workers. These strata of the working class are thereby won over to the side of capital. Their reasoning runs as follows: 'If "our" industry finds a market in the African colonies, so much the better; it will flourish all the more; the boss will make larger profits, and we shall have a finger in the pie.' Thus capital fetters its wage slaves to its own state, buying one section of them, who are attracted by a share in the colonial plunder.

The founders of scientific communism had already taken note of this phenomenon. Engels, for example, in a letter to Kautsky, wrote in the year 1882: 'You ask me what the British workers think about colonial policy. Very much the same as what they think about politics in general. Here there does not yet exist a labour party; there are only conservatives and liberal radicals; while the workers gladly participate in those advantages which accrue to the British in virtue of their monopoly on the world market and in the colonies.' Upon this soil has flourished a peculiar form of servility, an attachment of the workers to the bourgeoisie of their own country, an abasement before them. Engels wrote in 1889: 'The most repulsive phenomenon here in England is the bourgeois respectability which soaks into the very marrow of the workers... So deeply rooted is this inborn respect for "betters" and "superiors" that Mr Bourgeois finds it an easy matter to catch the workers in his nets. I really believe that, at the bottom of his heart, John Burns is more flattered by his popularity with Cardinal Manning and other notables, with the bourgeoisie generally, than by his popularity with his own class.'

The working masses were not accustomed to carry on a great fight upon the international scale. Indeed, they had no opportunity for anything of the sort. For the most part the activity of their organisations was confined within the limits of the state administered by their own bourgeoisie. 'Their own' bourgeoisie managed to interest in colonial policy a section of the working class, and chiefly the stratum of skilled workers. The same bait was swallowed by the leaders of the working-class organisations, by the working-class bureaucracy, and by the parliamentary representatives of the workers, these being all persons who had secured cosy corners, and were inclined to advocate 'peaceful', 'quiet' and 'law-abiding' methods. We have already pointed out that the bloodthirsty aspects of capitalism were especially displayed in the colonies. In Europe and the United States, industry was highly developed, and in these regions the struggle of the working class had assumed comparatively peaceful forms. Since 1871 there had been no great revolutions anywhere except in Russia, and in most countries there had been none since 1848. People were universally accustomed to the idea that the future development of capitalism would be peaceful, and even those who spoke of coming wars hardly believed their own words. A section of the workers, including the working-class leaders, was more and more inclined to accept the idea that the working class was interested in colonial policy and that the workers ought to join forces with their own bourgeoisie in order to promote, in this matter, 'the common national welfare'. Consequently, large numbers of the lower middle class flocked into the socialist parties. In Germany, for example, among the members of the social-democratic parliamentary group, there was quite a number of publicans and keepers of working-class restaurants. In 1892, out of 35 socialist MPs, there were 4 following these occupations; in 1905, there were 6 out of 81; in 1912, there were 12 out of 110.

It is not surprising that in critical moments their devotion to the imperialist robber state outweighed their devotion to international solidarity.

WE SEE, THEN, THAT THE CHIEF CAUSE OF THE BREAK-UP OF THE SECOND INTERNATIONAL WAS TO BE FOUND IN THE FACT THAT THE COLONIAL POLICY AND THE MONOPOLIST POSITION OF THE GREAT STATE CAPITALIST TRUSTS, HAD ATTACHED THE WORKERS — AND ESPECIALLY THE 'UPPER STRATA' OF THE WORKING CLASS — TO THE IMPERIALIST BOURGEOIS STATE.

In the history of the working-class movement it has often happened that the workers have made common cause with their oppressors. For example, in the very early stages of development, the worker who sat at the same table with his master, looked upon his master's workshop almost as if it had been his own, and regarded his master not as an enemy but as a 'giver of work'. Only in course of time did the workers in various factories come to unite one with another against all the masters. When the great countries had themselves been converted into 'state capitalist trusts', the workers continued to display towards these state capitalist trusts the same sort of devotion that in earlier days they had displayed towards individual masters.

Only the war has taught them that they must not take the side of their respective bourgeois states, but must join forces for the overthrow of these bourgeois states and for the realisation of the dictatorship of the proletariat.

The Watchwords 'National Defence' and 'Pacifism'

The leaders of the socialist parties and of the Second International justified their treason to the cause of the workers and to the common struggle of the working class by saying that it was essential to defend the fatherland.

We have seen that as far as the imperialist war was concerned this was pure nonsense. In that war not one of the Great Powers was on the defensive; all were aggressors. The slogan 'defence of the fatherland' (the defence of the bourgeois state) was humbug, and was shouted by the leaders in order to hide their treason.

Here it is necessary to consider the question in somewhat greater detail.

First of all, what is our fatherland? What is the real meaning of this word? Does it mean, people who all speak the same language; is it the same as 'nation'? No, is is not. Let us consider, for example, Tsarist Russia. When the Russian bourgeoisie clamoured for the defence of the fatherland, it was not thinking of the area in which people of one nationality were living, of the area, say, inhabited by the White Russians; it was referring to the peoples of various nationalities who are settled in Russia. What, in fact, did the bourgeoisie mean? Nothing else than the state authority of the Russian bourgeoisie and the landlords. This is what the capitalists wanted the Russian workers to defend. Really, of course, they were not thinking simply of defending it, but of extending its frontiers to include Constantinople and Cracow. When the German bourgeoisie sang the defence of the fatherland, what was the meaning in that case? Here, the reference was to the authority of the German bourgeoisie, to an extension of the boundaries of the robber state ruled by William II.

We have, then, to inquire whether, under capitalism, the working class has any fatherland at all. Marx, in *The Manifesto of the Communist Party*, replied to this question by saying: 'The workers have no country.' What he said was true. Why? The answer is very simple. Because under capitalism the workers have no power; because under capitalism everything is in the hands of the bourgeoisie; because under capitalism the state is merely an instrument for the suppression and oppression of the working class. We have already seen that the task of the proletariat is to destroy the bourgeois state, not to defend it. Then only will the proletariat have a country, when it has seized the state authority and has become master of the country. Then, and only then, will it be the duty of the proletariat to defend its fatherland; for then it will be defending its own authority and its own cause; it will not be defending the authority of its enemies, and will not be defending the robber policy of its oppressors.

The bourgeoisie is well aware of all this. Here is evidence of the fact. When the proletariat had effected the conquest of power in Russia, the

Russian bourgeoisie began to fight against Russia, forming an alliance with anyone who was willing — with the Germans, the Japanese, the British, the Americans, with all the world and his wife. Why? Because, having lost power in Russia, it had also lost the power of robbing and plundering, the power of bourgeois exploitation. The Russian capitalists were ready at any moment to destroy *proletarian* Russia, to destroy, that is, the Soviet power. Let us take Hungary for another example. When the bourgeois had the power in their own hands, they issued appeals for the defence of the fatherland; but in order to destroy proletarian Hungary they were prompt to enter into an alliance with the Rumanians, the Czecho-Slovaks, the Austrians, and the Entente. We see, then, that the bourgeoisie knows perfectly well what it is about. Under the plea of the defence of the fatherland, it appeals to all citizens to defend its own bourgeois power, and it sentences for high treason all who refuse to assist. On the other hand, when it is a question of destroying the proletarian fatherland, it assembles all its forces and sticks at nothing.

The proletariat must take a leaf out of the bourgeois book; it must destroy the *bourgeois* fatherland and must do nothing for its defence or enlargement; but the proletariat must defend its *own* fatherland with all its might and to the last drop of its blood.

To these considerations the objector may reply as follows. Do you not know, he will say, that colonial policy and imperialism have helped the industrial development of the Great Powers, and that, thanks to this, crumbs from the masters' table fall to the working class? Surely this means that the worker should defend his master, should help his master against competitors?

It means nothing of the kind. Let us suppose that there are two manufacturers whom we will call Schultz and Petrov. They are rivals in the market. Schultz says to his men: 'Friends, stand by me with all your strength. Do all the harm you can to the Petrov factory, to Petrov himself, to his workmen. Then my factory will flourish, for I shall have downed Petrov and my business will boom. I shall be able to give all you fellows a rise.' Petrov says just the same thing to his men. Now let us suppose that Schultz has the best of it. It is quite likely that in the flush of victory he will give his workers a rise. But after a time he will cut down wages to the old level. If now the workers in the Schultz factory go on strike, and would like those who had formerly worked in the Petrov factory to help them, the latter would say: 'Mighty fine! You did us all the harm you could, and now you come crawling to us for help! Clear out!' It would be impossible to arrange for a general strike. When the workers are disunited, the capitalist is strong. Now that he has overthrown his competitor, he is able to get the better of his disunited workers. For a brief space the workers in Schultz's factory enjoyed higher wages, but their gains were soon lost. Just the same thing happens in the international struggle. The bourgeois state is a masters' league. When one such league grows fat the the expense of the others, it is able to bribe the workers. The collapse of the Second International and the betrayal of socialism by the leaders of the working-class movement occurred because these leaders determined to 'defend' the crumbs that fell from the masters' table and hoped for an increase in the amount of these crumbs. During the war, when, owing to the aforesaid treason, the workers were disunited, capital in all countries imposed terrible burdens upon them. The workers came to realise their miscalculation; they came to understand that their leaders had sold them for the merest trifle. Thus began the rebirth of socialism. We can readily understand that the first protests came from the badly paid, unskilled workers. The 'aristocracy of labour' (the printers, for instance) and the old leaders, continued to play a traitor's game.

Not content with using the slogan of the defence of the (bourgeois) fatherland, the bourgeoisie has another means with which to cheat and befool the working masses. We refer to the so-called *pacifism*. This name is given to the view that within the framework of capitalism – without any revolution, without any revolt of the workers – a reign of universal peace can be established. It would suffice, we are told, to set up courts of arbitration between the various powers, to abolish secret diplomacy, to agree upon disarmament (at first, perhaps, only to a limited extent).With this and a few similar measures, all would be well.

The basic error of pacifism is that the bourgeoisie simply will not carry out any of these fine things like disarmament. It is absolutely absurd to preach disarmament in an era of imperialism and civil war. The bourgeoisie will take care to be well armed; and if the workers were to disarm or were to fail to arm themselves, they would be inviting destruction. We can thus realise how the pacifist watchwords cannot fail to lead the proletariat astray. PACIFISM TENDS TO PREVENT THE WORKERS FROM CONCENTRATING THEIR ATTENTION UPON THE ARMED STRUGGLE FOR COMMUNISM.

The best example of the fraudulent character of pacifism is furnished by the policy of Wilson, and by his fourteen points. Here, under a garnish of fine words, and in the name of the League of Nations, world-wide plunder and a civil war against the proletariat are promulgated. The following examples will show to what depths of baseness the pacifists can descend. Taft, sometime president of the USA, was one of the founders of the American Peace Society, and at the same time a rabid imperialist. Ford, the famous American motor-car manufacturer, financed entire expeditions to Europe in order to trumpet his pacifist views; but at the very same time he was netting millions of dollars from the work his factories were doing for the war. Fried, in his Handbook of the Peace Movement (*Handbuch der Friedensbewegung*, vol.ii, pp.149-50) assures his readers that the joint expedition of the imperialists against China in 1900 proved the 'brotherhood of the nations'. He writes as follows: 'The expedition to China furnished another proof of the ascendancy of the idea of peace in contemporary affairs. An *international association of armies* was displayed ... The armies marched, as a pacific force, under the command of a European generalissimo. We, the friends of peace, regard this world generalissimo' (he was writing about Count Waldersee, who was appointed generalissimo by William II) 'as merely the forerunner of that world statesman who will be in a position to realise our ideal of peaceful methods.' Here we see open and universal robbery designated 'the brotherhood of the nations'. In like manner, the robber League of Capitalists is dished up with the League of Nations's sauce.

Jingo Socialists

The false watchwords with which, day after day, the bourgeoisie deafened the masses, with which the newspapers were filled, and which clamoured from every hoarding, were also adopted as slogans by the traitors to socialism.

In nearly all countries, the old socialist parties were split up. Three trends were manifest. First of all, there were open and brazen-faced traitors, the jingo socialists. Secondly, there were secret and vacillating traitors, constituting the so-called centre. Thirdly, there were those who remained faithful to socialism. Out of the members of this third group, the communist parties were subsequently organised.

In nearly every country the leaders of the old socialist parties proved to be jingo socialists. Under the banner of socialism, they preached international hatred; under the lying watchword of the defence of the fatherland, they preached the support of the robber bourgeois states. Among the jingo socialists in Germany were Scheidemann, Noske, Ebert, David, Heine and others; in England, Henderson; in the USA, Russell, Gompers; in France, Renaudel, Albert-Thomas, Guesde, Jouhaux; in Russia, Plekhanov, Potresov, the right essers (Breshko-Breshkovskaya, Kerensky, Chernov), and the right mensheviks (Liber, Rosanov); in Austria, Renner, Seitz, Victor Adler; in Hungary, Garami, Buchinger, etc.

One and all they were for the 'defence' of the bourgeois fatherland. Many of them openly declared themselves in favour of the robber policy of annexations and indemnities, and advocated the seizure of the colonial possessions of other nations. These were usually spoken of as the imperialist socialists. Throughout the war, they supported it, not only by voting the war credits, but by propaganda. In Russia, Plekhanov's manifesto was widely posted on the hoardings by Hvostov, the Tsarist minister of state. General Kornilov made Plekhanov a member of his administration. Kerensky (the social revolutionary) and Tseretelli (the menshevik), concealed the Tsar's secret treaties from the people; in the July days, they bludgeoned the Petrograd proletariat; the social revolutionaries and the right mensheviks were members of Kolchak's administration; Rosanov was one of Yudenich's spies. In a word, like all the bourgeoisie, they stood for the support of the robber bourgeois fatherland, and for the destruction of the proletarian soviet fatherland. The French jingo socialists, Guesde and Albert-Thomas, entered the robber government; they supported all the predatory plans of the Entente; they stood for the suppression of the Russian revolution and for the sending of troops against the Russian workers. The German jingo socialists entered the ministry while William II was still on the throne (Scheidemann); they supported the emperor when he suppressed the Finnish revolution and when he ravaged Ukraine and Great Russia; members of the Social-Democratic Party (for instance, Winnig in Riga) conducted campaigns against the Russian and the Latvian workers; subsequently, the German jingo socialists murdered Karl Liebknecht and Rosa Luxemburg, and drowned in blood the risings of the communist workers of Berlin, Leipzig, Hamburg, Munich, etc. The Hungarian jingo socialists gave their support to the monarchical government as long as that was in power; afterwards they betrayed the Soviet Republic. IN A WORD, IN ALL COUNTRIES ALIKE, THE JINGO SOCIALISTS ASSUMED THE ROLE OF EXECUTIONERS AGAINST THE WORKING CLASS.

When Plekhanov was still a revolutionist, writing in the Russian newspaper *Iskra* (published in Switzerland) he declared that in the twentieth century, which was destined to witness the realisation of socialism, there would in all probability be a great split in the socialist ranks, and that a fierce struggle would ensue between the two factions. Just as, in the days of the French revolution (1789-93), the extremist revolutionary party (nicknamed the Mountain) carried on a civil war against the moderates who were later organised as a counter-revolutionary party (spoken of as the Gironde) so – said Plekhanov – in the twentieth century, those who had at one time been brothers in opinion would probably be split into two warring sections, for some of them would have taken sides with the bourgeoisie.

Plekhanov's prophecy was fulfilled. But when he wrote he did not foresee that he himself would be among the traitors.

In this way the jingo socialists (sometimes spoken of as opportunists) are transformed into the open class enemies of the proletariat. During the great world revolution they fight in the ranks of the Whites against the Reds; they march shoulder to shoulder with the military caste, with the great bourgeoisie and with the landlords. It is perfectly clear that we must wage as relentless a war against them as against the bourgeoisie, whose agents they are.

The remnants of the Second International, which the members of these parties have endeavoured to revive, form merely a branch office of the League of Nations. THE SECOND INTERNATIONAL IS NOW ONE

OF THE WEAPONS USED BY THE BOURGEOISIE IN ITS FIGHT
WITH THE PROLETARIAT.

The Centre

Another group of parties composed of those who were once socialists
constitutes the so-called 'Centre'. Persons of this trend are said to form the
'Centre' because they waver between the communists on one side and the
jingo socialists on the other. Of this complexion are: in Russia, the left
mensheviks under the leadership of Martov; in Germany, the
'independents' (the Independent Social Democratic Party), under the
leadership of Kautsky and Haase; in France, the group led by Jean
Longuet; in the USA, the Socialist Party of America, under the leadership
of Hilquit; in Great Britain, part of the British Socialist Party, the
Independent Labour Party; and so on.

At the outset of the war the centrists advocated the defence of the
fatherland (making common cause in this matter with the traitors to
socialism), and they opposed the idea of revolution. Kautsky wrote that the
'enemy invasion' was the most terrible thing in the world, and that the
class struggle must be postponed until everything was over. In Kautsky's
opinion, as long as the war lasted, there was nothing whatever for the
International to do. After the conclusion of 'peace', Kautsky began to write
that everything was now in a state of such great confusion that it was no
use dreaming about socialism. The reasoning amounts to this. While the
war was on, we must drop the class struggle, for it would be useless, and
we must wait until after the war; when peace has come, there is no use
thinking about the class war, for the imperialist war has entailed general
exhaustion. It is plain that Kautsky's theory is an avowal of absolute
impotence, that it is calculated to lead the proletariat utterly astray, and
that it is closely akin to rank treason. Worse still, when we were in the very
throes of revolution, Kautsky could find nothing better to do than to raise
the hunt against the bolsheviks. Forgetting Marx's teaching, he persisted
in a campaign against the proletarian dictatorship, the Terror, etc.,
ignoring the fact that in this way he was himself assisting the White Terror
of the bourgeoisie. His own hopes would appear to be now those of the
ordinary pacifist; he wants courts of arbitration, and things of that sort.
Thus he has come to resemble any bourgeois pacifist you care to name.

Although Kautsky's position is to the right of the Centre, we choose him
as an example rather than another because his theory is typical of the
centrist outlook.

The chief characteristic of centrist policy is the way in which it wobbles
between the bourgeoisie and the proletariat. The Centre is unsteady on its
legs; wants to reconcile irreconcilables; and at the critical moment betrays
the proletariat. During the Russian November Revolution, the Russian
Centre (Martov, etc.) vociferated against the use of force by the bolsheviks;

it endeavoured to 'reconcile' everybody, thus actually helping the White Guards, and reducing the energy of the proletariat in the hour of struggle. The mensheviks did not even exclude from their party those who had acted as spies and plotters for the military caste. In the crisis of the proletarian struggle, the Centre advocated a strike in the name of the Constituent Assembly against the dictatorship of the proletariat. During Kolchak's onslaught, some of these mensheviks, solidarising themselves with the bourgeois plotters, raised the slogan, 'Stop the civil war' (the menshevik Pleskov). In Germany the 'independents' played a treacherous part at the time of the rising of the Berlin workers, for they practised their policy of 'conciliation' while the fight was actually in progress, and thus contributed to the defeat. Among the independents there are many advocates of collaboration with the Scheidemannites. But the gravest charge against them is that they refrain from the advocacy of a mass rising against the bourgeoisie, and that they wish to drug the proletariat with pacifist hopes. In France and Britain, the Centre 'condemns' the counter-revolution; it 'protests' in words against the crushing of the revolution; but it displays utter incapacity for mass action.

At the present time the centrist group does quite as much harm as do the jingo socialists. The centrists, sometimes spoken of as the Kautskyites, are attempting, like the jingo socialists, to reanimate the corpse of the Second International and to 'reconcile' it with the communists. Unquestionably, a victory over the counter-revolution is impossible without a definite breach, and without a decisive struggle against them.

The attempts to revive the Second International took place under the benevolent patronage of the robber League of Nations. For, in fact, the jingo socialists are faithful supporters of the decaying capitalist order, and are its very last props. The imperialist war could never have continued to rage for five years but for the treachery of the socialist parties. Directly the period of revolution began, the bourgeoisie looked to the socialist traitors for help in crushing the proletarian movement. The sometime socialist parties were the chief obstacle in the way of the struggle of the working class for the overthrow of capitalism. Throughout the war, every one of the traitor socialist parties echoed all that the bourgeoisie said. After the peace of Versailles, when the League of Nations was founded, the remnants of the Second International (the Centre as well as the jingo socialists) began to re-echo all the slogans uttered by the League of Nations. The League accused the bolsheviks of terrorism, of violating democracy, of Red imperialism. The Second International repeated the accusations. Instead of engaging in a decisive struggle against the imperialists, it voiced the imperialist war-cries. Just as the various parties of socialist traitors had supported the respective bourgeois administrations, so did the Second International support the League of Nations.

The Third International

The jingo socialists and the Centre adopted as their watchword during the war, the defence of the (bourgeois) fatherland, this meaning the defence of the state organisation of the enemies of the proletariat. A logical sequel was the watchword of the 'party truce', which signified universal submission to the bourgeois state. The matter is perfectly clear. When Plekhanov or Scheidemann considered it necessary to 'defend' the Tsarist or kaiserist fatherland, they had, of course, to insist that the workers must do absolutely nothing to interfere with the defence of the robber state. Consequently, there must be no strikes, and still less must there be any talk of rising against the bourgeoisie. The socialist traitors reasoned as follows. First of all, they said, we must settle accounts with the 'foreign' enemy, and then we shall see. For example, Plekhanov declared in his manifesto that there must be no strikes now that Russia was in danger. The workers of all the belligerent lands were enslaved by the bourgeoisie in like manner. But from the first days of the war there were groups of trusty socialists who realised that the 'defence of the fatherland' and the 'truce of parties' tied the proletariat hand and foot, and that to utter these slogans was treason to the workers. The bolsheviks saw this from the outset. As early as 1914 they declared that there must be no truce with the bourgeoisie, but unceasing struggle against the capitalists − revolution. The first duty of the proletariat in any country is to overthrow its own bourgeoisie − such was the opinion voiced by our party in the early days of the war. In Germany, too, there was formed a group of comrades led by Karl Liebknecht and Rosa Luxemburg. This group took the name of International, declaring that the international solidarity of the proletariat was the first of all duties. Soon Karl Liebknecht openly proclaimed the need for civil war, and incited the workers to armed insurrection against the bourgeoisie. Such was the origin of the party of the German bolsheviks − the Spartacist group. In the other countries, too, there was a split in the old parties. In Sweden there were bolsheviks, who formed what was known as the Left Socialist Party; while in Norway the 'lefts' gained entire control of the party. The Italian socialists took a firm stand throughout. In a word, there gradually came into existence the parties which stood for the revolution. An attempt to secure unified action was now made in Switzerland. In two conferences, at Zimmerwald and Kienthhal respectively, were laid the foundations of the Third International. Soon, however, it became apparent that certain dubious elements from the Centre were adhering to the movement, and were in fact hindering it. Within the international union of Zimmerwald there was formed the so-called 'Zimmerwald Left' under the leadership of Comrade Lenin. The Zimmerwald Left was in favour of decisive action. It fiercely criticised the Zimmerwald Centre led by Kautsky.

After the November revolution and the establishment of the Soviet power in Russia, that country came to occupy the most important place in the international movement. In order to distinguish itself from the party of the traitors to socialism, and in order to return to the fine old fighting name, our party now called itself the Communist Party. Under the impulsion of the Russian revolution, communist parties were formed in other lands. The Spartacus League changed its name to the Communist Party of Germany. A communist party was formed in Hungary, headed by Bela Kun, who had at one time been a prisoner of war in Russia. Parties were also formed in Austria, Czecho-Slovakia, Finland, etc., and subsequently in France. In the United States, the centre expelled the left wing from the party, and the lefts thereupon organised themselves into a fighting communist party. In Britain, negotiations for the formation of a united communist party were begun in the autumn of 1919. To sum up, after the split between the Centre and the Left, the formation and active development of real revolutionary workers' parties began everywhere. The development of these parties led to the formation of a new International, the *Communist International*. In March 1919, at the Kremlin in Moscow, was held the first international communist congress, at which the Third, or Communist, International was formally constituted. The congress was attended by delegates from the German, Russian, Austrian, Hungarian, Swedish, Norwegian, and Finnish communists; communists from France, the USA, Britain, etc., were also present.

The platform put forward by the German and Russian communists was adopted by the congress with complete unanimity, this showing that the proletariat had planted its feet solidly under the banner of the dictatorship of the proletariat, soviet power and communism.

The Third International took the name of Communist International in conformity with that of the Communist Federation which had been headed by Karl Marx. In all its works the Third International shows that it is following in the footsteps of Marx, that it is on the revolutionary road towards the forcible overthrow of the capitalist system. It is not surprising that all who are live, trusty and revolutionary minded members of the international proletariat are turning more and more eagerly towards the new International, and are joining forces to form the workers' vanguard. The very name Communist International suffices to show that the organisation has absolutely nothing in common with the traitors to socialism.

Marx and Engels consider the name 'social democrat' unsuitable for the party of the revolutionary proletariat. 'Democrat' signifies one who advocates a particular form of rule. But, as we have previously seen, in the society of the future there will be no 'state' of any kind. During the transitional period there will have to be a dictatorship of the workers. Those who have betrayed the working class look no farther than a bourgeois republic. We are out for communism.

In the preface to the 1888 edition of the Communist Manifesto, Engels wrote that the name socialist had in 1847, when the manifesto was penned, signified 'men outside the working class movement, and looking rather to the "educated" classes for support'; but communism in 1847 was a working-class movement. We see the same thing today. The communists look for support to the rank and file of the workers; the social democrats look for support to the aristocracy of the workers, to the professional classes, to the small shopkeepers, and to the petty bourgeoisie in general.

THE COMMUNIST INTERNATIONAL HAS THUS REALISED MARX'S DOCTRINES IN ACTUAL FACT, FOR IT HAS FREED THEM FROM THE ACCRETIONS WHICH HAD FORMED UPON THEM DURING THE 'PEACEFUL' PERIOD OF CAPITALIST DEVELOPMENT. THAT WHICH THE GREAT TEACHER OF COMMUNISM WAS PREACHING SEVENTY YEARS AGO, IS BEING FULFILLED TODAY UNDER THE LEADERSHIP OF THE COMMUNIST INTERNATIONAL.

Sources and Bibliography

1. Sources

Marx, *The Historical Limits of Capitalism*, from Marx (1974) pp. 249-50

Lenin, *The Historical Destiny of the Doctrine of Karl Marx*, from Lenin (1969) pp. 17-19

Krupskaya, *In Exile, 1898-1901*, from Krupskaya (1970) pp. 32-50 (abridged)

Correspondence, from *Soviet Weekly* (1987)

Trotsky, *New York* from Trotsky (1975) pp. 279-88

Philips Price, *In the First All-Russian Congress of Soviets*, from Pethybridge (1964) pp. 162-5

Lenin, *State and Revolution* from Lenin (1969) pp. 264-351 (abridged)

Volia Naroda, Editorial, from Browder and Karensky (1961) p.1641

The Debate in the Council of the Republic, 24 October 1917, from Browder and Kerensky (1961) pp. 1772-80

The Minutes of the Bolshevik Central Committee, from Bone (1974) pp. 96-109

P. Malyantovich, *In the Winter Palace on 25-26 October 1917* from Knyazev and Konstantinov (1957) (abridged)

Mercy or Death to the Whites, from Rhys Williams (1967) pp. 134-55

Podvoisky, *Lenin, Organiser of the Victorious October Uprising* from Knyazev and Konstantinov (1957)

Lisinova, *Letters to her Family* from Sevruk (1973) pp.85-98

Zetkin, *The Battle for Power and Peace in Russia* from Zetkin (1984) pp. 136-41

Reisner, *The Front*, from Sevruk (1973) (abridged)

Kollontai, *Women and Revolution* (1) 'A Commission for Women', from Kollontai (1971) (abridged):, (2) 'On the History of the Movement of Women Workers in Russia', from Kollontai (1984)

Bukharin and Preobrazhensky, *Friends and False Friends of the Working Class* from Bukharin and Preobrazhensky (1969) pp.186-204

2. Bibliography

Bone, A. (trans) (1974) *The Bolsheviks and the October Revolution: Central Committee Minutes* (London, Pluto Press)

Browder, R. P. and Kerensky, A. F. (1961) *The Russian Provisional Government of 1917* (Documents) (3 vols) Stanford, Stanford University Press)

Bryant, L. (1919) *Six Red Months in Russia* (London, Heinemann)
_____ (1923) *Mirrors of Moscow* (New York, Thomas Seltzer)

Bukharin, N. and Preobrazhensky, E. (1969) *The ABC of Communism*

(Harmondsworth, Penguin Books)

Carr, E. H. (1966) *The Bolshevik Revolution*, vol. 1 (Harmondsworth, Penguin Books)

Chamberlin, W. H. (1935) *The Russian Revolution 1917-1921* (2 vols) (London, Macmillan)

Ferro, M. (1972) *The Russian Revolution of February 1917* (London, Routledge)

Gorky, M. (1967) *Lenin* (Edinburgh, University Texts)

Hasegawa, T. (1981) *The February Revolution, Petrograd 1917* (London)

Katkov, G. (1967) *Russia 1917: the February Revolution* (London)

Knyazev, S. P. and Konstantinov, A. P. (1957) *Petrograd, October 1917* (Moscow, FLPH)

Kollontai, A. M. (1971) *Women Workers Struggle for their Rights* (Bristol, Falling Wall Press)

(1984) *Selected Speeches and Articles* (Moscow, Progress Publishers)

Krupskaya, N. K. (1970) *Memories of Lenin* (London, Panther Books)

Lenin, V. I. (1964) vol. 22, *Collected Works* (Moscow, Progress)

_____ (1964) vol. 24, *Collected Works* (Moscow, Progress)

_____ (1964) vol. 26, *Collected Works* (Moscow, Progress)

_____ (1969) *Selected Works* (London, Lawrence and Wishart)

_____ (1979) *The Impending Catastrophe and How to Fight It* (Moscow, Progress)

_____ (1980) *Marxism and Insurrection* (Moscow, Progress)

_____ (1984) *On the Great October Socialist Revolution* (Moscow, Progress)

Liebman, M. (1974) *Leninism under Lenin* (London, Cape)

_____ (1970) *The Russian Revolution* (London, Cape)

Mandel, D. (1983) *The Petrograd Workers and the Fall of the Old Regime* (London, Macmillan)

_____ (1984) *The Petrograd Workers and the Soviet Seizure of Power* (London, Macmillan)

Marx K (1973) *Grundrisse* (Harmondsworth, Penguin)

_____ (1974) *Capital*, vol. 3 (London, Lawrence and Wishart)

Pethybridge, R. (ed) (1964) *Witnesses to the Russian Revolution* (Secaucus, Citadel Press)

Reed, J. (1966) *Ten Days That Shook the World* (Harmondsworth, Penguin)

Rhys Williams, A. (1967) *Through the Russian Revolution* (New York. Monthly Review Press)

Schapiro, L. (1983) 1917 *The Russian Revolutions* (Harmondsworth, Penguin)

Sevruk, V. (1973) *The Young in the Revolution* (Moscow, Progress)

Shlyapnikov, A. (1983) *On the Eve of 1917* (London, Allison and Busby)

Smith, S. A. (1985) *Red Petrograd: Revolution in the Factories, 1917-18* (Cambridge, Cambridge University Press)

Startsev, V. (1984) 27 Fevraliya *1917* (Moscow, Melodaya Gvardiya)

Sukhanov, M. (1955) *The Russian Revolution* (2 vols) (London, Oxford University Press)

Thompson, J. M. (1966) *Russia, Bolshevism and the Versailles Peace* (Princeton University Press)

Trotsky, L.D. (1975) *My Life* (Harmondsworth, Penguin Books)

Zetkin, C. (1984) *Selected Writings*, eds Foner, P.S. and Davis, A. Y. (New York, International Publishers)